STANDARD BRITISH POETS.

The Poems

OF

COLLINS, GRAY AND GOLDSMITH.

Collins Gray

Goldsmith

THE

COMPLETE

POETICAL WORKS

OF

WILLIAM COLLINS, THOMAS GRAY,

AND

OLIVER GOLDSMITH.

WITH

Biographical Sketches and Notes.

EDITED BY

EPES SARGENT.

BOSTON:
CROSBY, NICHOLS, LEE AND COMPANY.
1860.

RIVERSIDE, CAMBRIDGE:
PRINTED BY H. O. HOUGHTON AND COMPANY.

CONTENTS.

PREFACE.

IN pursuing the plan of an edition of the Standard British Poets, that should be, at the same time, so elegant as to be generally desirable, and so cheap as to be within the most moderate means, we have collected, in a single volume, the *Complete Poetical Works of Collins, Gray, and Goldsmith*, with notes, memoirs, and engraved portraits of the authors.

The memoirs are believed to be sufficiently full for a work of this kind. Nothing important in the lives, or in relation to the poetical works of the authors, has been designedly omitted. The original notes of all have been given, without omission or abbreviation, and from various sources such others have been added as in the editor's judgment were desirable in the way of explanation or commentary.

In settling the text of Collins, we have carefully collated the best editions; and the biographical sketch has been chiefly prepared from the materials collected by Mr. Dyce, with occasional reference to other sources of authentic information. We have omitted, without much reluctance, the critical dissertations of Dr. Langhorne, with which the editions of Collins have usually been swelled to the dimensions of a profitable book. At first they were, to some extent, useful in advertising the unacknowledged merits of the poet; but even then they were condemned as mere devices to enhance the size and price of the volume. For the first-named purpose they are no longer necessary, and it is therefore not uncharitable to believe that the extra "shilling" is the only inducement to their republication in late editions.

With regard to Gray, we have consulted the publications of Mason and Matthias, and have been much indebted to the editorial labors and researches of Mr. Mitford, as displayed, not only in the five volumes of the Aldine issue of Gray's writings, but more recently in the Eton edition of his poems, supervised by the Rev. Mr. Moultrie. The biographical sketch prefixed to the last-named volume is from the pen of Mr. Mitford, and is enriched with his latest gleanings in a field to which he has devoted himself with well-rewarded diligence. We have transferred to an appendix a few trifling productions attributed to Gray, which do not appear in the volume of the Aldine edition assigned to the poems. They may be found, however, in one of the later volumes, which have never been reprinted in this country.

We reprint all the poems of Goldsmith that are contained in any approved edition of his works; following chiefly the text adopted by Mr. Bolton Corney in the volume so beautifully illustrated by the Etching Club. This text we have compared carefully with that of the excellent edition of Goldsmith's works just published by Mr. Murray under the editorial charge of Mr. Peter Cunningham, and in some instances have adopted the version approved by the latter. In preparing the memoir, we have sometimes consulted Mr. Prior's materials, but have chiefly relied on the more recent work of Mr. Forster, which we cannot but commend as a valuable contribution to literature, as well as a most entertaining history of the life and adventures of Goldsmith.

We should do great injustice to Mr. Murray if we omitted to mention that we have also been indebted to his valuable edition for a poem which must constitute perhaps the most attractive, as it is the most novel feature of the volume now submitted to the public. We allude to the translation by Dr. Goldsmith of the celebrated poem by Vida, entitled *The Game of Chess.* This translation is as carefully elaborated as the best of his original poems. How it happens that it should so long have escaped the research of Goldsmith's editors, we cannot well comprehend; but of its authenticity we imagine there can be no doubt. We know that Dr. Percy mentions in one of his letters the existence of a manuscript poem of Goldsmith more considerable than any of his posthumous poems which had appeared. This may be the production alluded to by Dr. Percy, but its history is not given by Mr. Cunningham. At present, we only know on the authority of Mr. Forster, Mr. Corney, and Mr. Cunningham, that it exists in the handwriting of Goldsmith; and no one can for a moment imagine that he would have transcribed a production of such length if it were not his own. The ingenuity and skill with which the poem is translated prove that it must be from a hand not inferior to Goldsmith's,—and where should we look for such another?

We believe, therefore, that we have been successful in the effort to present an edition of the poets embraced in this volume which possesses some advantages, independently of beauty and cheapness, over any other extant; and which will fairly entitle it to the favor that has been extended to its predecessors in the same series.

THE

POETICAL WORKS

OF

WILLIAM COLLINS.

LIFE OF COLLINS.

William Collins was born at Chichester, in Sussex, on the 25th of December, 1721. His father was a respectable tradesman, and at that time Mayor of his native city. The maiden name of his mother was Elizabeth Martin. His parents intended to educate him for the church, and, with this design, sent him, in 1733, to Winchester College, where he was placed under the care of Dr. Burton. Here he remained for seven years. Here, many years afterwards, Sir Egerton Brydges saw his name written on a window-pane in his own hand; and so few are the personal memorials left of the poet, that this fact was thought of sufficient interest to record. Among his school-fellows was Joseph Warton, with whom he formed an intimacy that continued through life. While school-boys, they wrote poems which were published in the columns of the *Gentleman's Magazine*, where Collins's first printed production appeared in January, 1739. Another trifle of his appeared in the same journal in the October following, which is now inserted among his poems. This was sent by Collins, under the signature of Delicatulus, to the publisher, Edward Cave, Jr., at St. John's Gate, in a letter, with two other pieces from Winchester, — *Sappho's Advice*, by Monitorius, his friend Warton; *Beauty and Innocence*, by Tomkyns, as Auramantulus. At that time Johnson was Mr. Cave's reliable man for editorial aid in the *Magazine*, and in the following month there is a notice of the contents of the October number, said to be from his pen. It is curious enough, as containing, probably, the first word of encouragement Collins received, and the kindest that was ever spoken of him while he was in a situation to be moved by praise or censure. "We pass on," says Johnson, "to three more [poems] of the lyric kind, which might do honor to any collection. There belongs to them a happy facility of versification, and the way to the scope, or the striking part, is natural and well conducted. Whoever ventures to prefer one. must allow the other two worthy of the same hand. The least [Collins's] which is a favorite of mine, carries a force mixed with tenderness, and an uncommon elevation."

Whilst at school Collins wrote the Oriental Eclogues (which were not published till after he went to Oxford), and distinguished himself by his proficiency in English composition. To the studies of the school he must have devoted himself with diligence, for, in consideration of his merit, he came off from Winchester first on the roll, where Joseph Warton, who afterwards acquired so much distinction as a scholar and man of letters, was second. In 1740 he was entitled to fill the first vacancy at New College, but, none occurring, he was entered a commoner of Queen's, where he remained till he was elected a demy, or scholar of Magdalen, in July, 1741.

During his residence at Magdalen, it happened, one afternoon, at a tea visit, that several of his college friends were assembled at his rooms to enjoy each other's conversation, when entered Hampton, afterwards the translator of Polybius, as remarkable at that time for his brutal disposition as for his good scholarship, and, being determined to quarrel, lifted up his foot, and kicked the tea-table, and all its contents, to the other side of the room. Collins, though of a warm temper, was so confounded at the unexpected downfall, and so astonished at the unmerited insult, that he took no notice of the aggressor; but, getting up from his chair calmly, he began picking up the slices of bread and butter, and the fragments of his china, repeating, very mildly,

"Invenias etiam disjecti membra poetæ."

An academic career, however, had no attraction for Collins. Its discipline was irksome, and its studies failed to excite or interest him. But it was during his residence at Oxford that he published his Eclogues, under the title of *Persian Eclogues*, and his verses to Sir Thomas Hanmer on his edition of Shakspeare. To neither of these did he prefix his name. The latter appeared as the production of "a Gentleman of Oxford," in December, 1743.

He took his Bachelor's degree, and then suddenly left the university; "for what reason," says Dr. Johnson, "I know not that he told." We learn from other sources that the cause he assigned was his mortification at the loss of a fellowship for which he was a candidate. But a person who had a "particular friendship" for him has supplied the information considerately withheld by his biographer. Mr. John Ragsdale tells us that he had other reasons for quitting the place than he mentioned; that he was in arrears to his bookseller and tailor, but that his principal motive was a desire to partake of the dissipation and gayety of London. Some other motive than this may have mingled with the inducements that led him to the great metropolis, but none other presented itself to the charitable judgment of Mr. Ragsdale.

In London, then, we find him, in 1743 or 1744, as Johnson had gone before him, and as Goldsmith soon followed, a "literary adventurer, with many projects in his head, and very little money in his pocket." These words of Johnson apply equally well to any one of the illustrious trio, though it is probable that Collins was something better off than his biographer. Like Goldsmith, he, too, had a kind relative, — a sort of uncle Contarine, — but of the army, and not of the church. This uncle was on the mother's side, — Colonel Martin, who, when his sister's husband became embarrassed in his latter years, not only greatly aided the family, and supported young Collins at the university, but continued the supplies after his removal to London. When the poet left the university, he called on his uncle's agent, "cousin Payne," gayly dressed, and with a feather in his hat, the very ideal, probably, of a fine young fellow about town. Whereupon, cousin Payne was astonished; and not a little astonished Colonel Martin's nephew by telling him that his appearance was by no means that of a young man that had not a guinea he could call his own. Collins very naturally took offence at the liberty, but confined his resentment to the remark, in his private circles, that "he thought Payne a dull fellow." This was no great crime; but Payne held the purse-strings, and undertook to think that the young man called oftener for money than uncle Martin would approve. He declined to honor the nephew's drafts, and no doubt Collins thought him duller than ever.

"This resource being stopped," says Mr. John Ragsdale, in a letter to Mr. Hymers, of Queen's College, Oxford, dated July, 1783, "forced him to set about some work, of which his 'History of the Revival of Learning' was the first, and for which he printed proposals (one of which I have), and took the first subscription money from many of his particular friends: the work was begun, but soon stood still. Both Dr. Johnson and Mr. Langhorne are mistaken when they say the 'Translation of Aristotle' was never begun. I know the contrary, for some progress was made in both, but most in the latter. From the freedom subsisting between us, we took the liberty of saying anything to each other. I one day reproached him with idleness; when, to convince me my censure was unjust, he showed me many sheets of his 'Translation of Aristotle,' which he said he had so fully employed himself about, as to prevent him calling on many of his friends so frequently as he used to do. Soon after this he engaged with Mr. Manby, a bookseller on Ludgate-hill, to furnish him with some Lives for the 'Biographia Britannica,' which Manby was then publishing. He showed me some of the lives in embryo, but I do not recollect that any of them came to perfection. To raise a present subsistence, he set about writing his odes; and, having a general invitation to my house, he frequently passed whole days there, which he employed in writing them, and as frequently burning what he had written, after reading them to me: many of them, which pleased me, I struggled to preserve, but without effect, for, pretending he would alter them, he got them from me and thrust them into the fire. He was an acceptable companion everywhere; and, among the gentlemen who loved him for a genius, I may reckon the Doctors Armstrong, Barrowby and Hill, Messrs. Quin, Garrick and Foote, who frequently took his opinion on their pieces before they were seen by the public. He was particularly noticed by the geniuses who frequented the Bedford and Slaughter's Coffee Houses. From his knowledge of Garrick, he had the liberty of the scenes and green-room, where he made diverting observations on the vanity and false consequence of that class of people; and his manner of relating them to his particular friends was extremely entertaining."

This account agrees with that of a correspondent of the *Gentleman's Magazine* (January, 1781), who describes Collins as spending his time at "Ranelagh, Vauxhall, and the play-houses" — places which Gray loved to visit when in London. No very gross "dissipation" was this, as long as uncle Martin's money could be had to pay expenses, but rather a thriftless mode of squandering the hours which it now became necessary for him to coin into shillings and pounds, in whatever form of composition he could find his talents most available. He planned tragedies, but his situation was not favorable to a long-sustained effort. Shorter pieces were more easily produced, and, perhaps, were thought more available for that present subsistence, the need of which is said to have inspired the production of the odes. If this were so, it must have been a need with no relief and but little hope at that period. It was about this time that Dr. Johnson fell into his company. "His appearance," says the Doctor, "was decent and manly; his knowledge considerable, his views extensive, his conversation elegant, and his disposition cheerful. By degrees I gained his confidence; and one day was admitted to him when he was immured by a bailiff, that was prowling in the street. On this occasion recourse was had to the booksellers, who, on the credit of a translation of Aristotle's Poetics, which he engaged to write with a large commentary, advanced as much money as enabled him to escape into the country. He showed me the guineas safe in his hand."

Collins's first plan for the publication of his Odes was to issue them in a volume, the joint production of himself and his friend Joseph Warton. This contemplated enterprise was probably of the year 1745, or early in 1746, and is thus described in a letter of Warton to his brother:

"Dear Tom: You will wonder to see my name in an advertisement next week, so I thought I would apprize you of it. The case was this. Collins met me in Surrey, at Guildford races, when I wrote out for him my odes, and he likewise communicated some of his to me; and, being both in very high spirits, we took courage, resolved to join our forces, and to publish them immediately. I flatter myself that I shall lose no honor by this publication, because I believe these odes, as they now stand, are infinitely the best things I ever wrote. You will see a very pretty one of Collins's, on the Death of Colonel Ross before Tournay. It is addressed to a lady who was Ross's intimate acquaintance, and who, by the way, is Miss Bett Goddard. Collins is not to publish the odes unless he gets ten guineas for them. I returned from Milford last night, where I left Collins with my mother and sister, and he sets out to-day for London. I must now tell you that I have sent him your imitation of Horace's Blandusian Fountain, to be printed amongst ours, and which you shall own or not, as you think proper. I would not have done this without your consent, but because I think it very poetically and correctly done, and will get you honor. You will let me know what the Oxford critics say. Adieu, dear Tom,

"I am your most affectionate brother,

"J. WARTON."

Collins very likely could not get the ten guineas, without which there was to be no publication, for the joint enterprise seems to have been abandoned. In the beginning of December, 1746, however, a shilling pamphlet was published by Millar, containing the *Odes* of Collins. Never did a volume of poems excite less attention. It would have been some consolation to the author, no doubt, if they had been well abused; but nobody would take the trouble to criticize them. Joseph Warton published about the same time, and with more success. His lyrics went to a second edition in the course of a year. Both volumes fell under the eye of Gray, and their merits seem to have struck him forcibly. Before the end of December he had read them both, and called the attention of his friend, Dr. Wharton, to them. "Have you seen," he wrote, "the work of two young authors, a Mr. Warton and Mr. Collins, both writers of Odes? It is odd enough, but each is the half of a considerable man, and one the counterpart of the other. The first has but little invention, very poetical choice of expression, and a good ear; the second, *a fine fancy, modelled upon the antique, a bad ear, great variety of words and images, and no choice at all.* They both deserve to last some years, but will not."

In 1748, he wrote the Ode on the Death of Thomson, and about the same time the Dirge in Cymbeline. The failure of his poems, however, wounded him deeply; and he was no doubt glad to escape from the "gayety of London" on a visit to his uncle Martin, who was stationed with the British army in Flanders. While on this tour he wrote several letters to his Oxford friends, but none of them have appeared in print, or are now known to exist. Soon after his arrival, his uncle died, and left his property to Collins and his sisters. The poet's legacy amounted to about two thousand pounds. And now he was able, at all events, to cancel his obligations with the booksellers. Forthwith he returned the money he had received for the copyright of the unwritten translation of Aristotle. Now, too, he was able to possess himself of the unsold copies of his *Odes*, and make a bonfire of them. This anecdote has been frequently alluded to, and sometimes as of doubtful authority; but we have good evidence of its truth, seemingly from the publisher himself.

When Mr. Langhorne, several years after the poet's death, edited a collection of his works, he had alluded in this connection to Collins's publisher, Mr. Millar, as having issued the *Odes* "on the author's account," a mode, well understood by the trade, of absorbing all the profits of a salable work, and throwing the expense of a losing one on the writer. This Mr. Millar thought a misstatement of sufficient consequence to be corrected; and the *Monthly Review* (Griffiths) for April, 1765, contains an explanatory paragraph that is well worth transcribing:

"It is certainly a reflection on the discernment and taste of the age in which Mr. Collins's Odes first made their appearance, that they met with no success — no, not so much as to answer the charge of printing the little volume in which they were comprised. This reflection, however, is by our present editor sarcastically extended to Mr. Millar, the bookseller who first printed these Odes, and who is here said to have warily published them on the author's account. This, we are assured, was by no means the case; for the bookseller actually *purchased* the copy, *at a very handsome price* (for those times), and, at his own expense and risk, did all in his power to introduce Mr. Collins to the notice of the public. In this instance, therefore, Mr. Millar ought, by no means, to be pointed out as 'a favorer of genius when *once it has made its way to fame*.' The sequel of this little anecdote is greatly to the honor of our poet's memory. At the time when he sold his Odes to Mr. Millar, his circumstances were too narrow to have allowed him to print at his own expense; and the copy-money was then, to him, a considerable object. Afterwards, when he came to the possession of an easy fortune, by the death of his uncle, Colonel Martin, he recollected that the publisher of his poems was a *loser* by them. His spirit was too great to submit to this circumstance, when he found himself enabled to do justice to his own delicacy; and therefore he desired his bookseller to balance the account of that unfortunate publication, declaring he himself would make good the deficiency; the bookseller readily acquiesced in the proposal, and gave up to Mr. Collins the remainder of the impression, which the generous, resentful bard immediately consigned to the flames."

Collins's better fortunes came too late to be of any essential service. From poverty and neglect he had sought relief in dissipation, and the result had been a nervous disorder, with an unconquerable depression of spirits. His vital powers became feeble and exhausted, and he at last fell into a state of intellectual torpor, now and then lit up with a gleam of vigor and intelligence, but verging continually to actual mental alienation. "The approaches of this dreadful malady," says Johnson, "he began to feel soon after his uncle's death; and with the usual weakness of men so diseased, eagerly snatched that temporary relief with which the table and the bottle flatter and seduce. But his health continually declined, and he grew more and more burthensome to himself."

It was not till after the autumn of 1750 that he fell into this state; for the only letter of Collins's known to be extant shows that he had produced about that time an Ode on the Music of the Grecian Theatre, which is unfortunately lost. This circumstance renders the letter one of peculiar interest. The honor to which it alludes was the setting to music of his Ode on the Passions.

"TO DR. WILLIAM HAYES, PROFESSOR OF MUSIC, OXFORD.

"SIR: Mr. Blackstone, of Winchester, some time since informed me of the honor you had done me at Oxford last summer; for which I return you my sincere thanks. I have another more perfect copy of the ode; which, had I known your obliging design, I would have communicated to you. Inform me by a line, if you should think one of my better judgment acceptable. In such case I could send you one written on a nobler subject; and which, though I have been persuaded to bring it forth in London, I think more calculated for an audience in the university. The subject is the Music of the Grecian Theatre; in which I have, I hope naturally, introduced the various characters with which the chorus was concerned, as Œdipus, Medea, Electra, Orestes, etc. etc. The composition, too, is probably more correct, as I have chosen the ancient tragedies for my models, and only copied the most affecting passages in them.

"In the mean time, you will greatly oblige me by sending the score of the last. If you can get it written, I will readily answer the expense. If you send it with a copy or two of the ode (as printed at Oxford) to Mr. Clarke, at Winchester, he will forward it to me here. I am, sir,

"With great respect, your obliged humble servant,

"WILLIAM COLLINS.

"*Chichester*, *Sussex*, *November* 8, 1750."

"P. S. Mr. Clarke past some days here while Mr. Worgan was with me; from whose friendship, I hope, he will receive some advantage."

Among the papers of Mr. Hymers, a communication was found from Mr. Thomas Warton, which contains a very interesting account of the poet's latter days.

"I often saw Collins in London in 1750. This was before his illness. He then told me of his intended History of the Revival of Learning, and proposed a scheme of a review, to be called the *Clarendon Review*, and to be printed at the university press, under the conduct and authority of the university. About Easter, the next year, I was in London; when, being given over, and supposed to be dying, he desired to see me, that he might take his last leave of me; but he grew better; and in the summer he sent me a letter on some private business, which I have now by me, dated Chichester, June 9, 1751, written in a fine hand, and without the least symptom of a disordered or debilitated understanding. In 1754, he came to Oxford for change of air and amusement, where he stayed a month; I saw him frequently, but he was so weak and low that he could not bear conversation. Once he walked from his lodgings, opposite Christ Church, to Trinity College, but supported by his servant. The same year, in September, I and my brother visited him at Chichester, where he lived, in the cathedral cloisters, with his sister. The first day he was in high spirits at intervals, but exerted himself so much that he could not see us the second. Here he showed us an Ode to Mr. John Home, on his leaving England for Scotland. . . . . Mr. Home has no copy of it. He also showed us another ode, of two or three four-lined stanzas, called the Bell of Arragon; on a tradition that, anciently, just before the King of Spain died, the great bell of the cathedral of Sarragossa, in Arragon, tolled spontaneously. It began thus:

'The bell of Arragon, they say,
Spontaneous speaks the fatal day.'

Soon afterwards were these lines:

'Whatever dark, aërial power,
Commissioned, haunts the gloomy tower.'

The last stanza consisted of a moral transition to his own death and knell, which he called 'some simpler bell.' I have seen all his odes already published in his own handwriting; they had the marks of repeated correction: he was perpetually changing his epithets. Dr. Warton, my brother, has a few fragments of some other odes, but too loose and imperfect for publication, yet containing traces of high imagery. In the Ode to Pity, the idea of a Temple of Pity, of its situation, construction and groups of paintings, with which its walls were decorated, was borrowed from a poem, now lost, entitled The Temple of Pity, written by my brother, while he and Collins were school-fellows at Winchester College. . . . .

"In illustration of what Dr. Johnson has related, that during his last malady he was a greater reader of the Bible, I am favored with the following anecdote from the Reverend Mr. Shenton, Vicar of St. Andrews, at Chichester, by whom Collins was buried: 'Walking in my vicarial garden one Sunday evening, during Collins's last illness, I heard a female (the servant, I suppose) reading the Bible in his chamber. Mr. Collins had been accustomed to rave much, and make great moanings; but while she was reading, or rather attempting to read, he was not only silent but attentive likewise, correcting her mistakes, which indeed were very frequent, through the whole of the twenty-seventh chapter of Genesis.' I have just been informed, from undoubted authority, that Collins had finished a Preliminary Dissertation to be prefixed to his History of the Restoration of Learning, and that it was written with great judgment, precision and knowledge of the subject."

The ode referred to by Warton was long supposed to be lost. Dr. Johnson alludes to it as a poem which the Wartons thought superior to Collins's other works, "but which no search has yet found." Nearly forty years after it was written it first appeared in print; a most remarkable proof of the little interest that attached to the memory of the writer. At a meeting of the Royal Society of Edinburgh, on the 19th of April, 1784, the Rev. Dr. Carlyle, minister of Inveresk, read the copy of an unpublished ode written "by the late Mr. William Collins." The committee appointed to superintend the publication of the Society's Transactions judged this ode "extremely deserving of a place in that collection," and requested Mr. Alexander Fraser Tytler, one of their number, to procure from Dr. Carlyle every degree of information which he could give concerning it. In reply to a communication to this effect, Dr. Carlyle sent his original MS. to Mr. Tytler, with the following statement:

"The manuscript is in Mr. Collins's handwriting, and fell into my hands among the papers of a friend of mine and Mr. John Home's, who died as long ago as the year 1754. Soon after I found the poem, I showed it to Mr. Home, who told me that it had been addressed to him by Mr. Collins on his leaving London, in 1749; that it was hastily composed and incorrect; but that he would one day find leisure to look it over with care. Mr. Collins and Mr. Home had been made acquainted by Mr. John Barrow (the *cordial* youth mentioned in the first stanza), who had been, for some time, at the university of Edinburgh; had been a volunteer, along with Mr. Home, in the year 1746; had been taken prisoner with him at the battle of Falkirk, and had escaped, together with him and five or six other gentlemen, from the castle of Donn. Mr. Barrow resided, in 1749, at Winchester, where Mr. Collins and Mr. Home were for a week or two together on a visit. Mr. Barrow was paymaster in America in the war that commenced in 1756, and died in that country. I thought no more of the poem till a few years ago, when, on reading Dr. Johnson's Life of Collins, I conjectured it might be the very copy of verses which he mentions, which he says was much prized by some of his friends, and for the loss of which he expresses regret. I sought for it among my papers; and perceiving that a stanza and a half were wanting, I made the most diligent search I could for them, but in vain. Whether or not this great chasm was in the poem when it first came into my hands, is more than I can remember at this distance of time."

As a "curious and valuable" fragment, he thought it could not appear with more advantage than in the collection of the Royal Society; in which it was published accordingly, in 1789. As it then appeared, the fifth stanza and one half of the sixth, contained on a lost leaf of the manuscript, were ingeniously supplied by Mr. Henry Mackenzie, at the request of Mr. Tytler. The manuscript was evidently the first rough draft, as was apparent from the erasures and substitutions of words, and the new modelling of the twelfth stanza. The following original passages in that stanza, compared with the text as it now appears, show how much it had been improved by the second thoughts of the author :

VARIATIONS.

Ver. 5. How have I trembled, when, at Tancred's side,
Like him I stalked, and all his passions felt ;
When, charmed by Ismen, through the forest wide
Barked in each plant a talking spirit dwelt !

Ver. 13. Hence, sure to charm, his early numbers flow,
Though strong, yet sweet ——
Though faithful, sweet ; though strong, of simple kind,
Hence, with each theme, he bids the bosom glow,
While his warm lays an easy passage find,
Poured through each inmost nerve, and lull the harmonious ear.

Ver. 16. Melting it flows, pure, numerous, strong and clear.

The publication of the ode drew forth from a correspondent of the *St. James's Chronicle* a statement that the copy seen by the Wartons at Chichester, in 1754, was without one interpolation or hiatus, and was evidently prepared for the press. Soon afterwards the ode appeared in the form which it still retains in the best editions, and which is claimed to be its complete and authentic text. It was inscribed by the anonymous editor to the Wartons, and was issued in quarto by a respectable bookseller. Sir Egerton Brydges, on internal evidence, is disposed to denounce this version as a fabrication ; but the general acceptance of it by all the editors of Collins as supplying most successfully the chasm in Dr. Carlyle's copy, would seem to warrant a belief in its genuineness.

Collins is described, by a person who knew him well, (the correspondent, already cited, of the *Gentleman's Magazine*,) as being of the middle size, with a bright and clear complexion, and gray eyes, so weak as not always to bear the light of a candle without pain. Langhorne represents him with a tall figure, brown complexion, keener eyes, and a fixed, sedate aspect, which from intense thinking had contracted an habitual frown. In the London *Morning Chronicle*, some time in the year 1799, there was an advertisement of a portrait of Collins for sale. It was stated to be the only one in existence, and to have belonged to his sister. The only engraved portrait of him is from a drawing formerly in the possession of Mr. William Seward and is prefixed to Pickering's Aldine edition of the poet, and represents him at the age of fourteen years. Whether or not this pleasing and bright boy's face is from the same portrait which is said to have belonged to his sister, we have no means of ascertaining. So much interest, however, has been excited of late years in tracing every memorial of Collins, that if any other portrait than this is in existence, it will some time be brought to light again.

Collins was an accomplished classical scholar, an accurate linguist, and well versed in early English poetry and literature. In his History of English Poetry, Mr. T. Warton refers more than once to black-letter treasures in the "dispersed library of the late Mr. William Collins," and speaks of the fidelity, judgment and industry, with which he had pursued these studies. He was well acquainted with the best authors of Spain, Italy and France. He sometimes handled the pencil, though without much skill. Of music he is said to have been passionately fond.

Besides the fragments of poetry said to have been in the possession of Dr. Warton, there were extant, some seventy years ago, other fragments and letters in the possession of his friend Mr. Ragsdale, the fate of which he thus describes:

"I had formerly several scraps of his poetry, which were suddenly written on particular occasions. These I lent among our acquaintance, who were never civil enough to return them; and, being then engaged in extensive business, I forgot to ask for them, and they are lost: all I have remaining of his are about twenty lines, which would require a little history to be understood, being written on trifling subjects. I have a few of his letters, the subjects of which are chiefly on business, but I think there are in them some flights which strongly mark his character; for which reason I preserved them."

It is not likely that we shall ever hear again of these remains. It is as little likely that the History of Learning will ever be recovered, for it is said that his sister, in his last days, not only repressed all she could of his remaining enthusiasm for poetry, but destroyed all his papers, in a paroxysm of resentment because he squandered what little money he had, or gave it away to the boys in the cloisters. This anecdote rests on the authority of a son of her second husband, Dr. Durnford, who related it to Mr. Park. For the honor of human nature we must refuse our belief to it.

Johnson was attached to Collins, and during his illness was a frequent inquirer after his health. His correspondence with Joseph Warton contains several allusions to his friend, which are preserved in the following extracts:

"March 8, 1754.

"But how little can we venture to exult in any intellectual powers or literary attainments, when we consider the condition of poor Collins! I knew him a few years ago, full of hopes and full of projects, versed in many languages, high in fancy, and strong in retention. This busy and forcible mind is now under the government of those who lately would not have been able to comprehend the least and most narrow of its designs. What do you hear of him? are there hopes of his recovery? or is he to pass the remainder of his life in misery and degradation? perhaps with complete consciousness of his calamity."

"December 24, 1754.

"Poor dear Collins! Let me know whether you think it would give him pleasure if I should write to him. I have often been near his state, and therefore have it in great commiseration."

"April 15, 1756.

"What becomes of poor dear Collins? I wrote him a letter, which he never answered. I suppose writing is very troublesome to him. That man is no common loss. The moralists all talk of the uncertainty of fortune, and the transitoriness of beauty; but it is yet more dreadful to consider that the powers of the mind are equally liable to change, that understanding may make its appearance and depart, that it may blaze and expire."

We hear nothing of Collins's life after the visit of the Wartons, except that he passed his last year in a state bordering on insanity, till he was released from his sufferings on the 12th of June, 1759 He was buried in the church of St. Andrew, at Chichester, where a monument by Flaxman was long afterwards erected, by subscription, to his memory. In this Collins is represented in a reclining posture, with his lyre and a neglected poem lying upon the ground, and the

Gospel open on a table before him. On the pediment ideal pictures of Love and Pity embracing are placed in relief. This monument was completed in 1795. It was projected not only to do honor to Collins, but to afford an early field for the talents of Flaxman. The son of the poet Hayley, then a student of the sculptor, sat for the figure; and the epitaph was the joint production of two Sussex poets, W. Hayley and J. Sargent.

> "Ye who the merits of the dead revere,
> Who hold misfortune's sacred genius dear,
> Regard this tomb, where Collins, hapless name,
> Solicits kindness with a double claim.
> Though nature gave him, and though science taught
> The fire of fancy, and the reach of thought,
> Severely doomed to penury's extreme,
> He passed in maddening pain life's feverish dream,
> While rays of genius only served to show
> The thickening horror, and exalt his woe.
> Ye walls that echoed to his frantic moan,
> Guard the due records of this grateful stone;
> Strangers to him, enamored of his lays,
> This fond memorial to his talents raise.
> For this the ashes of a bard require,
> Who touched the tenderest notes of pity's lyre;
> Who joined pure faith to strong poetic powers;
> Who, in reviving reason's lucid hours,
> Sought on one book his troubled mind to rest,
> And rightly deemed the book of God the best.'

"The neglected author of the Persian Eclogues," wrote Goldsmith, in 1759, "which, however inaccurate, excel any in our language, is still alive; happy, if insensible of our neglect, not raging at our ingratitude." Within four months afterwards, the poet was in his grave. Six years later Dr. Langhorne published an edition of his collected poems, with commentaries and a biographical notice. But thirty-eight years after the appearance of his Odes, Cowper first heard of their author through the memoir in Dr. Johnson's Collection — one of his most remarkable and inexplicable productions.

A few years after the death of Collins, Johnson communicated to the Poetical Calendar a critical notice, which renders ample justice to its subject:

"Mr. Collins was a man of extensive literature, and of vigorous faculties. He was acquainted not only with the learned tongues, but with the Italian, French and Spanish languages. He had employed his mind chiefly upon works of fiction, and subjects of fancy; and, by indulging some peculiar habits of thought, was eminently delighted with those flights of imagination which pass the bounds of nature, and to which the mind is reconciled only by a passive acquiescence in popular traditions. He loved fairies, genii, giants and monsters; he delighted to rove through the meanders of enchantment, to gaze on the magnificence of golden palaces, to repose by the water-falls of Elysian gardens.

"This was, however, the character rather of his inclination than his genius; the grandeur of wildness, and the novelty of extravagance, were always desired by him, but were not always attained. Yet, as diligence is never wholly lost, if his efforts sometimes caused harshness and obscurity, they likewise produced in happier moments sublimity and splendor. This idea which he had formed of excellence led him to oriental fictions and allegorical imagery; and, perhaps, while he was intent upon description, he did not sufficiently cultivate sentiment. His poems are the productions of a mind not deficient in fire, nor unfurnished with knowledge either of books or life, but somewhat obstructed in its progress by deviation in quest of mistaken beauties.

"His morals were pure, and his opinions pious; in a long continuance of poverty, and long habits of dissipation, it cannot be expected that any character should be exactly uniform. There is a degree of want by which the freedom of agency is almost destroyed, and long association with fortuitous companions will at last relax the strictness of truth, and abate the fervor of sincerity. That this man, wise and virtuous as he was, passed always unentangled through the snares of life, it would be prejudice and temerity to affirm; but it may be said that at least he preserved the source of action unpolluted, that his principles were never shaken, that his distinctions of right and wrong were never confounded, and that his faults had nothing of malignity or design, but proceeded from some unexpected pressure or casual temptation.

"The latter part of his life cannot be remembered but with pity and sadness. He languished some years under that depression of mind which enchains the faculties without destroying them, and leaves reason the knowledge of right without the power of pursuing it. These clouds, which he perceived gathering on his intellects, he endeavored to disperse by travel, and passed into France; but found himself constrained to yield to his malady, and returned. He was for some time confined in a house of lunatics, and afterwards returned to the care of his sister in Chichester, where death, in 1759, came to his relief.

"After his return from France, the writer of this character paid him a visit at Islington, where he was waiting for his sister, whom he had directed to meet him; there was then nothing of disorder discernible in his mind by any but himself; but he had withdrawn from study, and travelled with no other book than an English Testament, such as children carry to the school; when his friend took it into his hand, out of curiosity to see what companion a man of letters had chosen, 'I have but one book,' said Collins, 'but that is the best.'"

When preparing the life for his edition of the poets, Johnson extracted this account of Collins as having been written when his character was, perhaps, more deeply impressed on his memory, and speaks of him as a man with whom he once delighted to converse, and whom he still remembered with tenderness. He then proceeds in the following severe strain of censure:

"To what I have formerly said of his writings may be added, that his diction was often harsh, unskilfully labored, and injudiciously selected. He affected the obsolete when it was not worthy of revival; and he puts his words out of the common order, seeming to think, with some later candidates for fame, that not to write prose is certainly to write poetry. His lines commonly are of slow motion, clogged and impeded with clusters of consonants. As men are often esteemed who cannot be loved, so the poetry of Collins may sometimes extort praise when it gives little pleasure."

But in spite of the neglect of his contemporaries, and the sweeping condemnation of Dr. Johnson, Collins has risen in the estimation of critics and the literary world, till his poems are now universally acknowledged, as Southey says, "to be the best of their kind in the language." We have studied them to discover the faults pointed out by Dr. Johnson, and we must acknowledge without the least success. To us they give unmixed delight, and we regard the author with an admiration that grows as we contemplate and dwell upon his works. It has been usual to mention *Alexander's Feast* as the first ode in the English language, and Gray's Odes as only second to it. And yet the magnificent lyric of Dryden is justly liable to the objection that it sometimes sinks to the level of a drinking-song ; and even the poet's annotations do not render *The Bard* and *The Progress of Poetry* intelligible altogether to any other than readers of considerable culture. No such criticism applies to the Ode on the Passions. It sustains the lyric dignity in every line and sentiment, and does not require a note of illustration. For pictorial effects, variety and harmony of versification, energy and beauty of expression, it is inferior to none of the master-pieces to which we have referred ; and is in one respect, at least, superior to Gray's, — that it does not betray the art with which it is constructed. We cannot but assent most heartily to the remark of Campbell, that the lyrics of Collins will abide comparison with whatever Milton wrote under the age of thirty ; and we are willing even to venture the opinion that there is no English poet since Milton who so nearly approaches him in that affluent diction, that splendid imagery, and that elevation and solemnity of tone, which are the characteristics of his genius.

ORIENTAL ECLOGUES.

WRITTEN ORIGINALLY FOR THE ENTERTAINMENT OF THE LADIES OF TAURIS,

AND NOW TRANSLATED.

——Ubi primus equis Oriens adflavit anhelis.

VIRG.

PREFACE.

It is with the writings of mankind, in some measure, as with their complexions or their dress ; each nation hath a peculiarity in all these, to distinguish it from the rest of the world.

The gravity of the Spaniard, and the levity of the Frenchman, are as evident in all their productions as in their persons themselves ; and the style of my countrymen is as naturally strong and nervous, as that of an Arabian or Persian is rich and figurative.

There is an elegancy and wildness of thought which recommends all their compositions ; and our geniuses are as much too cold for the entertainment of such sentiments, as our climate is for their fruits and spices. If any of these beauties are to be found in the following Eclogues, I hope my reader will consider them as an argument of their being original. I received them at the hands of a merchant, who had made it his business to enrich himself with the learning, as well as the silks and carpets, of the Persians. The little information I could gather concerning their author was, that his name was Abdallah, and that he was a native of Tauris.

It was in that city that he died of a distemper fatal in those parts, whilst he was engaged in celebrating the victories of his favorite monarch, the great Abbas.* As to the Eclogues themselves, they give a very just view of the miseries and inconveniences, as well as the felicities, that attend one of the finest countries in the East.

The time of writing them was probably in the beginning of Sha Sultan Hosseyn's reign, the successor of Sefi or Solyman the Second.

Whatever defects, as, I doubt not, there will be many, fall under the reader's observation, I hope his candor will incline him to make the following reflection :

That the works of Orientals contain many peculiarities, and that, through defect of language, few European translators can do them justice.

* In the Persian tongue, Abbas signifieth "the father of the people."

ORIENTAL ECLOGUES.

ECLOGUE I.

SELIM; OR, THE SHEPHERD'S MORAL.

SCENE, A valley near Bagdat.

TIME, The morning.

"YE Persian maids, attend your poet's lays,
And hear how shepherds pass their golden days.
Not all are blest whom Fortune's hand sustains
With wealth in courts, nor all that haunt the plains:
Well may your hearts believe the truths I tell;
'T is virtue makes the bliss, where'er we dwell."

Thus Selim sung, by sacred Truth inspired;
Nor praise, but such as Truth bestowed, desired:
Wise in himself, his meaning songs conveyed
Informing morals to the shepherd maid;
Or taught the swains that surest bliss to find,
What groves nor streams bestow, a virtuous mind.

When sweet and blushing, like a virgin bride,
The radiant morn resumed her orient pride;

When wanton gales along the valleys play,
Breathe on each flower, and bear their sweets away;
By Tigris' wandering waves he sat, and sung
This useful lesson for the fair and young.

"Ye Persian dames," he said, "to you belong—
Well may they please—the morals of my song:
No fairer maids, I trust, than you are found,
Graced with soft arts, the peopled world around!
The morn that lights you, to your loves supplies
Each gentler ray delicious to your eyes:
For you those flowers her fragrant hands bestow;
And yours the love that kings delight to know.
Yet think not these, all beauteous as they are,
The best kind blessings Heaven can grant the fair!
Who trust alone in beauty's feeble ray
Boast but the worth Bassora's pearls display:
Drawn from the deep we own their surface bright,
But, dark within, they drink no lustrous light:
Such are the maids, and such the charms they boast,
By sense unaided, or to virtue lost.
Self-flattering sex! your hearts believe in vain
That love shall blind, when once he fires, the swain;
Or hope a lover by your faults to win,
As spots on ermine beautify the skin:
Who seeks secure to rule, be first her care
Each softer virtue that adorns the fair;
Each tender passion man delights to find,
The loved perfections of a female mind!

"Blest were the days when Wisdom held her reign,
And shepherds sought her on the silent plain!

With Truth she wedded in the secret grove,
Immortal Truth, and daughters blessed their love.
O haste, fair maids! ye Virtues, come away!
Sweet Peace and Plenty lead you on your way!
The balmy shrub, for you shall love our shore,
By Ind excelled, or Araby, no more.

"Lost to our fields, for so the Fates ordain,
The dear deserters shall return again.
Come thou, whose thoughts as limpid springs are clear,
To lead the train, sweet Modesty, appear:
Here make thy court amidst our rural scene,
And shepherd girls shall own thee for their queen:
With thee be Chastity, of all afraid,
Distrusting all, a wise suspicious maid,
But man the most: — not more the mountain doe
Holds the swift falcon for her deadly foe.
Cold is her breast, like flowers that drink the dew;
A silken veil conceals her from the view.
No wild desires amidst thy train be known;
But Faith, whose heart is fixed on one alone:
Desponding Meekness, with her downcast eyes,
And friendly Pity, full of tender sighs;
And Love the last: by these your hearts approve;
These are the virtues that must lead to love."

Thus sung the swain; and ancient legends say
The maids of Bagdat verified the lay:
Dear to the plains, the Virtues came along,
The shepherds loved, and Selim blessed his song.

ECLOGUE II.

HASSAN; OR, THE CAMEL-DRIVER.

SCENE, The desert. TIME, Midday.

IN silent horror o'er the boundless waste
The driver Hassan with his camels passed:
One cruise of water on his back he bore,
And his light scrip contained a scanty store;
A fan of painted feathers in his hand,
To guard his shaded face from scorching sand.
The sultry sun had gained the middle sky,
And not a tree and not an herb was nigh;
The beasts with pain their dusty way pursue;
Shrill roared the winds, and dreary was the view!
With desperate sorrow wild, the affrighted man
Thrice sighed, thrice struck his breast, and thus began:
"Sad was the hour, and luckless was the day,
When first from Schiraz' walls I bent my way!

"Ah! little thought I of the blasting wind,
The thirst or pinching hunger, that I find!
Bethink thee, Hassan, where shall thirst assuage,
When fails this cruise, his unrelenting rage?
Soon shall this scrip its precious load resign;
Then what but tears and hunger shall be thine?

"Ye mute companions of my toils, that bear
In all my griefs a more than equal share!
Here, where no springs in murmurs break away,
Or moss-crowned fountains mitigate the day,

In vain ye hope the green delights to know,
Which plains more blest, or verdant vales, bestow:
Here rocks alone, and tasteless sands, are found,
And faint and sickly winds forever howl around.
  Sad was the hour, and luckless was the day,
  When first from Schiraz' walls I bent my way!

"Curst be the gold and silver which persuade
Weak men to follow far-fatiguing trade!
The lily peace outshines the silver store,
And life is dearer than the golden ore:
Yet money tempts us o'er the desert brown,
To every distant mart and wealthy town.
Full oft we tempt the land, and oft the sea;
And are we only yet repaid by thee?
Ah! why was ruin so attractive made?
Or why fond man so easily betrayed?
Why heed we not, whilst mad we haste along,
The gentle voice of peace, or pleasure's song?
Or wherefore think the flowery mountain's side,
The fountain's murmurs, and the valley's pride,
Why think we these less pleasing to behold
Than dreary deserts, if they lead to gold?
  Sad was the hour, and luckless was the day,
  When first from Schiraz' walls I bent my way!

"O cease, my fears! — all frantic as I go,
When thought creates unnumbered scenes of woe,
What if the lion in his rage I meet! —
Oft in the dust I view his printed feet:
And, fearful! oft, when day's declining light
Yields her pale empire to the mourner night,
By hunger roused, he scours the groaning plain,
Gaunt wolves and sullen tigers in his train:

Before them Death with shrieks directs their way,
Fills the wild yell, and leads them to their prey.
Sad was the hour, and luckless was the day,
When first from Schiraz' walls I bent my way!

"At that dead hour the silent asp shall creep,
If aught of rest I find, upon my sleep:
Or some swoln serpent twist his scales around,
And wake to anguish with a burning wound.
Thrice happy they, the wise contented poor,
From lust of wealth and dread of death secure!
They tempt no deserts, and no griefs they find;
Peace rules the day, where reason rules the mind.
Sad was the hour, and luckless was the day,
When first from Schiraz' walls I bent my way!

"O hapless youth! — for she thy love hath won,
The tender Zara will be most undone!
Big swelled my heart, and owned the powerful maid.
When fast she dropt her tears, as thus she said:
'Farewell the youth whom sighs could not detain;
Whom Zara's breaking heart implored in vain!
Yet, as thou go'st, may every blast arise
Weak and unfelt as these rejected sighs!
Safe o'er the wild, no perils mayst thou see,
No griefs endure, nor weep, false youth, like me.'
O, let me safely to the fair return,
Say, with a kiss, she must not, shall not mourn;
O! let me teach my heart to lose its fears,
Recalled by Wisdom's voice, and Zara's tears."

He said, and called on Heaven to bless the day,
When back to Schiraz' walls he bent his way.

ECLOGUE III.

ABRA; OR, THE GEORGIAN SULTANA.

SCENE, A forest. TIME, The evening.

IN Georgia's land, where Tefflis' towers are seen,
In distant view, along the level green,
While evening dews enrich the glittering glade,
And the tall forests cast a longer shade,
What time 't is sweet o'er fields of rice to stray,
Or scent the breathing maize at setting day;
Amidst the maids of Zagen's peaceful grove,
Emyra sung the pleasing cares of love.

Of Abra first began the tender strain,
Who led her youth with flocks upon the plain.
At morn she came those willing flocks to lead,
Where lilies rear them in the watery mead;
From early dawn the livelong hours she told,
Till late at silent eve she penned the fold.
Deep in the grove, beneath the secret shade,
A various wreath of odorous flowers she made:
Gay-motleyed pinks and sweet jonquils she chose,
The violet blue that on the moss-bank grows;
All sweet to sense, the flaunting rose was there;
The finished chaplet well adorned her hair.

Great Abbas chanced that fated morn to stray,
By love conducted from the chase away;

Among the vocal vales he heard her song,
And sought the vales and echoing groves among;
At length he found, and wooed the rural maid;
She knew the monarch, and with fear obeyed.
  Be every youth like royal Abbas moved,
  And every Georgian maid like Abra loved!

  The royal lover bore her from the plain;
Yet still her crook and bleating flock remain:
Oft, as she went, she backward turned her view,
And bade that crook and bleating flock adieu.
Fair, happy maid! to other scenes remove,
To richer scenes of golden power and love!
Go leave the simple pipe and shepherd's strain;
With love delight thee, and with Abbas reign!
  Be every youth like royal Abbas moved,
  And every Georgian maid like Abra loved!

  Yet, 'midst the blaze of courts, she fixed her love
On the cool fountain, or the shady grove;
Still, with the shepherd's innocence, her mind
To the sweet vale, and flowery mead, inclined;
And oft as spring renewed the plains with flowers,
Breathed his soft gales, and led the fragrant hours,
With sure return she sought the sylvan scene,
The breezy mountains, and the forests green.
Her maids around her moved, a duteous band!
Each bore a crook, all rural, in her hand:
Some simple lay, of flocks and herds, they sung;
With joy the mountain and the forest rung.
  Be every youth like royal Abbas moved,
  And every Georgian maid like Abra loved!

And oft the royal lover left the care
And thorns of state, attendant on the fair;
Oft to the shades and low-roofed cots retired,
Or sought the vale where first his heart was fired:
A russet mantle, like a swain, he wore,
And thought of crowns, and busy courts, no more.
Be every youth like royal Abbas moved,
And every Georgian maid like Abra loved!

Blest was the life that royal Abbas led:
Sweet was his love, and innocent his bed.
What if in wealth the noble maid excel?
The simple shepherd girl can love as well.
Let those who rule on Persia's jewelled throne
Be famed for love, and gentlest love alone;
Or wreathe, like Abbas, full of fair renown,
The lover's myrtle with the warrior's crown.
O happy days! the maids around her say:
O haste, profuse of blessings, haste away!
Be every youth like royal Abbas moved,
And every Georgian maid like Abra loved!

4*

ECLOGUE IV.

AGIB AND SECANDER; OR, THE FUGITIVES.

SCENE, A mountain in Circassia.

TIME, Midnight.

IN fair Circassia, where, to love inclined,
Each swain was blest, for every maid was kind;
At that still hour, when awful midnight reigns,
And none, but wretches, haunt the twilight plains;
What time the moon had hung her lamp on high,
And past in radiance through the cloudless sky;
Sad, o'er the dews, two brother shepherds fled,
Where wildering fear and desperate sorrow led:
Fast as they pressed their flight, behind them lay
Wide ravaged plains, and valleys stole away:
Along the mountain's bending sides they ran,
Till, faint and weak, Secander thus began.

SECANDER.

O stay thee, Agib, for my feet deny,
No longer friendly to my life, to fly.
Friend of my heart, O turn thee and survey!
Trace our sad flight through all its length of way,
And first review that long extended plain,
And yon wide groves, already past with pain!
Yon ragged cliff, whose dangerous path we tried!
And, last, this lofty mountain's weary side!

AGIB.

Weak as thou art, yet, hapless, must thou know
The toils of flight, or some severer woe!
Still, as I haste, the Tartar shouts behind,
And shrieks and sorrows load the saddening wind:
In rage of heart, with ruin in his hand,
He blasts our harvests, and deforms our land.
Yon citron grove, whence first in fear we came,
Droops its fair honors to the conquering flame:
Far fly the swains, like us, in deep despair,
And leave to ruffian bands their fleecy care.

SECANDER.

Unhappy land, whose blessings tempt the sword,
In vain, unheard, thou call'st thy Persian lord!
In vain thou court'st him, helpless, to thine aid,
To shield the shepherd, and protect the maid!
Far off, in thoughtless indolence resigned,
Soft dreams of love and pleasure soothe his mind:
'Midst fair sultanas lost in idle joy,
No wars alarm him, and no fears annoy.

AGIB.

Yet these green hills, in summer's sultry heat,
Have lent the monarch oft a cool retreat.
Sweet to the sight is Zabran's flowery plain,
And once by maids and shepherds loved in vain!
No more the virgins shall delight to rove
By Sargis' banks, or Irwan's shady grove;
On Tarkie's mountain catch the cooling gale,
Or breathe the sweets of Aly's flowery vale:
Fair scenes! but, ah! no more with peace possest,

With ease alluring, and with plenty blest!
No more the shepherds' whitening tents appear,
Nor the kind products of a bounteous year;
No more the date, with snowy blossoms crowned!
But ruin spreads her baleful fires around.

SECANDER.

In vain Circassia boasts her spicy groves,
Forever famed for pure and happy loves:
In vain she boasts her fairest of the fair,
Their eyes' blue languish, and their golden hair!
Those eyes in tears their fruitless grief must send;
Those hairs the Tartar's cruel hand shall rend.

AGIB.

Ye Georgian swains, that piteous learn from far
Circassia's ruin, and the waste of war;
Some weightier arms than crooks and staves prepare,
To shield your harvests, and defend your fair:
The Turk and Tartar like designs pursue,
Fixed to destroy, and steadfast to undo.
Wild as his land, in native deserts bred,
By lust incited, or by malice led,
The villain Arab, as he prowls for prey,
Oft marks with blood and wasting flames the way;
Yet none so cruel as the Tartar foe,
To death inured, and nursed in scenes of woe.

He said; when loud along the vale was heard
A shriller shriek, and nearer fires appeared:
The affrighted shepherds, through the dews of night,
Wide o'er the moonlight hills renewed their flight.

ODES.

ON SEVERAL DESCRIPTIVE AND ALLEGORICAL SUBJECTS.

Ειην
Ευρησιεπης αναγει
Προσφορος εν Μοισαν Διφρω
Τολμα δε και αμφιλαφης Δυναμις
Εσπυιτο. *Πινδαρ. Ολυμπ. Θ.*

ODES.

ODE TO PITY.

O THOU, the friend of man, assigned
With balmy hands his wounds to bind,
   And charm his frantic woe :
When first Distress, with dagger keen,
Broke forth to waste his destined scene,
   His wild unsated foe !

By Pella's bard, a magic name,
By all the griefs his thought could frame
   Receive my humble rite :
Long, Pity, let the nations view
Thy sky-worn robes of tenderest blue,
   And eyes of dewy light !

But wherefore need I wander wide
To old Ilissus' distant side,
   Deserted stream, and mute ?
Wild Arun too has heard thy strains,
And Echo, 'midst my native plains,
   Been soothed by Pity's lute.

There first the wren thy myrtles shed
On gentlest Otway's infant head,
  To him thy cell was shown;
And while he sung the female heart,
With youth's soft notes unspoiled by art,
  Thy turtles mixed their own.

Come, Pity, come, by Fancy's aid,
E'en now my thoughts, relenting maid,
  Thy temple's pride design:
Its southern site, its truth complete,
Shall raise a wild enthusiast heat
  In all who view the shrine.

There Picture's toils shall well relate
How chance, or hard involving fate,
  O'er mortal bliss prevail:
The buskined Muse shall near her stand,
And sighing prompt her tender hand,
  With each disastrous tale.

There let me oft, retired by day,
In dreams of passion melt away,
  Allowed with thee to dwell:
There waste the mournful lamp of night,
Till, Virgin, thou again delight
  To hear a British shell!

ODE TO FEAR.

Thou, to whom the world unknown,
With all its shadowy shapes, is shown;
Who seest, appalled, the unreal scene,
While Fancy lifts the veil between:
  Ah Fear! ah frantic Fear!
  I see, I see thee near.
I know thy hurried step, thy haggard eye!
Like thee I start; like thee disordered fly.
For, lo, what monsters in thy train appear!
Danger, whose limbs of giant mould
What mortal eye can fixed behold?
Who stalks his round, an hideous form,
Howling amidst the midnight storm;
Or throws him on the ridgy steep
Of some loose hanging rock to sleep:
And with him thousand phantoms joined,
Who prompt to deeds accursed the mind:
And those, the fiends, who, near allied,
O'er Nature's wounds, and wrecks, preside;
Whilst Vengeance, in the lurid air,
Lifts her red arm, exposed and bare:
On whom that ravening brood of Fate,
Who lap the blood of sorrow, wait:
Who, Fear, this ghastly train can see,
And look not madly wild, like thee?

EPODE.

In earliest Greece, to thee, with partial choice,
  The grief-full Muse addrest her infant tongue;

The maids and matrons on her awful voice,
  Silent and pale, in wild amazement hung.

Yet he, the bard who first invoked thy name,
  Disdained in Marathon its power to feel:
For not alone he nursed the poet's flame,
  But reached from Virtue's hand the patriot's steel.

But who is he whom later garlands grace,
  Who left a while o'er Hybla's dews to rove,
With trembling eyes thy dreary steps to trace,
  Where thou and furies shared the baleful grove?

Wrapt in thy cloudy veil, the incestuous queen
  Sighed the sad call her son and husband heard,
When once alone it broke the silent scene,
  And he the wretch of Thebes no more appeared.

O Fear, I know thee by my throbbing heart:
  Thy withering power inspired each mournful line:
Though gentle Pity claim her mingled part,
  Yet all the thunders of the scene are thine!

ANTISTROPHE.

Thou who such weary lengths hast past,
Where wilt thou rest, mad Nymph, at last?
Say, wilt thou shroud in haunted cell,
Where gloomy Rape and Murder dwell?
    Or, in some hollowed seat,
    'Gainst which the big waves beat,
Hear drowning seamen's cries, in tempests brought?
Dark power, with shuddering meek submitted thought,
Be mine to read the visions old
Which thy awakening bards have told:

And, lest thou meet my blasted view,
Hold each strange tale devoutly true;
Ne'er be I found, by thee o'erawed,
In that thrice hallowed eve, abroad,
When ghosts, as cottage maids believe,
Their pebbled beds permitted leave;
And goblins haunt, from fire, or fen,
Or mine, or flood, the walks of men!

O thou, whose spirit most possest
The sacred seat of Shakspeare's breast!
By all that from thy prophet broke,
In thy divine emotions spoke;
Hither again thy fury deal,
Teach me but once like him to feel:
His cypress wreath my meed decree,
And I, O Fear, will dwell with thee!

ODE TO SIMPLICITY.

O THOU, by Nature taught
To breathe her genuine thought,
In numbers warmly pure, and sweetly strong;
Who first, on mountains wild,
In Fancy, loveliest child,
Thy babe, and Pleasure's, nursed the powers of song!

Thou, who, with hermit heart,
Disdain'st the wealth of art,

And gauds, and pageant weeds, and trailing pall;
  But comest a decent maid,
  In Attic robe arrayed,
O chaste, unboastful Nymph, to thee I call!

  By all the honeyed store
  On Hybla's thymy shore;
By all her blooms, and mingled murmurs dear;
  By her whose lovelorn woe,
  In evening musings slow,
Soothed sweetly sad Electra's poet's ear:

  By old Cephisus deep,
  Who spread his wavy sweep,
In warbled wanderings, round thy green retreat;
  On whose enamelled side,
  When holy Freedom died,
No equal haunt allured thy future feet.

  O sister meek of Truth,
  To my admiring youth,
Thy sober aid and native charms infuse!
  The flowers that sweetest breathe,
  Though beauty culled the wreath,
Still ask thy hand to range their ordered hues.

  While Rome could none esteem,
  But virtue's patriot theme,
You loved her hills, and led her laureate band:
  But staid to sing alone
  To one distinguished throne;
And turned thy face, and fled her altered land.

No more, in hall or bower,
The Passions own thy power,
Love, only Love her forceless numbers mean:
For thou hast left her shrine;
Nor olive more, nor vine,
Shall gain thy feet to bless the servile scene.

Though taste, though genius, bless
To some divine excess,
Faint 's the cold work till thou inspire the whole:
What each, what all supply,
May court, may charm, our eye;
Thou, only thou, canst raise the meeting soul!

Of these let others ask,
To aid some mighty task,
I only seek to find thy temperate vale;
Where oft my reed might sound
To maids and shepherds round,
And all thy sons, O Nature, learn my tale.

ODE ON THE POETICAL CHARACTER.

As once,—if, not with light regard,
I read aright that gifted bard,
—Him whose school above the rest
His loveliest elfin queen has blest;—
One, only one, unrivalled fair,
Might hope the magic girdle wear,

At solemn tourney hung on high,
The wish of each love-darting eye;

— Lo! to each other nymph, in turn, applied,
As if, in air unseen, some hovering hand,
Some chaste and angel friend to virgin fame,
With whispered spell had burst the starting band,
It left unblest her loathed, dishonored side;
Happier, hopeless Fair, if never
Her baffled hand, with vain endeavor,
Had touched that fatal zone to her denied!
Young Fancy thus, to me divinest name,
To whom, prepared and bathed in heaven,
The cest of amplest power is given:
To few the godlike gift assigns,
To gird their blest prophetic loins,
And gaze her visions wild, and feel unmixed her flame!
The band, as fairy legends say,
Was wove on that creating day,
When He, who called with thought to birth
Yon tented sky, this laughing earth,
And dressed with springs and forests tall,
And poured the main engirting all,
Long by the loved enthusiast wooed,
Himself in some diviner mood,
Retiring, sat with her alone,
And placed her on his sapphire throne;
The whiles, the vaulted shrine around,
Seraphic wires were heard to sound,
Now sublimest triumph swelling,
Now on love and mercy dwelling;
And she, from out the veiling cloud,
Breathed her magic notes aloud:

And thou, thou rich-haired youth of morn,
And all thy subject life was born!
The dangerous passions keep aloof,
Far from the sainted growing woof:
But near it sat ecstatic Wonder,
Listening the deep applauding thunder;
And Truth, in sunny vest arrayed,
By whose the tarsel's eyes were made;
All the shadowy tribes of mind,
In braided dance, their murmurs joined,
And all the bright uncounted powers
Who feed on heaven's ambrosial flowers.
— Where is the bard whose soul can now
Its high presuming hopes avow?
Where he who thinks, with rapture blind,
This hallowed work for him designed?

High on some cliff, to heaven up-piled,
Of rude access, of prospect wild,
Where, tangled round the jealous steep,
Strange shades o'erbrow the valleys deep,
And holy genii guard the rock,
Its glooms embrown, its springs unlock,
While on its rich ambitious head
An Eden, like his own, lies spread:
I view that oak, the fancied glades among,
By which, as Milton lay, his evening ear,
From many a cloud that dropped ethereal dew,
Nigh sphered in heaven, its native strains could hear,
On which that ancient trump he reached was hung:
Thither oft, his glory greeting,
From Waller's myrtle shades retreating,

With many a vow from Hope's aspiring tongue,
My trembling feet his guiding steps pursue;
  In vain — such bliss to one alone,
  Of all the sons of soul, was known;
  And Heaven, and Fancy, kindred powers,
  Have now o'erturned the inspiring bowers;
Or curtained close such scene from every future view.

ODE,

WRITTEN IN THE BEGINNING OF THE YEAR 1746.

How sleep the brave, who sink to rest,
By all their country's wishes blest!
When Spring, with dewy fingers cold,
Returns to deck their hallowed mould,
She there shall dress a sweeter sod
Than Fancy's feet have ever trod.

By fairy hands their knell is rung;
By forms unseen their dirge is sung;
There Honor comes, a pilgrim gray,
To bless the turf that wraps their clay;
And Freedom shall a while repair,
To dwell a weeping hermit there!

ODE TO MERCY.

STROPHE.

O THOU, who sitt'st a smiling bride
By Valor's armed and awful side,
Gentlest of sky-born forms, and best adored;
Who oft with songs, divine to hear,
Winn'st from his fatal grasp the spear,
And hidest in wreaths of flowers his bloodless sword!
Thou who, amidst the deathful field,
By godlike chiefs alone beheld,
Oft with thy bosom bare art found,
Pleading for him the youth who sinks to ground:
See, Mercy, see, with pure and loaded hands,
Before thy shrine my country's genius stands,
And decks thy altar still, though pierced with many a wound.

ANTISTROPHE.

When he whom even our joys provoke,
The fiend of nature joined his yoke,
And rushed in wrath to make our isle his prey;
Thy form, from out thy sweet abode,
O'ertook him on his blasted road,
And stopped his wheels, and looked his rage away.
I see recoil his sable steeds,
That bore him swift to savage deeds,
Thy tender melting eyes they own;
O, maid, for all thy love to Britain shown,

Where Justice bars her iron tower,
To thee we build a roseate bower;
Thou, thou shalt rule our queen, and share our monarch's throne!

ODE TO LIBERTY.

STROPHE.

Who shall wake the Spartan fife,
And call in solemn sounds to life
The youths, whose locks divinely spreading,
Like vernal hyacinths in sullen hue,
At once the breath of fear and virtue shedding,
Applauding Freedom loved of old to view?
What new Alcæus, fancy-blest,
Shall sing the sword, in myrtles drest,
At Wisdom's shrine a while its flame concealing,
(What place so fit to seal a deed renowned?)
Till she her brightest lightnings round revealing,
It leaped in glory forth, and dealt her prompted wound!
O Goddess, in that feeling hour,
When most its sounds would court thy ears,
Let not my shell's misguided power
E'er draw thy sad, thy mindful tears.
No, Freedom, no, I will not tell
How Rome, before thy weeping face,
With heaviest sound, a giant-statue, fell,
Pushed by a wild and artless race
From off its wide ambitious base,

When Time his northern sons of spoil awoke,
  And all the blended work of strength and grace,
  With many a rude repeated stroke,
And many a barbarous yell, to thousand fragments broke.

EPODE.

Yet, even where'er the least appeared,
The admiring world thy hand revered;
Still, 'midst the scattered states around,
Some remnants of her strength were found;
They saw, by what escaped the storm,
How wondrous rose her perfect form;
How in the great, the labored whole,
Each mighty master poured his soul!
For sunny Florence, seat of art,
Beneath her vines preserved a part,
Till they, whom Science loved to name,
(O who could fear it?) quenched her flame.
And, lo, an humbler relic laid
In jealous Pisa's olive shade!
See small Marino joins the theme,
Though least, not last in thy esteem:
Strike, louder strike the ennobling strings
To those whose merchant sons were kings;
To him, who, decked with pearly pride,
In Adria weds his green-haired bride;
Hail, port of glory, wealth, and pleasure,
Ne'er let me change this Lydian measure:
Nor e'er her former pride relate,
To sad Liguria's bleeding state.
Ah, no! more pleased thy haunts I seek,
On wild Helvetia's mountains bleak

(Where, when the favored of thy choice,
The daring archer, heard thy voice,
Forth from his eyrie roused in dread,
The ravening eagle northward fled) :
Or dwell in willowed meads more near,
With those to whom thy stork is dear :
Those whom the rod of Alva bruised,
Whose crown a British queen refused!
The magic works, thou feel'st the strains,
One holier name alone remains;
The perfect spell shall then avail,
Hail, Nymph, adored by Britain, hail!

ANTISTROPHE.

Beyond the measure vast of thought,
The works the wizard Time has wrought!
The Gaul, 't is held of antique story,
Saw Britain linked to his now adverse strand,
No sea between, nor cliff sublime and hoary,
He passed with unwet feet through all our land.
To the blown Baltic then, they say,
The wild waves found another way,
Where Orcas howls, his wolfish mountains rounding;
Till all the banded west at once 'gan rise,
A wide wild storm, even Nature's self confounding,
Withering her giant sons with strange uncouth surprise.
This pillared earth so firm and wide,
By winds and inward labors torn,
In thunders dread was pushed aside,
And down the shouldering billows borne.
And see, like gems, her laughing train,
The little isles on every side.

Mona, once hid from those who search the main,
  Where thousand elfin shapes abide,
And Wight who checks the westering tide,
  For thee consenting Heaven has each bestowed,
A fair attendant on her sovereign pride:
  To thee this blest divorce she owed,
For thou hast made her vales thy loved, thy last abode!

SECOND EPODE.

Then, too, 't is said, an hoary pile,
'Midst the green navel of our isle,
Thy shrine in some religious wood,
O soul-enforcing Goddess, stood!
There oft the painted native's feet
Were wont thy form celestial meet:
Though now with hopeless toil we trace
Time's backward rolls, to find its place;
Whether the fiery-tressèd Dane,
Or Roman's self, o'erturned the fane,
Or in what Heaven-left age it fell,
'T were hard for modern song to tell.
Yet still, if Truth those beams infuse,
Which guide at once and charm the Muse,
Beyond yon braided clouds that lie,
Paving the light embroidered sky,
Amidst the bright pavilioned plains,
The beauteous model still remains.
There, happier than in islands blest,
Or bowers by Spring or Hebe drest,
The chiefs who fill our Albion's story,
In warlike weeds, retired in glory,
Hear their consorted Druids sing
Their triumphs to the immortal string.

How may the poet now unfold
What never tongue or numbers told?
How learn delighted, and amazed,
What hands unknown that fabric raised?
Even now before his favored eyes,
In Gothic pride, it seems to rise!
Yet Græcia's graceful orders join,
Majestic, through the mixed design:
The secret builder knew to choose
Each sphere-found gem of richest hues;
Whate'er heaven's purer mould contains,
When nearer suns emblaze its veins;
There on the walls the patriot's sight
May ever hang with fresh delight,
And, graved with some prophetic rage,
Read Albion's fame through every age.
  Ye forms divine, ye laureate band,
That near her inmost altar stand!
Now soothe her to her blissful train
Blithe Concord's social form to gain;
Concord, whose myrtle wand can steep
Even Anger's bloodshot eyes in sleep;
Before whose breathing bosom's balm
Rage drops his steel, and storms grow calm:
Here let our sires and matrons hoar
Welcome to Britain's ravaged shore;
Our youths, enamored of the fair,
Play with the tangles of her hair,
Till, in one loud applauding sound,
The nations shout to her around,
O, how supremely art thou blest,
Thou, Lady — thou shalt rule the west!

ODE TO A LADY,

ON THE DEATH OF COLONEL ROSS, IN THE ACTION OF FONTENOY.

Written in May, 1745.

WHILE, lost to all his former mirth,
Britannia's genius bends to earth,
And mourns the fatal day:
While stained with blood he strives to tear
Unseemly from his sea-green hair
The wreaths of cheerful May:

The thoughts which musing Pity pays,
And fond Remembrance loves to raise,
Your faithful hours attend;
Still Fancy, to herself unkind,
Awakes to grief the softened mind,
And points the bleeding friend.

By rapid Scheld's descending wave
His country's vows shall bless the grave,
Where'er the youth is laid:
That sacred spot the village hind
With every sweetest turf shall bind,
And Peace protect the shade.

Blest youth, regardful of thy doom,
Aërial hands shall build thy tomb,
With shadowy trophies crowned;
Whilst Honor bathed in tears shall rove
To sigh thy name through every grove,
And call his heroes round.

The warlike dead of every age,
Who fill the fair recording page,
Shall leave their sainted rest;
And, half reclining on his spear,
Each wondering chief by turns appear,
To hail the blooming guest:

Old Edward's sons, unknown to yield,
Shall crowd from Cressy's laurelled field,
And gaze with fixed delight;
Again for Britain's wrongs they feel,
Again they snatch the gleamy steel,
And wish the avenging fight.

But, lo! where, sunk in deep despair,
Her garments torn, her bosom bare,
Impatient Freedom lies!
Her matted tresses madly spread,
To every sod, which wraps the dead,
She turns her joyless eyes.

Ne'er shall she leave that lowly ground
Till notes of triumph bursting round
Proclaim her reign restored:
Till William seek the sad retreat,
And, bleeding at her sacred feet,
Present the sated sword.

If, weak to soothe so soft a heart,
These pictured glories naught impart,
To dry thy constant tear:
If yet in Sorrow's distant eye
Exposed and pale thou seest him lie,
Wild War insulting near:

Where'er from time thou court'st relief,
The Muse shall still, with social grief,
    Her gentlest promise keep;
Even humbled Harting's cottaged vale
Shall learn the sad repeated tale,
    And bid her shepherds weep.

ODE TO EVENING.

If aught of oaten stop, or pastoral song,
May hope, chaste Eve, to soothe thy modest ear,
    Like thy own brawling springs,
    Thy springs, and dying gales;

O, Nymph reserved, while now the bright-haired sun
Sits in yon western tent, whose cloudy skirts,
    With brede ethereal wove,
    O'erhang his wavy bed:

Now air is hushed, save where the weak-eyed bat
With short shrill shriek flits by on leathern wing;
    Or where the beetle winds
    His small but sullen horn,

As oft he rises 'midst the twilight path,
Against the pilgrim borne in heedless hum:
    Now teach me, maid composed,
    To breathe some softened strain,

Whose numbers, stealing through thy darkening vale,
May not unseemly with its stillness suit·
As, musing slow, I hail
Thy genial loved return!

For when thy folding-star arising shows
His paly circlet, at his warning lamp
The fragrant Hours, and Elves
Who slept in buds the day,

And many a Nymph who wreathes her brows with sedge,
And sheds the freshening dew, and, lovelier still,
The pensive Pleasures sweet,
Prepare thy shadowy car.

Then let me rove some wild and heathy scene;
Or find some ruin, 'midst its dreary dells,
Whose walls more awful nod
By thy religious gleams.

Or, if chill blustering winds, or driving rain,
Prevent my willing feet, be mine the hut,
That, from the mountain's side,
Views wilds, and swelling floods,

And hamlets brown, and dim-discovered spires;
And hears their simple bell, and marks o'er all
Thy dewy fingers draw
The gradual dusky veil.

While Spring shall pour his showers, as oft he wont,
And bathe thy breathing tresses, meekest Eve!
While Summer loves to sport
Beneath thy lingering light;

While sallow Autumn fills thy lap with leaves;
Or Winter, yelling through the troublous air,
Affrights thy shrinking train,
And rudely rends thy robes;

So long, regardful of thy quiet rule,
Shall Fancy, Friendship, Science, smiling Peace,
Thy gentlest influence own,
And love thy favorite name!

ODE TO PEACE.

O THOU, who badest thy turtles bear
Swift from his grasp thy golden hair,
And sought'st thy native skies;
When War, by vultures drawn from far,
To Britain bent his iron car,
And bade his storms arise!

Tired of his rude tyrannic sway,
Our youth shall fix some festive day,
His sullen shrines to burn:
But thou who hear'st the turning spheres,
What sounds may charm thy partial ears,
And gain thy blest return!

O Peace, thy injured robes up-bind!
O rise! and leave not one behind
Of all thy beamy train!
The British Lion, goddess sweet,
Lies stretched on earth to kiss thy feet,
And own thy holier reign.

Let others court thy transient smile,
But come to grace thy western isle,
By warlike Honor led;
And, while around her ports rejoice,
While all her sons adore thy choice,
With him forever wed!

THE MANNERS.

AN ODE.

Farewell, for clearer ken designed,
The dim-discovered tracts of mind;
Truths which, from action's paths retired,
My silent search in vain required!
No more my sail that deep explores;
No more I search those magic shores;
What regions part the world of soul,
Or whence thy streams, Opinion, roll:
If e'er I round such fairy field,
Some power impart the spear and shield,
At which the wizard Passions fly;
By which the giant Follies die!

Farewell the porch whose roof is seen
Arched with the enlivening olive's green:
Where Science, pranked in tissued vest,
By Reason, Pride, and Fancy drest,
Comes, like a bride, so trim arrayed,
To wed with Doubt in Plato's shade!

Youth of the quick uncheated sight,
Thy walks, Observance, more invite!

O thou who lovest that ampler range,
Where life's wide prospects round thee change,
And, with her mingling sons allied,
Throwest the prattling page aside,
To me, in converse sweet, impart
To read in man the native heart;
To learn, where Science sure is found,
From Nature as she lives around;
And, gazing oft her mirror true,
By turns each shifting image view!
Till meddling Art's officious lore
Reverse the lessons taught before;
Alluring from a safer rule,
To dream in her enchanted school:
Thou, Heaven, whate'er of great we boast,
Hast blest this social science most.

Retiring hence to thoughtful cell,
As Fancy breathes her potent spell,
Not vain she finds the charmful task,
In pageant quaint, in motley mask;
Behold, before her musing eyes,
The countless Manners round her rise;
While, ever varying as they pass,
To some Contempt applies her glass:
With these the white-robed maids combine;
And those the laughing Satyrs join!
But who is he whom now she views,
In robe of wild contending hues?
Thou by the Passions nursed, I greet
The comic sock that binds thy feet!

O Humor, thou whose name is known
To Britain's favored isle alone:
Me too amidst thy band admit;
There where the young-eyed healthful Wit
(Whose jewels in his crispéd hair
Are placed each other's beams to share;
Whom no delights from thee divide),
In laughter loosed, attends thy side.

By old Miletus, who so long
Has ceased his love-inwoven song;
By all you taught the Tuscan maids,
In changed Italia's modern shades;
By him whose knight's distinguished name
Refined a nation's lust of fame;
Whose tales e'en now, with echo sweet,
Castilia's Moorish hills repeat;
Or him whom Seine's blue nymphs deplore,
In watchet weeds on Gallia's shore;
Who drew the sad Sicilian maid,
By virtues in her sire betrayed.

O Nature boon, from whom proceed
Each forceful thought, each prompted deed;
If but from thee I hope to feel,
On all my heart imprint thy seal!
Let some retreating cynic find
Those oft-turned scrolls I leave behind:
The Sports and I this hour agree,
To rove thy scene-full world with thee!

THE PASSIONS.

AN ODE FOR MUSIC.

When Music, heavenly maid, was young,
While yet in early Greece she sung,
The Passions oft, to hear her shell,
Thronged around her magic cell,
Exulting, trembling, raging, fainting,
Possessed beyond the Muse's painting:
By turns they felt the glowing mind
Disturbed, delighted, raised, refined;
Till once, 't is said, when all were fired,
Filled with fury, rapt, inspired,
From the supporting myrtles round
They snatched her instruments of sound;
And, as they oft had heard apart
Sweet lessons of her forceful art,
Each (for Madness ruled the hour)
Would prove his own expressive power.

First Fear his hand, its skill to try,
Amid the chords bewildered laid,
And back recoiled, he knew not why,
Even at the sound himself had made.

Next Anger rushed; his eyes on fire,
In lightnings owned his secret stings:
In one rude clash he struck the lyre,
And swept with hurried hand the strings.

With woful measures wan Despair
Low, sullen sounds his grief beguiled,

A solemn, strange, and mingled air;
'T was sad by fits, by starts 't was wild.

But thou, O Hope, with eyes so fair,
What was thy delighted measure?
Still it whispered promised pleasure,
And bade the lovely scenes at distance hail!
Still would her touch the strain prolong;
And from the rocks, the woods, the vale,
She called on Echo still, through all the song;
And, where her sweetest theme she chose,
A soft responsive voice was heard at every close,
And Hope enchanted smiled, and waved her golden hair.
And longer had she sung; — but, with a frown,
Revenge impatient rose:
He threw his blood-stained sword, in thunder, down;
And, with a withering look,
The war-denouncing trumpet took,
And blew a blast so loud and dread,
Were ne'er prophetic sounds so full of woe!
And, ever and anon, he beat
The doubling drum, with furious heat;
And though sometimes, each dreary pause between,
Dejected Pity, at his side,
Her soul-subduing voice applied,
Yet still he kept his wild unaltered mien,
While each strained ball of sight seemed bursting from his head.

Thy numbers, Jealousy, to naught were fixed;
Sad proof of thy distressful state;
Of differing themes the veering song was mixed;
And now it courted Love, now raving called on Hate.

With eyes upraised, as one inspired,
Pale Melancholy sate retired;
And, from her wild sequestered seat,
In notes by distance made more sweet,
Poured through the mellow horn her pensive soul:
  And, dashing soft from rocks around,
  Bubbling runnels joined the sound;
Through glades and glooms the mingled measure stole,
  Or o'er some haunted stream, with fond delay,
    Round an holy calm diffusing,
    Love of Peace, and lonely musing,
  In hollow murmurs died away.

But, O! how altered was its sprightlier tone,
When Cheerfulness, a nymph of healthiest hue,
  Her bow across her shoulder flung,
  Her buskins gemmed with morning dew,
Blew an inspiring air, that dale and thicket rung,
  The hunter's call, to Faun and Dryad known!
The oak-crowned Sisters, and their chaste-eyed Queen,
  Satyrs and Sylvan Boys, were seen,
  Peeping from forth their alleys green:
  Brown Exercise rejoiced to hear;
  And Sport leapt up, and seized his beechen spear.
  Last came Joy's ecstatic trial:
  He, with viny crown advancing,
    First to the lively pipe his hand addrest;
  But soon he saw the brisk awakening viol,
    Whose sweet entrancing voice he loved the best;
  They would have thought who heard the strain
    They saw, in Tempe's vale, her native maids,
    Amidst the festal sounding shades,
  To some unwearied minstrel dancing,

While, as his flying fingers kissed the strings,
Love framed with Mirth a gay fantastic round:
Loose were her tresses seen, her zone unbound;
And he, amidst his frolic play,
As if he would the charming air repay,
Shook thousand odors from his dewy wings.

O Music! sphere-descended maid,
Friend of Pleasure, Wisdom's aid!
Why, goddess! why, to us denied,
Lay'st thou thy ancient lyre aside?
As, in that loved Athenian bower,
You learned an all-commanding power,
Thy mimic soul, O Nymph endeared,
Can well recall what then it heard;
Where is thy native simple heart,
Devote to Virtue, Fancy, Art?
Arise, as in that elder time,
Warm, energic, chaste, sublime!
Thy wonders, in that godlike age,
Fill thy recording Sister's page —
'T is said, and I believe the tale,
Thy humblest reed could more prevail,
Had more of strength, diviner rage,
Than all which charms this laggard age;
Even all at once together found,
Cecilia's mingled world of sound —
O, bid our vain endeavors cease;
Revive the just designs of Greece:
Return in all thy simple state!
Confirm the tales her sons relate!

ODE ON THE DEATH OF THOMSON.

THE SCENE IS SUPPOSED TO LIE ON THE THAMES, NEAR RICHMOND

In yonder grave a Druid lies,
  Where slowly winds the stealing wave;
The year's best sweets shall duteous rise
  To deck its poet's sylvan grave.

In yon deep bed of whispering reeds
  His airy harp shall now be laid,
That he, whose heart in sorrow bleeds,
  May love through life the soothing shade.

Then maids and youths shall linger here,
  And while its sounds at distance swell,
Shall sadly seem in Pity's ear
  To hear the woodland pilgrim's knell.

Remembrance oft shall haunt the shore
  When Thames in summer wreaths is drest,
And oft suspend the dashing oar,
  To bid his gentle spirit rest!

And oft, as ease and health retire
  To breezy lawn, or forest deep,
The friend shall view yon whitening spire
  And 'mid the varied landscape weep.

But thou, who own'st that earthy bed,
  Ah! what will every dirge avail!
Or tears, which Love and Pity shed,
  That mourn beneath the gliding sail!

Yet lives there one, whose heedless eye
  Shall scorn thy pale shrine glimmering near?
With him, sweet bard, may Fancy die,
  And Joy desert the blooming year!

But thou, lorn stream, whose sullen tide
  No sedge-crowned sisters now attend,
Now waft me from the green hill's side,
  Whose cold turf hides the buried friend!

And see, the fairy valleys fade;
  Dun night has veiled the solemn view!
Yet once again, dear parted shade,
  Meek Nature's child again adieu!

The genial meads, assigned to bless
  Thy life, shall mourn thy early doom;
Their hinds and shepherd-girls shall dress,
  With simple hands, thy rural tomb.

Long, long, thy stone and pointed clay
  Shall melt the musing Briton's eyes:
O! vales and wild woods, shall he say,
  In yonder grave your Druid lies!

ODE ON THE POPULAR SUPERSTITIONS OF THE HIGHLANDS OF SCOTLAND;

CONSIDERED AS THE SUBJECT OF POETRY; INSCRIBED TO MR. JOHN HOME.

I.

HOME, thou return'st from Thames, whose Naiads long
Have seen thee lingering with a fond delay,
'Mid those soft friends, whose hearts, some future day,
Shall melt, perhaps, to hear thy tragic song.
Go, not unmindful of that cordial youth
Whom, long endeared, thou leavest by Lavant's side;
Together let us wish him lasting truth,
And joy untainted with his destined bride.
Go! nor regardless, while these numbers boast
My short-lived bliss, forget my social name;
But think, far off, how, on the southern coast,
I met thy friendship with an equal flame!
Fresh to that soil thou turn'st, where every vale
Shall prompt the poet, and his song demand:
To thee thy copious subjects ne'er shall fail;
Thou need'st but take thy pencil to thy hand,
And paint what all believe, who own thy genial land.

II.

There must thou wake perforce thy Doric quill;
'T is Fancy's land to which thou sett'st thy feet;
Where still, 't is said, the fairy people meet,
Beneath each birken shade, on mead or hill;

There, each trim lass, that skims the milky store,
  To the swart tribes their creamy bowls allots;
By night they sip it round the cottage door,
  While airy minstrels warble jocund notes.
There, every herd, by sad experience, knows
  How, winged with fate, their elf-shot arrows fly,
When the sick ewe her summer food foregoes,
  Or, stretched on earth, the heart-smit heifers lie.
Such airy beings awe the untutored swain:
  Nor thou, though learned, his homelier thoughts neglect;
Let thy sweet muse the rural faith sustain;
  These are the themes of simple, sure effect,
That add new conquests to her boundless reign,
And fill, with double force, her heart-commanding strain.

III.

Even yet preserved, how often may'st thou hear,
  Where to the pole the Boreal mountains run,
  Taught by the father, to his listening son,
Strange lays, whose power had charmed a Spenser's ear
At every pause, before thy mind possest,
  Old Runic bards shall seem to rise around,
With uncouth lyres, in many-colored vest,
  Their matted hair with boughs fantastic crowned:
Whether thou bidd'st the well-taught hind repeat
  The choral dirge, that mourns some chieftain brave,
When every shrieking maid her bosom beat,
  And strewed with choicest herbs his scented grave!
Or whether, sitting in the shepherd's shiel,
  Thou hear'st some sounding tale of war's alarms;
When at the bugle's call, with fire and steel,
  The sturdy clans poured forth their brawny swarms,
And hostile brothers met, to prove each other's arms.

IV.

'T is thine to sing, how, framing hideous spells,
In Sky's lone isle, the gifted wizard seer,
Lodged in the wintry cave with Fate's fell spear,
Or in the depth of Uist's dark forest dwells:
How they, whose sight such dreary dreams engross,
With their own visions oft astonished droop,
When, o'er the watery strath, or quaggy moss,
They see the gliding ghosts unbodied troop.
Or, if in sports, or on the festive green,
Their destined glance some fated youth descry,
Who now, perhaps, in lusty vigor seen,
And rosy health, shall soon lamented die.
For them the viewless forms of air obey;
Their bidding heed, and at their beck repair:
They know what spirit brews the stormful day,
And heartless, oft like moody madness, stare
To see the phantom train their secret work prepare.

V.

To monarchs dear, some hundred miles astray,
Oft have they seen Fate give the fatal blow!
The seer, in Skye, shrieked as the blood did flow,
When headless Charles warm on the scaffold lay!
As Boreas threw his young Aurora forth,
In the first year of the first George's reign
And battles raged in welkin of the North,
They mourned in air, fell, fell Rebellion slain!
And as, of late, they joyed in Preston's fight,
Saw, at sad Falkirk, all their hopes near crowned!
They raved! divining, through their second sight,
Pale, red Culloden, where these hopes were drowned!

Illustrious William! Britain's guardian name!
  One William saved us from a tyrant's stroke;
He, for a sceptre, gained heroic fame,
  But thou, more glorious, Slavery's chain hast broke,
To reign a private man, and bow to Freedom's yoke!

VI.

These, too, thou'lt sing! for well thy magic muse
  Can to the topmost heaven of grandeur soar;
  Or stoop to wail the swain that is no more!
Ah, homely swains! your homeward steps ne'er lose;
Let not dank Will mislead you to the heath;
  Dancing in murky night, o'er fen and lake,
He glows, to draw you downward to your death,
  In his bewitched, low, marshy, willow brake!
What though far off, from some dark dell espied,
  His glimmering mazes cheer the excursive sight,
Yet turn, ye wanderers, turn your steps aside,
  Nor trust the guidance of that faithless light;
For watchful, lurking 'mid the unrustling reed,
  At those mirk hours the wily monster lies,
And listens oft to hear the passing steed,
  And frequent round him rolls his sullen eyes,
If chance his savage wrath may some weak wretch surprise.

VII.

Ah, luckless swain, o'er all unblest, indeed!
  Whom late bewildered in the dank, dark fen,
  Far from his flocks, and smoking hamlet, then!
To that sad spot where hums the sedgy weed:
On him, enraged, the fiend, in angry mood,
  Shall never look with pity's kind concern,

But instant, furious, raise the whelming flood
O'er its drowned banks, forbidding all return!
Or, if he meditate his wished escape
To some dim hill, that seems uprising near,
To his faint eye the grim and grisly shape,
In all its terrors clad, shall wild appear.
Meantime the watery surge shall round him rise,
Poured sudden forth from every swelling source!
What now remains but tears and hopeless sighs?
His fear-shook limbs have lost their youthful force,
And down the waves he floats, a pale and breathless corse!

VIII.

For him in vain his anxious wife shall wait,
Or wander forth to meet him on his way;
For him in vain at to-fall of the day,
His babes shall linger at the unclosing gate!
Ah, ne'er shall he return! Alone, if night
Her travelled limbs in broken slumbers steep,
With drooping willows dressed, his mournful sprite
Shall visit sad, perchance, her silent sleep:
Then he, perhaps, with moist and watery hand,
Shall fondly seem to press her shuddering cheek,
And with his blue swollen face before her stand,
And, shivering cold, these piteous accents speak:
"Pursue, dear wife, thy daily toils pursue,
At dawn or dusk, industrious as before;
Nor e'er of me one helpless thought renew,
While I lie weltering on the osiered shore,
Drowned by the Kelpie's wrath, nor e'er shall aid thee more!"

IX.

Unbounded is thy range; with varied skill
Thy muse may, like those feathery tribes which spring

From their rude rocks, extend her skirting wing
Round the moist marge of each cold Hebrid isle,
To that hoar pile which still its ruins shows :
In whose small vaults a pigmy folk is found,
Whose bones the delver with his spade upthrows,
And culls them, wondering, from the hallowed ground !
Or thither, where, beneath the showery west,
The mighty kings of three fair realms are laid ;
Once foes, perhaps, together now they rest,
No slaves revere them, and no wars invade :
Yet frequent now, at midnight's solemn hour,
The rifted mounds their yawning cells unfold,
And forth the monarchs stalk with sovereign power,
In pageant robes, and wreathed with sheeny gold,
And on their twilight tombs aërial council hold.

X.

But, O, o'er all, forget not Kilda's race,
On whose bleak rocks, which brave the wasting tides,
Fair Nature's daughter, Virtue, yet abides.
Go ! just, as they, their blameless manners trace !
Then to my ear transmit some gentle song,
Of those whose lives are yet sincere and plain,
Their bounded walks the rugged cliffs along,
And all their prospect but the wintry main.
With sparing temperance, at the needful time,
They drain the scented spring ; or, hunger-prest,
Along the Atlantic rock undreading climb,
And of its eggs despoil the solan's nest.
Thus, blest in primal innocence, they live
Sufficed, and happy with that frugal fare
Which tasteful toil and hourly danger give.

Hard is their shallow soil, and bleak and bare;
Nor ever vernal bee was heard to murmur there!

XI.

Nor need'st thou blush that such false themes engage
Thy gentle mind, of fairer stores possest;
For not alone they touch the village breast,
But filled, in elder time, the historic page.
There, Shakspeare's self, with every garland crowned,
Flew to those fairy climes his fancy sheen,
In musing hour; his wayward sisters found,
And with their terrors dressed the magic scene.
From them he sung, when, 'mid his bold design,
Before the Scot, afflicted, and aghast!
The shadowy kings of Banquo's fated line
Through the dark cave in gleamy pageant passed.
Proceed! nor quit the tales which, simply told,
Could once so well my answering bosom pierce;
Proceed, in forceful sounds, and colors bold,
The native legends of thy land rehearse;
To such adapt thy lyre, and suit thy powerful verse.

XII.

In scenes like these, which, daring to depart
From sober truth, are still to nature true,
And call forth fresh delight to Fancy's view,
The heroic Muse employed her Tasso's art!
How have I trembled, when, at Tancred's stroke,
Its gushing blood the gaping cypress poured!
When each live plant with mortal accents spoke,
And the wild blast upheaved the vanished sword!
How have I sat, when piped the pensive wind,
To hear his harp by British Fairfax strung!

Prevailing poet! whose undoubting mind
  Believed the magic wonders which he sung!
Hence, at each sound, imagination glows!
  Hence, at each picture, vivid life starts here!
Hence his warm lay with softest sweetness flows!
  Melting it flows, pure, murmuring, strong, and clear,
And fills the impassioned heart, and wins the harmonious ear!

XIII.

All hail, ye scenes that o'er my soul prevail!
  Ye splendid friths and lakes, which, far away,
  Are by smooth Annan filled, or pastoral Tay,
Or Don's romantic springs, at distance hail!
The time shall come, when I, perhaps, may tread
  Your lowly glens, o'erhung with spreading broom;
Or, o'er your stretching heaths, by Fancy led;
  Or, o'er your mountains creep, in awful gloom!
Then will I dress once more the faded bower,
  Where Jonson sat in Drummond's classic shade;
Or crop, from Teviotdale, each lyric flower,
  And mourn, on Yarrow's banks, where Willy 's laid!
Meantime, ye powers that on the plains which bore
  The cordial youth, on Lothian's plains, attend!
Where'er Home dwells, on hill, or lowly moor,
  To him I lose your kind protection lend,
And, touched with love like mine, preserve my absent friend!

MISCELLANEOUS POEMS.

8

MISCELLANEOUS POEMS.

AN EPISTLE,

ADDRESSED TO SIR THOMAS HANMER, ON HIS EDITION OF SHAKSPEARE'S WORKS.

SIR,

WHILE, born to bring the Muse's happier days,
A patriot's hand protects a poet's lays,
While nursed by you she sees her myrtles bloom,
Green and unwithered o'er his honored tomb;
Excuse her doubts, if yet she fears to tell
What secret transports in her bosom swell:
With conscious awe she hears the critic's fame,
And blushing hides her wreath at Shakspeare's name.
Hard was the lot those injured strains endured,
Unowned by Science, and by years obscured:
Fair Fancy wept; and echoing sighs confessed
A fixed despair in every tuneful breast.
Not with more grief the afflicted swains appear,
When wintry winds deform the plenteous year;
When lingering frosts the ruined seats invade
Where Peace resorted, and the Graces played.

Each rising art by just gradation moves,
Toil builds on toil, and age on age improves:

The Muse alone unequal dealt her rage,
And graced with noblest pomp her earliest stage.
Preserved through time, the speaking scenes impart
Each changeful wish of Phædra's tortured heart;
Or paint the curse that marked the Theban's reign,
A bed incestuous, and a father slain.
With kind concern our pitying eyes o'erflow,
Trace the sad tale, and own another's woe.

To Rome removed, with wit secure to please,
The comic Sisters kept their native ease:
With jealous fear, declining Greece beheld
Her own Menander's art almost excelled;
But every Muse essayed to raise in vain
Some labored rival of her tragic strain:
Ilissus' laurels, though transferred with toil,
Drooped their fair leaves, nor knew the unfriendly soil.

As Arts expired, resistless Dulness rose;
Goths, Priests, or Vandals, — all were Learning's foes.
Till Julius first recalled each exiled maid,
And Cosmo owned them in the Etrurian shade:
Then, deeply skilled in Love's engaging theme,
The soft Provençal passed to Arno's stream:
With graceful ease the wanton lyre he strung;
Sweet flowed the lays — but Love was all he sung.
The gay description could not fail to move,
For, led by Nature, all are friends to Love.

But Heaven, still various in its works, decreed
The perfect boast of time should last succeed.
The beauteous union must appear at length,
Of Tuscan fancy, and Athenian strength:
One greater Muse Eliza's reign adorn,
And even a Shakspeare to her fame be born!

Yet, ah! so bright her morning's opening ray,
In vain our Britain hoped an equal day!
No second growth the western isle could bear,
At once exhausted with too rich a year.
Too nicely Jonson knew the critic's part;
Nature in him was almost lost in art.
Of softer mould the gentle Fletcher came,
The next in order, as the next in name;
With pleased attention, 'midst his scenes we find
Each glowing thought that warms the female mind;
Each melting sigh, and every tender tear;
The lover's wishes, and the virgin's fear.
His every strain the Smiles and Graces own;
But stronger Shakspeare felt for man alone:
Drawn by his pen, our ruder passions stand
The unrivalled picture of his early hand.

With gradual steps and slow, exacter France
Saw Art's fair empire o'er her shores advance:
By length of toil a bright perfection knew,
Correctly bold, and just in all she drew:
Till late Corneille, with Lucan's spirit fired,
Breathed the free strain, as Rome and he inspired:
And classic judgment gained to sweet Racine
The temperate strength of Maro's chaster line.

But wilder far the British laurel spread,
And wreaths less artful crown our poet's head.
Yet he alone to every scene could give
The historian's truth, and bid the manners live.
Waked at his call I view, with glad surprise,
Majestic forms of mighty monarchs rise.

There Henry's trumpets spread their loud alarms,
And laurelled Conquest waits her hero's arms.
Here gentler Edward claims a pitying sigh,
Scarce born to honors, and so soon to die!
Yet shall thy throne, unhappy infant, bring
No beam of comfort to the guilty king:
The time shall come when Glo'ster's heart shall bleed,
In life's last hours, with horror of the deed;
When dreary visions shall at last present
Thy vengeful image in the midnight tent:
Thy hand unseen the secret death shall bear,
Blunt the weak sword, and break the oppressive spear'

Where'er we turn, by Fancy charmed, we find
Some sweet illusion of the cheated mind.
Oft, wild of wing, she calls the soul to rove
With humbler nature in the rural grove;
Where swains contented own the quiet scene,
And twilight fairies tread the circled green;
Dressed by her hand, the woods and valleys smile,
And Spring diffusive decks the enchanted isle.

O, more than all in powerful genius blest,
Come, take thine empire o'er the willing breast!
Whate'er the wounds this youthful heart shall feel,
Thy songs support me, and thy morals heal!
There every thought the poet's warmth may raise,
There native music dwells in all the lays.
O might some verse with happiest skill persuade
Expressive Picture to adopt thine aid!
What wondrous draughts might rise from every page!
What other Raphaels charm a distant age!

Methinks even now I view some free design,
Where breathing nature lives in every line:
Chaste and subdued the modest lights decay,
Steal into shades, and mildly melt away.
And see where Anthony, in tears approved,
Guards the pale relics of the chief he loved:
O'er the cold corse the warrior seems to bend,
Deep sunk in grief, and mourns his murdered friend!
Still, as they press, he calls on all around,
Lifts the torn robe, and points the bleeding wound.

But who is he, whose brows exalted bear
A wrath impatient, and a fiercer air?
Awake to all that injured worth can feel,
On his own Rome he turns the avenging steel;
Yet shall not war's insatiate fury fall
(So Heaven ordains it) on the destined wall.
See the fond mother, 'midst the plaintive train,
Hung on his knees, and prostrate on the plain!
Touched to the soul, in vain he strives to hide
The son's affection in the Roman's pride:
O'er all the man conflicting passions rise;
Rage grasps the sword, while Pity melts the eyes.

Thus, generous Critic, as thy Bard inspires,
The sister Arts shall nurse their drooping fires;
Each from his scenes her stores alternate bring,
Blend the fair tints, or wake the vocal string:
Those Sibyl leaves, the sport of every wind
(For poets ever were a careless kind),
By thee disposed, no further toil demand,
But, just to Nature, own thy forming hand.

So spread o'er Greece, the harmonious whole unknown,
Even Homer's numbers charmed by parts alone.

Their own Ulysses scarce had wandered more,
By winds and waters cast on every shore:
When, raised by Fate, some former Hanmer joined
Each beauteous image of the boundless mind;
And bade, like thee, his Athens ever claim
A fond alliance with the Poet's name.

Oxford, Dec. 3, 1743.

DIRGE IN CYMBELINE,

SUNG BY GUIDERUS AND ARVIRAGUS OVER FIDELE, SUPPOSED TO BE DEAD.

To fair Fidele's grassy tomb
  Soft maids and village hinds shall bring
Each opening sweet of earliest bloom,
  And rifle all the breathing spring.

No wailing ghost shall dare appear
  To vex with shrieks this quiet grove;
But shepherd lads assemble here,
  And melting virgins own their love.

No withered witch shall here be seen;
  No goblins lead their nightly crew:
The female fays shall haunt the green,
  And dress thy grave with pearly dew!

The redbreast oft, at evening hours,
  Shall kindly lend his little aid,
With hoary moss, and gathered flowers,
  To deck the ground where thou art laid.

When howling winds, and beating rain,
  In tempests shake the sylvan cell;
Or 'midst the chase, on every plain,
  The tender thought on thee shall dwell;

Each lonely scene shall thee restore;
  For thee the tear be duly shed;
Beloved till life can charm no more,
  And mourned till Pity's self be dead.

VERSES

WRITTEN ON A PAPER WHICH CONTAINED A PIECE OF BRIDE-CAKE, GIVEN TO THE AUTHOR BY A LADY.

Ye curious hands, that, hid from vulgar eyes,
  By search profane shall find this hallowed cake,
With Virtue's awe forbear the sacred prize,
  Nor dare a theft, for Love and Pity's sake!

This precious relic, formed by magic power,
  Beneath her shepherd's haunted pillow laid,
Was meant by Love to charm the silent hour,
  The secret present of a matchless maid.

The Cyprian queen, at Hymen's fond request,
  Each nice ingredient chose with happiest art;
Fears, sighs, and wishes of the enamored breast,
  And pains that please, are mixed in every part.

With rosy hand the spicy fruit she brought,
  From Paphian hills and fair Cythera's isle;
And tempered sweet with these the melting thought,
  The kiss ambrosial, and the yielding smile.

Ambiguous looks, that scorn and yet relent,
  Denials mild, and firm unaltered truth;
Reluctant pride, and amorous faint consent,
  And meeting ardors, and exulting youth.

Sleep, wayward god! hath sworn, while these remain,
  With flattering dreams to dry his nightly tear,
And cheerful Hope, so oft invoked in vain,
  With fairy songs shall soothe his pensive ear.

If, bound by vows to Friendship's gentle side,
  And fond of soul, thou hopest an equal grace,
If youth or maid thy joys and griefs divide,
  O, much entreated, leave this fatal place!

Sweet Peace, who long hath shunned my plaintive day,
  Consents at length to bring me short delight,
Thy careless steps may scare her doves away,
  And Grief with raven note usurp the night.

TO MISS AURELIA C——R,

ON HER WEEPING AT HER SISTER'S WEDDING.

Cease, fair Aurelia, cease to mourn,
  Lament not Hannah's happy state;
You may be happy in your turn,
  And seize the treasure you regret.

With Love united Hymen stands,
  And softly whispers to your charms,
"Meet but your lover in my bands,
  You'll find your sister in his arms."

SONNET.

WHEN Phœbe formed a wanton smile,
My soul! it reached not here:
Strange, that thy peace, thou trembler, flies
Before a rising tear!
From 'midst the drops my love is born
That o'er those eyelids rove:
Thus issued from a teeming wave
The fabled queen of love.

SONG.

THE SENTIMENTS BORROWED FROM SHAKSPEARE.

YOUNG Damon of the vale is dead,
Ye lowly hamlets, moan;
A dewy turf lies o'er his head,
And at his feet a stone.

His shroud, which Death's cold damps destroy,
Of snow-white threads was made:
All mourned to see so sweet a boy
In earth forever laid.

Pale pansies o'er his corpse were placed,
Which, plucked before their time,
Bestrewed the boy, like him to waste
And wither in their prime.

But will he ne'er return, whose tongue
Could tune the rural lay?
Ah, no! his bell of peace is rung,
His lips are cold as clay.

They bore him out at twilight hour,
   The youth who loved so well:
Ah, me! how many a true love shower
   Of kind remembrance fell!

Each maid was woe — but Lucy chief,
   Her grief o'er all was tried;
Within his grave she dropped in grief,
   And o'er her loved one died.

NOTES TO COLLINS.

ORIENTAL ECLOGUES.

Page 30, line 16. — Bassora, the gulf of that name, famous for the pearl fishery.

Page 33, line 4.

"In this line he does not merely seem to describe the sultry desert, but brings it home to the senses." — *Campbell.*

Page 35, line 17.

That these flowers are found in very great abundance in some of the provinces of Persia, see the "Modern History" of the ingenious Mr. Salmon. — *Collins.*

Ode to Pity.

Page 43, line 7.

Pella's bard, Euripides, of whom Aristotle pronounces, on a comparison of him with Sophocles, that he was the greater master of the tender passions, ἦν τραγικώτερος. — *Collins.*

Page 43, line 16.

The river Arun runs by the village of Trotton, in Sussex, where Otway had his birth. — *Collins.*

Ode to Fear.

Page 45, line 22.

Alluding to the Κύνας ἀφύκτους of Sophocles. See the Electra.

Page 46, line 3. — The bard — Æschylus.

Page 46, line 11. — The incestuous queen — Jocasta.

Page 46, line 12.

——— οὐδ' ἔτ' ὠρώρει βοή,
'Ην μὲν σιωπή· φθέγμα δ' ἐξαίφνης τινὸς
Θώϋξεν αὐτόν, ὥστε πάντας ὀρθίας
Στῆσαι φόβω δείσαντας ἐξαίφνης τρίχας.

See the Œdip. Colon. of Sophocles.

Page 46, line 18.

"It may be remarked, that when we are anxious to communicate the highest possible character of sublimity to anything we are describing, we generally contrive, either directly, or by means of some strong and obvious association, to introduce the image of the heavens, or of the clouds; or, in other words, of sublimity, properly so called. In Collins' Ode to Fear, the happy use of a single word (*thunders*) identifies at once the physical with the moral sublime, and concentrates the effect of their united force." — *Dugald Stewart.*

Ode to Simplicity.

Page 48, line 8.

The ἀηδών, or nightingale, for which Sophocles seems to have entertained a peculiar fondness.

Ode on the Poetical Character.

Page 49, line 23.

One, only one, unrivalled fair ——

Florimel. See Spenser, Leg. 4th.

Page 51, line 8. — *The tarsel.* — The male falcon.

Ode written in 1746.

Page 52.

"What a quantity of thought is here condensed in the compass of twelve lines, like a cluster of rock crystals, sparkling and distinct, yet receiving and reflecting lustre by their combination. The stanzas themselves are almost unrivalled in the association of poetry with picture, pathos with fancy, grandeur with simplicity, and romance with reality. The melody of the verse leaves nothing for the ear to desire, except a continuance of the strain, or rather the repetition of a strain which cannot tire by repetition. The imagery is of the most delicate and exquisite character." — *James Montgomery's Lectures.*

Ode to Mercy.

Page 53.

Probably written on the occasion of the then recent rebellion, like the shorter ode; the latter being, as Langhorne supposed, consecrated to the memory of those who fell; the former, designed to awaken compassion for the unfortunate prisoners.

Ode to Liberty.

Page 53, line 11.

Alluding to that beautiful fragment of Alcæus:

Εν μύρτου κλαδὶ τὸ ξίφος φορήσω,
Ωσπερ Αρμόδιος κ' Αριστογείτων,
Οτε τὸν τύραννον κτανέτην,
Ισονόμους τ' Αθήνας εποιησάτην.
Φιλταθ' Αρμόδι' οὔ τι που τέθνηκας,
Νήσοις δ' ἐν μακάρων σε φασὶν εἶναι,
Ινα περ ποδώκης Αχιλεύς,
Τυδέιδην τε φασιν Διομήδεα.
Εν μύρτου κλαδὶ τὸ ξίφος φορήσω,
Ωσπερ Αρμόδιος κ' Αριστογείτων,
Οτ' Αθηναίης ἐν θυσίαις
Ανδρα τύραννον Ιππαρχον ἐκαινέτην.
Αεὶ σφῶν κλέος ἔσσεται κατ' αἶαν,
Φίλταθ' Αρμόδιε, κ' Αριστόγειτων,
Οτι τόν τύραννον κτάνετον,
Ισονόμους τ' Αθήνας ἐποιήσατον.

This fragment, we believe, is an entire poem. It has been thus translated.

Hymn

On Harmodius and Aristogiton.

My sword I'll hang upon the myrtle-bough;
Aristogiton and Harmodius brave,
All hail! for since the tyrant fell by you,
A man of Athens is no more a slave.

Beloved Harmodius! but thou art not dead;
To thee those blest isles yield a happier seat,

Where the great soul of swift Achilles fled,
  And brave Tydides found a last retreat.

My sword I'll hang upon the myrtle-bough,
  And once, once more, my country's heroes hail;
Pierced in the public sacrifice by you,
  The tyrant bled, the base Hipparchus fell.

O, live your fame through each revolving age!
  Aristogiton and Harmodius brave!
You sunk in death the ruthless tyrant's rage,
  'T was yours your country's suffering rights to save.

Page 54, line 19.

Let not my shell's misguided power ——

Μὴ μὴ ταῦτα λέγωμες, ἃ δάκρυον ἤγαγε Δηοῖ.

Callimach. *Ὕμνος εἰς Δήμητρα.*

Page 55, line 15. — "*They whom Science loved to name.*" — The family of the Medici.

Page 55, line 19. — The little republic of San Marino.

Page 55, line 22. — The Venetians.

Page 55, line 23. — The Doge of Venice.

Page 55, line 28. — *Liguria* — Genoa.

Page 55, line 30. — *Helvetia* — Switzerland.

Page 56, line 6.

"*Thy stork.*"

The Dutch, amongst whom there are very severe penalties for those who are convicted of killing this bird. They are kept tame in almost all their towns, and particularly at the Hague, of the arms of which they make a part. The common people of Holland are said to entertain a superstitious sentiment, that if the whole species of them should become extinct they should lose their liberties. — *Collins.*

Page 56, line 8. — Queen Elizabeth.

Page 56, line 16.

This tradition is mentioned by several of our old historians. Some naturalists, too, have endeavored to support the probability of the fact by arguments drawn from the correspondent disposition of the two opposite coasts. I do not remember that any poetical use has been hitherto made of it. — *Collins.*

Page 57, line 1.

There is a tradition in the Isle of Man, that a mermaid, becoming enamored of a young man of extraordinary beauty, took an opportunity of meeting him one day, as he walked on the shore, and opened her passion to him, but was received with a coldness occasioned by his horror and surprise at her appearance. This, however, was so misconstrued by the sea-lady, that, in revenge for his treatment of her, she punished the whole island, by covering it with a mist; so that all who attempted to carry on any commerce with it either never arrived at it, but wandered up and down the sea, or were, on a sudden, wrecked upon its cliffs. — *Collins.*

Ode to a Lady.

Page 59.

The lady is believed to have been Miss Elizabeth Goddard, who was then staying at the house of Lord Tankerville, near Chichester, and overlooking the village of Harting. Of this lady, who was engaged to Colonel Ross, Collins is said to have been enamored. She was one day older than himself, and he playfully complained that he came into the world a day after the fair. The ode was printed, without the seventh and eighth stanzas, in *Dodsley's Museum* for June 7, 1746. T. Warton had seen the original manuscript, with many interlineations and alterations. The fourth stanza stood thus:

"Even now, regardless of his doom,
Applauding Honor haunts his tomb,
With shadowy trophies crowned;
While Freedom's form beside her roves,
Majestic, through the twilight groves,
And calls her heroes round."

Ode to Evening.

Page 61.

In an article on Dr. Sayer's works, in the *London Quarterly Review* (vol. xxxv., p. 211), Southey speaks of the unrhymed lyrical measures which had been tried by Milton with unhappy success, and says that his translation of "*Quis multa gracilis te puer in rosa*" — uncouth in syntax, as well as sound — bears no other resemblance to the Latin measure, which it was designed to imitate, than that it consists of two long and two short lines. He adds, however, that it "presents the only example of a rhymeless stanza which can fairly be said to have become naturalized in our language. Collins saw what could be made of it, and few poems have been more frequently imitated than the 'Ode to Evening,' to which he has so finely and beautifully applied its slow and solemn movement."

Another writer, in the same journal (vol. li., p. 25), cites the translation from Horace, alluded to above, as a proof that it is not true that "rhyme is indispensable to the perfection of some kinds of lyric verse in English." He adds that, in his judgment, this rhymeless ode of Collins' "is not surpassed for musical effect in any language in Europe." We certainly know nothing sweeter or more musical in the whole range of English poetry.

The Manners.

Page 66, line 9. — Alluding to the Milesian tales, some of the earliest romances.

Page 66, line 13. — Cervantes.

Page 66, line 17.

Monsieur Le Sage, author of the incomparable Adventures of Gil Blas de Santillane, who died in Paris, in the year 1745. — *Collins.*

The Passions.

Page 67.

The Ode to the Passions is, by universal consent, the noblest of Collins' productions, because it exhibits a much more extended invention, not of one passion only, but of all the passions combined, acting, according to the powers of each, to one end. The execution, also, is the happiest; — each particular passion is drawn with inimitable force and compression. Let us take only Fear and Despair; — each dashed out in four lines, of which every word is like inspiration. * * * And surely there is not a single figure in Collins' Ode to the Passions which is not perfect, both in conception and language. He has had many imitators, but no one has ever approached him in his own department." — *Sir Egerton Brydges*

Ode on the Death of Thomson.

Page 71.

Thomson died on the 27th of August, 1748, and in the following June the ode appeared. No other memorial of the friendship of the poets has been preserved.

Page 71, line 6.

The harp of Æolus, of which see a description in the "Castle of Indolence." - *Collins.*

Page 71, line 19. — Richmond church, in which Thomson was buried.

Page 72, line 4.

"When Thomson died, Collins breathed forth his regrets in an elegiac poem, in which he pronounces a poetical curse upon him who should regard with insensibility the place where the poet's remains were deposited. The poems of the mourner himself have now passed through innumerable editions, and are universally known; but if, when Collins died, the same kind of imprecation had been pronounced by a surviving admirer, small is the number whom it would not have comprehended." — *Wordsworth.*

Page 72, line 13.

Mr. Thomson resided in the neighborhood of Richmond some time before his death. — *Collins.*

ODE ON THE SUPERSTITIONS OF THE HIGHLANDS.

Page 73, line 5.

The cordial youth was Mr. Barrow, by whom Home was introduced to Collins. Barrow and Home were volunteers in 1746, and, being taken prisoners at the battle of Falkirk, "escaped by cutting their bed-clothes into ropes, and letting themselves down from the window of the room in which they were confined." In this enterprise Barrow broke his leg. Adam Ferguson informed Mackenzie that Home's interest with Lord Bute procured for Barrow the office of paymaster to the army during the American war, from which he returned nearly as poor as he went.

Page 74, line 27.

Shiel — A summer hut, built in the high part of the mountains, for the shepherds to tend their flocks in the warm season, when the pasture is fine.

Page 75, line 22.

By young Aurora, Collins is supposed to have meant the first appearance of the northern lights, which happened about the year 1715.

Page 75, line 28.

Second sight is the term that is used for the divination of the Highlanders.

Page 76, line 1.

The late Duke of Cumberland, who defeated the Pretender, at the battle of Culloden. — *Collins.*

Page 76, line 10.

A fiery meteor, called by various names, such as Will with the Wisp, Jack with the Lantern, &c. It hovers in the air over marshy and fenny places. — *Collins.*

Page 77, line 28. —*Kelpie* — the water-fiend.

Page 78, line 5.

One of the Hebrides is called the Isle of Pigmies, where it is reported that several miniature bones of the human species have been dug up in the ruins of a chapel.

Page 78, line 7.

"The haze and darkness of the atmosphere seem to render it dubious if we can proceed, as we intended, to Staffa to-day; for mist among these islands is rather unpleasant. . . . . The haze is fast degenerating into downright rain, and that right heavy; verifying the words of Collins." — *Walter Scott.*

Page 78, line 15.

"In one of the Hebrides, called Ikolmkill, there are near sixty, it is said, of the ancient Scottish, Irish and Norwegian kings, interred; and the people believe that frequently during the night-time, these venerable monarchs appear, and, in conformity to their former terrestrial employments, meet in council together. This striking superstition Collins has recorded." — *Drake*, "*Literary Hours*," *No.* 31. Sir Walter Scott, who visited this spot in the summer of 1814, remarks that the graves of the kings can scarcely be said to exist, although their site is pointed out. He adds: "Macbeth is said to have been the last King of Scotland here buried. Sixty preceded him, all, doubtless, as powerful, in their day, but now unknown. A few weeks' labor of Shakspeare, an obscure player, has done more for the memory of Macbeth than all the gifts, wealth and monuments, of this cemetery of princes, have been able to secure to the rest of its inhabitants."

Page 78, line 27.

An aquatic bird, like a goose, on the eggs of which the inhabitants of St. Kilda, another of the Hebrides, chiefly subsist.

Page 80, lines 10, 11. — Annan — Tay — Don — three rivers in Scotland.

Page 80, line 17.

Ben Jonson paid a visit, on foot, in 1619, to the Scotch poet Drummond, at his seat of Hawthornden, within four miles of Edinburgh.

Page 80, line 21.

Barrow was at the Edinburgh University, which is in the county of Lothian.

An Epistle.

Page 83.

Sir Thomas Hanmer (born 1676, died 1746) was speaker of the House of Commons during the last parliament of Queen Anne.

"Hanmer, whose eloquence the unbiassed sways,"

was the panegyric of Gay, in his pleasing congratulation of Pope upon completing his translation of the Iliad.

Page 84, line 5. — The Œdipus of Sophocles.

Page 84, line 19. — Julius II., immediate predecessor of Leo X.

Page 85, line 13. — Their characters are thus distinguished by Mr. Dryden. — *Collins.*

Page 85, line 17.

About the time of Shakspeare, the poet Hardy was in great repute in France. He wrote, according to Fontenelle, six hundred plays. The French poets after him applied themselves, in general, to the correct improvement of the stage, which was almost totally disregarded by those of our own country, Jonson excepted. — *Collins.*

Page 85, line 21. — Lucan — The favorite author of the elder Corneille.

Page 86, line 7.

"Turno tempus erit, magno cum optaverit emptum
Intactum Pallanta," etc. — *Virg.*

Page 87, line 5. — See the tragedy of Julius Cæsar.

Page 87, line 11.

Coriolanus. See Mr. Spence's "Dialogue on the Odyssey." — *Collins.*

To Miss Aurelia C——r.

Page 90.

"This is the earliest composition of Collins that has reached us. It was printed in the *Gentleman's Magazine*, January, 1739, with the signature of 'Amasius.' It is, however, not improbable that he was the author of a poem on the 'Royal Nuptials,' which was published by the same bookseller who afterwards sent forth the Eclogues. Mr. Dyce sought a copy in vain. Collins was then in his fourteenth year." — *Willmott.*

Sonnet.

Page 91.

Collins wrote this Sonnet at Winchester College, and it appeared in the *Gentleman's Magazine*, October, 1739, accompanied by the "Sappho's Advice" of J. Warton, and the "Beauty and Innocence" of Tomkyns.

Song.

Page 91.

"When this Song was written, or in what publication it originally appeared, I am unable to inform the reader. Mr. Park (who inserts it on an additional leaf) observes to me that he has now forgotten on what authority he gave it as the production of Collins, but that he must have been satisfied of its genuineness at the time he reprinted it." — *Dyce.*

THE
POETICAL WORKS
OF
THOMAS GRAY.

CONTENTS.

LIFE OF GRAY.

THOMAS GRAY, the fifth child of Philip Gray, a money-scrivener, in London, was born in Cornhill, the 26th of December, 1716. The maiden name of his mother was Dorothy Antrobus. Of twelve children, he was the only one who survived; the rest dying in their infancy from suffocation, produced by fulness of blood. The poet would have shared their fate, but for the courage and firmness of the mother in opening a vein with her own hand. This was not her only claim to his affection, for she supported him from the proceeds of her own industry, both at Eton and Cambridge; the father not only refusing all assistance, but neglecting and abusing his family to an extent not at all consistent with the character of a "respectable citizen," ascribed to him by one of the poet's biographers. His unkindness bound the son and mother more closely together, and we can readily believe that after her death he never mentioned her name without a sigh, and deemed it, as he records in her epitaph, a misfortune to survive her.

At the age of thirteen he was sent to Eton, where one of his maternal uncles was an usher. We learn from Horace Walpole that his relative took prodigious pains with him, which "answered exceedingly." He was then a handsome boy with fine hair and good complexion; a pretty good scholar, with love enough for Virgil to read him in his play-hours for entertainment. Here his most intimate friends were Horace Walpole, and a more congenial spirit, Richard West. The latter was a grandson of the celebrated Bishop Burnet. He was a youth of uncommon promise, and was thought to exhibit more brilliant talents than Gray; but the most affectionate relations existed between them, which were disturbed by no jealousies. Walpole often asserted that "Gray was never a boy," in allusion to his feminine manners, which led his school-fellows to call him Miss Gray. Of his boyish days we know literally nothing, though we are told that his juvenile letters were full of wit and humor.

The uncle who superintended his education at Eton was a fellow of St. Peter's College, Cambridge, to which place Gray removed, and was admitted a pensioner in the year 1734; when Walpole went to King's College, in the same university, and West to Christ Church, at Oxford. Neither the studies nor the amusements of Cambridge were much to Gray's taste, for he found no pleasure in hard drinking or the mathematics. He became aware, too, that he had nerves, and was subject to low spirits; bad signs in a youth, and partly to be ascribed, perhaps, to a fancy of his uncle for teaching him the "virtues of simples," which had led to a habit of self-doctoring even worse than the perpetual recourse to a physician. Gray was at this early period a victim to the gloomy disposition inherited from his father. He found no resources out of his books in a place which was to him what Oxford was to his friend West, "a strange country, inhabited by things that call themselves doctors and masters of arts; a country flowing with syllogisms and ale, where Horace and Virgil are equally unknown." His life was monotonous and cheerless. "When you have seen one of my days," he wrote at this time, "you have seen a whole year of my life; they go round and round, like the blind horse in the mill, only he has the satisfaction of fancying he makes a progress and gets some ground; my eyes are open enough to see the same dull prospect, and to know that, having made four-and-twenty steps more, I shall be just where I was." He wrote, during this period, letters to his friends so full of humor and elegance that we may well regret we have not more of them; clever translations from the classics, and Latin verses of various merit, which continue to be republished, as proof of his accomplished scholarship, and from the desire to preserve everything from his classical pen. It is said to have been his first ambition to excel in Latin poetry; but it was bitter irony in Dr. Johnson to say, "Perhaps it were reasonable to wish that he had prosecuted his design." We are not aware that a poem has ever been written in any other than the mother tongue of an author which possesses interest except as a literary curiosity.

Gray left Cambridge in September, 1738, and lived at his father's house in London till the month of March following, when Horace Walpole invited him to become the companion of his continental travels. In letters to his family and to West we have an interesting though imperfect account of this tour. They travelled through France, crossed the Alps, visited the principal towns of Italy, and passed the winter in Florence, where they returned, after some short excursions, and remained for eleven months, during which Gray began the composition of his Latin poem, "De Principiis Cogitandi." In April, 1741, Gray set off with Walpole for Reggio, where they had a violent quarrel, and parted company. The fault of this outbreak was not with Gray. Walpole attributed it to the difference of their tastes and pursuits. "I had just broke loose from the restraint of the university, with as much money as I could spend; and I was willing to indulge myself. Gray was for antiquities, &c., whilst I was for perpetual balls and plays; the fault was mine." In a letter to Mr. Bentley, some years afterwards, Walpole says: "I was accustomed to flattery enough when my father was minister: at his fall I lost it all at once: and since that I have lived with Mr. Chute, who is all vehemence; with Mr. Fox, who is all disputation; with Sir C. Williams, who has no time from flattery, himself; *and with Gray, who does not hate to find fault with me.*" Whatever was the cause of this quarrel, it was more serious than Walpole was willing to confess. Isaac Reed states, on the information of a gentleman likely to be well informed, that his offence was clandestinely opening a letter of Gray's, from a suspicion that his companion spoke ill of him in his correspondence. It is difficult to believe this even of a person like Walpole; but it is certain that Gray regarded the cause of quarrel as one that forbade entire reconciliation. An interview took place between them, four years afterwards, at Strawberry Hill, when Gray emphatically declared that, while he was willing that civility should be restored, it must be understood that their friendship was totally cancelled. A letter which he addressed to Mr. Wharton immediately after the meeting affords further proof that he received the advances with coldness. "I went to see the *party* (as Mrs. Foible says), and was something abashed at his confidence: he came to meet me, kissed me on both sides with all the ease of one who receives an acquaintance just come out of the country, squatted me into a fauteuil, began to talk of the town, and this, and that, and t' other, and continued, with little interruption, for three hours, when I took my leave very indifferently pleased, but treated with monstrous good breeding." Two days afterwards they breakfasted together, "when," says the poet, "we had all the *éclaircissement* I ever expected, and I left him far better satisfied than I have been hitherto."

When the quarrel took place, Gray immediately returned to Venice, and retraced his steps to England nearly by the same route through France which he had travelled before. In November, two months after his arrival in London, his father died of gout in the stomach; and his mother, with means much impaired by her husband's folly, retired with a maiden sister to the house of another sister, Mrs. Rogers, at Stoke, near Windsor. At the time of going abroad, Gray intended to enter the Temple, and prepare himself for the practice of the law. This pursuit was but little adapted to his tastes and temperament. He now easily persuaded himself that his patrimony was insufficient to bear the charges of a long apprenticeship, and abandoned without reluctance all thoughts of the profession.

On his return to England, Gray found Mr. West rapidly declining in health, and oppressed by family misfortunes. He was in the habit of communicating all his compositions to his friend, and now sent him a part of the tragedy of Agrippina. West objected to the length of Agrippina's speech, which Gray himself thought so long that the tragedy, if ever finished, would be in the nature of Nat. Lee's Bedlam tragedy, which had twenty-five acts and some odd scenes. Mr. Mason tells us, with great *naïveté*, that he has obviated this objection by putting part of the speech into the mouth of Aceronia, and breaking it in a few other places. It was originally, he says, too long for the lungs of any actress; and, he might have added, for the patience of any audience. West's criticism discouraged Gray, and he laid Agrippina "up to sleep" till next summer. There is no reason to regret that her sleep was never disturbed. Four years afterwards, he tried Walpole with the same specimens, and was gratified with the compliments he received for them. "I had a mind," he writes, "to send you the remainder of Agrippina, that was lost in a wilderness of papers. Certainly you do her too much honor;

she seemed to me to talk like an old boy, all in figures and mere poetry, instead of nature and the language of real passion." There is more merit in Gray's criticism of it than in the specimens extant of the tragedy. Walpole seems to have been as frank in his mode of treating the matter as West, for Gray wrote him soon afterwards: "Agrippina can stay very well, she thanks you, and be damned at leisure: I hope you have not mentioned, or showed to anybody, that scene (for, trusting in its badness, I forgot to caution you concerning it); but I heard, the other day, that I was writing a play, and was told the name of it, which nobody here could know, I am sure." It is fortunate that the tragedy was thus arrested. Dr. Johnson says that it was certainly no loss to the English stage that *Agrippina* was never finished. This is almost the only judgment of the literary Goliath on Gray's writings in which we can concur. It must be confessed, however, that the specimens we have of it give us reason to believe that *Agrippina*, completed as begun, would have proved of as little interest for the stage or the closet as the Doctor's own *Irene*.

Gray now devoted himself to the study of the ancient authors. He read the Greek historians and poets, and in pursuing his Italian studies cultivated Petrarch. He translated and wrote Latin epistles and Greek epigrams. These he continued to send to his friend West, and to him also, when Gray was on a visit to his family at Stoke, in 1742, he sent his Ode to Spring, which was written there, but which did not reach Hertfordshire till after the death of his beloved friend. The letter enclosing it was returned unopened. West's loss was never supplied. Gray had attached friends in after life, but none for whom he seems to have cherished so warm and confiding a friendship.

During this visit to Stoke, the muse of Gray was "in flower." In the autumn of that year he composed the Ode on the Distant Prospect of Eton College, and the Hymn to Adversity; and Mason ascribes to this period the greater part of the Elegy written in a Country Church-yard. His relatives being desirous that he should fulfil his original intention of pursuing a profession, he had compromised the matter by taking a degree of bachelor of civil law, and fixing his residence at Cambridge. Here he pursued his classical studies so assiduously, that in six years he had gone through nearly the whole range of Greek authors, with a digest of their contents, and a running commentary, to say nothing of a chronological table which he compiled with a vast expenditure of labor. A number of his critical commonplace books are preserved in the library of Pembroke College; and many others exist, showing very minute erudition, and all written in a very delicate penmanship. On the margins of his classical books he inserted various critical notices and many conjectural emendations. In 1747 he thus reports progress: "I have read Pausanias and Athenæus all through, and Æschylus again. I am now in Pindar and Lysias; for I take verse and prose together, like bread and cheese." He gave much attention to Strabo and geography. Thucydides he thought the model of history, and the Retreat before Syracuse among the choicest pieces of writing in the world. Of Aristotle he said, that he was the hardest author he ever meddled with; that he had a dry conciseness, which rather resembled a table of contents than a book, and, to crown all, an abundance of fine, uncommon things, which were worth the trouble it cost to get at them. He had the highest admiration of Socrates; and ranked the Memorabilia of Xenophon among the most valuable works on morality. But his favorite author was Plato. "What he admired in him," he said, in conversation, "was, not his mystic doctrines, which he did not pretend to understand, nor his sophistry, but his excellent sense, sublime morality, elegant style, and the perfect dramatic propriety of his dialogues."

More than four years thus rolled on, after his flowering season at Stoke, which produced no fruit of his studies, unless the satirical fragment which Mason has entitled a Hymn to Ignorance may be referred to this period. It was probably written soon after his return to Cambridge. By the autumn of 1747 he was ready to venture before the public with the Ode to Eton College, which was published in folio by Dodsley. It was the first English production of Gray that appeared in print; and we are told, in Joseph Warton's Essay on Pope, that it attracted little notice. It was also published in Dodsley's Collection, with the verses which have been dignified with the style of Ode, but which Gray mentions, in a letter to Dr. Wharton, as "a Pôme on the Uncommon Death of Mr. Walpole's Cat." In the same collection the Ode to Spring was published with the simple title of Ode.

It was two or three years previous to this time that Gray made the acquaintance of Mr. Mason, then a bachelor scholar of St. John's, and subsequently elected to a vacant fellowship at Pembroke through the influence of the poet and Dr. Heberden. Mason was devoted and deferential to Gray during his lifetime, and became his literary executor and biographer; but he was artificial and conceited, and repaid Gray's confidence by mutilating his correspondence, and "completing" one of his unfinished poems. The latter, being an open offence, was comparatively venial; but there can be no apology for the liberties taken by Mr. Mason with the poet's letters. Mr. Mitford asserts, and furnishes abundant proof, that "there is scarcely a genuine letter of Gray in the whole of Mason's work." Besides Mason, the intimate friends of Gray in his riper years were Dr Wharton, Mr. Chute, Mr. Brown (the president of Pembroke College), Mr. Stonhewer, and the Rev. Mr. Nicholls.

In the August of 1748, Gray "fills up" a letter to Dr. Wharton with "the beginning of a sort of an essay." "What name to give to it," he adds, "I know not; but the subject is the alliance of education and government. I mean to show that they must necessarily concur, to produce great and useful men." He asked his friend's judgment on it, and begged him to show the fragment to no one, except Stonhewer, who had seen it already. It always remained a fragment. Gibbon calls it an exquisite specimen of a philosophic poem; and Dr. Johnson admits that it has many excellent lines. Gray was the best judge of his own powers, and probably did not think it worth while to provoke a comparison with Pope in that style of composition where he is still without a rival. The thesis which Gray proposed to himself might, perhaps, be better worked out in prose; and we would not part with one of his odes for all the philosophical essays in rhyme that he could have written in a lifetime. We are inclined to think that Gray gave the true reason for not finishing the poem, when he told his friend, Mr. Nicholls, that "*he could not.*" This he explained by adding that, being used to write only lyrical poems, he accustomed himself and was able to polish every part; but that the labor of this in a long poem would be intolerable.

In June, 1750, from Stoke, where he had written the greater part of the "Elegy," eight years before, Gray sent it in a finished state to Walpole. "I have been here at Stoke a few days," he says, "where I shall continue a good part of the summer; and, having put an end to a thing whose beginning you have seen long ago, I immediately send it you. You will, I hope, look upon it in the light of a thing with an end to it; a merit that most of my writings have wanted, and are like to want." It was handed about in manuscript by Walpole, and was received with great favor. Copies were taken, and one of them at last fell into the hands of "certain gentlemen" who were conductors of the *Magazine of Magazines.* They wrote to the fastidious scholar, informing him that his "ingenious poem" was about to be printed under their auspices, for which they beg his *indulgence*, and the *honor* of his correspondence. Gray was horrified at the idea of such a connection, and entreated Walpole to "make Dodsley print it immediately," "which may be done," he adds in a parenthesis, "*in less than a week's time.*" He gives special charge that it should be printed without his name, but on the bookseller's best paper and character. "He must correct the press himself, and print it without any interval between the stanzas, because the sense is in some places continued beyond them; and the title must be, Elegy written in a Country Church-yard. If he would add a line or two, to say it came into his hands by accident, I should like it better. If you behold the *Magazine of Magazines* in the light that I do, you will not refuse to give yourself this trouble on my account, which you have taken of your own accord before now. If Dodsley do not do this immediately, he may as well let it alone."

The elegy was received with delight, and soon ran through eleven editions. Gray was surprised at its popularity. "It spread," said Mr. Mason, in his Life of Whitehead, "at first, on account of the affecting and pensive cast of the subject, just like Hervey's Meditations on the Tombs. Soon after its publication, I remember sitting with Mr. Gray in his college apartment; he expressed to me his surprise at the rapidity of its sale. I replied,

'Sunt lacrymæ rerum, et mentem mortalia tangunt.'

He paused a while, and, taking his pen, wrote the line on a printed copy of it lying on his table. 'This,' said he, 'shall be its future motto.' 'Pity,' cried I, 'that Dr. Young's Night Thoughts have preöccupied it.' 'So,' replied he, 'indeed it is.'"

The elegy proved to be no less popular with scholars than with the multitude, and became a favorite subject for the exercise of skill and ingenuity in translation. Many Latin versions of it have appeared, among which may be mentioned those of Christopher Anstey and Gilbert Wakefield. It has been translated into Greek by sundry bishops and professors; and into Hebrew by G. Venturi, the celebrated Italian Orientalist. There were many French translations of it forty years ago; and others besides Chateaubriand have since added to the number. Boulard rendered it in the Portuguese tongue. Half-a-dozen German poets have naturalized it in their own language, and twice as many Italians have turned it into verse or prose. Polyglott editions have been issued in Italy as well as in England — Van Voorst's in London, and Torri's in Verona and Livorno. It gave birth, also, to a swarm of imitations, one of which was composed by the adventurous Mason, as a daylight companion-piece to the evening scene.

It is related that the night before the capture of Quebec, as the British troops were drifting in darkness and silence down the St. Lawrence, Wolfe repeated this elegy to his companions. On concluding its recitation, he exclaimed, "Now, gentlemen, I would prefer being the author of that poem to the glory of beating the French to-morrow!" Such was the impression Gray produced when he handled subjects that touched the feelings and passions of men. Even Dr. Johnson was compelled to "concur with the common reader" in regard to the character of the elegy. Nor should we omit to mention that a great statesman of our own country, — Mr. Webster, — when upon his death-bed, called upon his son to read him the elegy of Gray, and derived consolation and pleasure from its familiar stanzas.

There has been much diversity of opinion as to the locality described in the elegy. One tradition assigns the precincts of the church of Granchester, about two miles from Cambridge; and the curfew is supposed to have been the great bell of St. Mary's. Jacob Bryant says that when Gray visited Stoke House, on returning, late in the evening, he was obliged to pass by the church-yard, which was almost close to the house, and that he would sometimes deviate into it and spend a few melancholy moments. There it was, he says, that the elegy was certainly conceived, and that many of the stanzas were composed. The Earl of Carlisle, in his lecture on Gray, leans decidedly to this opinion. Though the claim of the church-yard of Stoke Pogeis to be the actual scene of the elegy is disputed with a neighboring village, "I cannot question," he says, "that the one which was nearest to his place of residence, answering adequately as it does to all the touches in his description, and which has since received his mother's remains and his own, was the real theatre of inspiration."

As a proof of the undiminished interest which still attaches to it, we may mention that at a sale in London, in 1845, of books and manuscripts which had belonged to the poet, a copy of the elegy in his own hand-writing, upon two small half-sheets of paper, in a mutilated condition, was sold for one hundred pounds sterling. It was purchased by Mr. Penn, of Stoke Pogeis, though he had Eton College for a competitor. The same gentleman bought a large portion of the collection, which he offered for sale again at auction in London in August, 1854, when the elegy brought an advance of thirty-one pounds on its previous price.

Gray's poetical reputation had attracted the attention of Lady Cobham, who occupied the mansion-house at Stoke Pogeis, in his neighborhood, and led to one of the few friendships which Gray seems to have cultivated with the other sex. Desirous of making his acquaintance, her ladyship one morning despatched two friends who were visiting her to make a call upon the poet. These were Lady Schaub and Miss Harriot Speed, both persons of no little wit and vivacity. Not finding him at home, they entered the house, called for ink and paper, and left an invitation for him from Lady Cobham to dine with her the next day. He accepted the invitation; and this incident was not only the origin of "The Long Story," but of a very agreeable acquaintance. From this time, when he was in the country Gray was continually at Stoke House. Miss Speed afterwards married Count Very, of Savoy; and we are indebted to her not merely for this humorous effort, but for Gray's only love-song, which was written at her request. Gray used to say that the Long Story was never intended for the public, and was only suffered to appear in "that pompous edition" of Dodsley's because of Mr. Bentley's designs, which were not intelligible without it.

At the suggestion of Walpole, Mr. Bentley, the son of the "slashing doctor," employed his pencil in the illustration of Gray's poems which at that time consisted of four little odes, the Elegy, and the Long Story. With his keen sensitiveness to ridicule, Gray was afraid that he might seem to give too much importance to these pieces by publishing them with designs in illustration, and he therefore insisted that the title of "Poems" should be dropped, and that the book should be styled "*Designs* by Mr. R. Bentley for Six Poems by Mr. T. Gray." On this point he was very solicitous, and one of his most characteristic letters was written to Dodsley in regard to it. He was willing that his plain Christian and surname should appear, without a Mr. before them, though this was bad enough; but he would not give up the question of the title, which was finally arranged as he desired.

In connection with this volume, he narrowly escaped a shock that would have been more serious than the surreptitious appearance of the elegy, or than seeing his plain name without the Mr. He learned that his portrait had been engraved for the frontispiece. He was horror-struck. "Sure you are not out of your wits!" he wrote to Walpole. "This I know, if you suffer my head to be printed, you will infallibly put me out of mine. I conjure you immediately to put a stop to any such design. Who is at the expense of engraving, I know not; but if it be Dodsley, I will make up the loss to him. The thing as it was, I know, will make me ridiculous enough; but, to appear in proper person at the head of my works, consisting of half-a-dozen ballads in thirty pages, would be worse than the pillory. I do assure you, if I had received such a book, with such a frontispiece, without any warning, I believe it would have given me a palsy."

The volume made a quarto of four-and-thirty pages; thin enough, though the paper was nearly as thick as pasteboard, and printed only on one side. This was probably for the sake of the engravings, but Dr. Johnson says it was that the poems might, in some form or other, make a book. The designs are as grotesque and tasteless as can well be imagined. Cumberland, in his memoirs, speaks the truth for once at least, when he says that the artist had "completely libelled both his poet and his patron" in these etchings; for grosser libels on the taste of both their worst enemy could hardly have invented. And yet Gray, with all his fastidiousness, was pleased with them, and addressed some complimentary verses to Mr. Bentley on his success.

A proof of one of these engravings which represented a village funeral, was sent to Gray at Stoke. His aunts saw him taking it from a letter, and, supposing it to be a burying-ticket, asked him if anybody had left him a ring. "Heaven forbid," he said, "they should suspect it to belong to any verses of mine; they would burn me for a poet." At this time his mother was ill in bed, and, in March, 1753, she died, "after a long and painful struggle for life," at the age of sixty-seven. The poet placed over her remains an inscription which aptly expresses his affection and sorrow:

BESIDE HER FRIEND AND SISTER,
HERE SLEEP THE REMAINS OF
Dorothy Gray,
WIDOW, THE CAREFUL, TENDER MOTHER
OF MANY CHILDREN, ONE OF WHOM ALONE
HAD THE MISFORTUNE TO SURVIVE HER.

In December, 1754, Gray completed his ode on "The Progress of Poetry." It was commenced two or three years before, but was arrested by a remark of Mason, who told him that it was not of a nature to suit the public taste. Whenever Mason afterwards urged him to complete it, he answered, "You have thrown cold water on it.' Indeed, we are informed by Walpole that Mason's cavils "on his two beautiful and sublime odes" almost induced the poet to destroy them. In 1755 the first part of The Bard was communicated to Mr Stonhewer and Dr. Wharton; but it remained unfinished for two years, when the accident of hearing a blind Welshman perform on the harp at Cambridge led to its completion. "Odicle" for a long time did not "grow a bit," though it was "fine mild open weather;" but, under the genial glow which the old harper inspired, it started, flourished, and bloomed, a consummate flower. His friend, Mr. Nicholls, asked him how he felt while composing it. He replied, "Why, I felt myself the bard."

In 1756 Gray left Peter-house, where he had resided above twenty years; and this he says was an "era in a life so barren of events.' The apartments adjoining his own were occupied by riotous under-graduates. Gray was very apprehensive of fire; and we find him requesting Dr. Wharton to bespeak for him a rope-ladder, thirty feet long, light and manageable, " easy to unroll, and not likely to entangle ; " and this he kept by him, affixed to two iron bars, which he placed there for the purpose, and which are still shown at the window of the chamber he occupied. The story got wind, and some of the collegians were determined to " have him out," and observe the practical working of the machine. They raised the cry of " Fire," one morning, and brought Gray to the window in a " delicate white night-cap ; " but, finding it a false alarm, he returned to his couch.

Gray was not so much amused at this practical joke as the reverend gentleman seems to have been who records it, and he made complaint to the college authorities. They treated it as a " boyish frolic ; " and the poet, indignant that his remonstrance was disregarded, removed to Pembroke College, where his principal friends resided. Here, some years afterwards, the chambers opposite his own were burned ; and, in describing the occurrence, he says, " I assure you, it is not amusing to be waked between two and three in the morning, and to hear, ' Don't be frightened, sir, but the college is all of a fire.' "

In July, 1757, Gray went to London with his two great odes, and sold them to Dodsley for forty guineas ; the poet's receipt for which is now in the possession of Mr. Samuel Rogers. Walpole was on the alert, however, and " snatched them out of Dodsley's hands," that they might be the first fruits of his press at Strawberry Hill, where an edition was printed of one thousand copies. These were speedily sold ; but the odes, Dr. Wharton tells us, were not liked by twenty persons in England. Garrick called them the best in our own or any other language. Shenstone and Lyttleton admired, but wished they were clearer. Mr. Fox, afterwards Lord Holland, thought that Edward I. would not have understood the song or a single hearing. When this was told to Gray, he said, " If he had recited it twenty times, Edward would not have been a bit wiser ; but that was no reason why Mr. Fox should not." Owen Cambridge told Walpole that Lord Chesterfield heard one Stanley read the odes, and thought he was the author. Walpole suggested that his lordship's deafness probably led him into the mistake. " Perhaps," rejoined Cambridge, " they are Stanley's, and, not caring to own them, he gave them to Gray." Lord Barrington believed that the last stanza of

The Bard related to Charles I. and Oliver Cromwell. "Mr. Beddington," the poet wrote to Dr. Wharton, "in a golden shower of panegyric, writes me word that, at York Races, he overheard three people, whom by their dress and manner he takes for lords, say that I was impenetrable and inexplicable, and they wished I had told them in prose what I meant in verse; and then they bought me (which was what most displeased him) and put me in their pocket. Dr. Warburton is come to town, and likes them extremely. He says the world never passed so just an opinion upon anything as upon them; for that in other things they have affected to like or dislike, whereas here they own they do not understand, which he looks upon to be very true; but yet thinks they understand them as well as they do Milton or Shakspeare, whom they are obliged by fashion to admire. Mr. Garrick's compliment you have seen; I am told it was printed in the *Chronicle* of last Saturday. The *Review* I have read, and admire it, particularly that observation that The Bard is taken from *Pastor cum traheret*. And the advice, to be more *original*, and in order to be so the way is (he says) to cultivate the native flowers of the soil, and not introduce the exotics of another climate."

The critique at which Gray sneers was written by an obscure adventurer in London, performing task-work in the service of R. Griffiths, in Paternoster Row, the publisher of *The Monthly Review, or Literary Journal*, conducted, as we learn from the title-page, "by several hands." One of these hands was Goldsmith, then and for some years afterwards far removed from any circle where he could by chance become acquainted with the friend of Horace Walpole, the learned scholar of Pembroke Hall. But his works he regarded in no ungenial or ungentle spirit; and we know of nothing ever written on Gray's poetry more philosophical, more true, or more sincere, than the article to which we refer. Not that Gray could, under any circumstances, have profited by its advice, for you cannot train a sensitive plant to become a pine-tree; but it points out Gray's real weakness, and shows why he failed to become as popular as he became eminent.

It is now nearly one hundred years since Griffiths handed the handsome shilling quarto from Strawberry Hill, with Dodsley's imprint, and the title, "Odes, by Mr. Gray," to his literary apprentice. Goldsmith was prompt in attending to them. The odes appeared in August, and the review in the following month. If to be "early" was to be "kind," Goldsmith certainly was not disposed to be unfriendly; but he was obliged to temper his praise with suggestions which were not agreeable to the poet.

"As this publication," says Goldsmith, "seems designed for those who have formed their tastes by the models of antiquity, the generality of readers cannot be supposed adequate judges of its merit; nor will the poet, it is presumed, be greatly disappointed if he finds them backward in commending a performance not entirely suited to their apprehensions. We cannot, however, without some regret, behold those talents, so capable of giving pleasure to all, exerted in efforts that, at best, can amuse only the few; we cannot behold this rising poet seeking fame among the learned, without hinting to him the same advice that Isocrates used to give his scholars, *Study the people.* This study it is that has conducted the great masters of antiquity up to immortality. Pindar himself, of whom our modern lyrist is an imitator, appears entirely guided by it. He adapted his works exactly to the dispositions of his countrymen. Irregular, enthusiastic, and quick in transition, he wrote for a people inconstant, of warm imaginations, and exquisite sensibility. He chose the most popular subjects, and all his allusions are to customs well known, in his days, to the meanest person."

"It is, by no means, our design," he adds, after showing how ill suited are Pindaric imitations to the English character, "to detract from the merit of our author's present attempt; we would only intimate that an English poet, one whom the Muse has *marked for her own*, could produce a more luxuriant bloom of flowers by cultivating such as are natives of the soil, than by endeavoring to force the exotics of another climate; or, to speak without a metaphor, such a genius as Gray might give greater pleasure, and acquire a larger portion of fame, if, instead of being an imitator, he did justice to his talents, and ventured to be more original." Goldsmith awards the palm of merit to the second of the odes, *The Bard*, which he thinks likely to give as much pleasure to those who relish this style of composition as the odes of Dryden himself. After Goldsmith became famous himself, and looked upon Gray more in the light of a rival, he regarded his poetry with less favor. Mr. Cradock mentions, in his memoirs, that he once said to him, "You are so attached to Hurd,

Gray and Mason, that you think nothing good can proceed but out of that formal school. Now, I'll mend Gray's Elegy by leaving out an idle word in every line."

About three years after the publication of the odes, the parodies by Colman the elder and Robert Lloyd appeared, addressed "To Obscurity," and "To Oblivion;" the latter aimed at Mason, and the first at Gray. They were laughed at for a day, and are forgotten, though Southey says they are "among the very best of their kind." The poet was amused by them, and sent a copy of the quarto pamphlet to Mason, as containing a "bloody satire against no less persons than *you and I* by name." The parodies were attributed to Colman, and Gray says, "What have you done to him? for I never heard his name before. He makes very tolerable fun with me where I understand him (which is not everywhere); but seems more angry with you. Lest people should not understand the humor of the thing (which indeed to do they must have our lyricisms at their fingerends), letters came out in Lloyd's *Evening Post*, to tell them who and what it was that he meant, and says it is like to produce a great combustion in the literary world. So, if you have any mind to *combustle* about it, well and good; for me, I am neither so literary nor so combustible."

At the close of 1757, the laureateship became vacant by the death of Cibber, and it was offered to Gray, with the intimation that he would not be called on for the customary odes. Looking upon this proffered honor in the light in which it was subsequently regarded by Walter Scott, he declined it without hesitation. Even as a sinecure Gray would not accept it. "Though I very well know," he wrote to Mason, "the bland emollient saponaceous qualities both of sack and silver, yet, if any great man would say to me, 'I make you ratcatcher to his majesty, with a salary of three hundred pounds a year and two butts of the best Malaga; and, though it has been usual to catch a mouse or two for form's sake, in public, once a year, yet to you, sir, we shall not stand upon these things,' I cannot say that I should jump at it; nay, if they would drop the very name of the office, and call me Sinecure to the King's Majesty, I should still feel a little awkward, and think everybody I saw smelt a rat about me."

After the loss of his mother, Gray spent the greater part of his summer vacations in the country: during which he visited the old houses, cathedrals, tombs, and other objects of interest to the antiquary in England and Wales, and made a catalogue of them on the blank pages of Kitchen's English Atlas. He was interested, also, in genealogical researches; and, in his copy of Dugdale's Origines, he filled in and described in the margin the arms of all the families mentioned. When the British Museum was opened to the public, in 1759, Gray went to London, and lived for nearly three years in the neighborhood, reading and transcribing historical documents with the diligence of a copying clerk. A folio volume of these transcripts was in Mason's hands, but they seem to have been made to little or no purpose. When tired of this aimless toil, Gray turned to natural history, and made notes in an interleaved Linnæus, with Latin descriptions of the living things and plants he met with in his tours. He watched the weather and the progress of the seasons, and devoured travels and novels, and commenced a history of English poetry, which was abandoned before it was fairly begun. While in London at this time he lodged in Southampton Row, then commanding a view of the country; but in general he took rooms, at half-a-guinea a week, with Roberts the hosier, or Frisby the oilman, in Jermyn-street, receiving his dinners from a neighboring coffee-house.

In 1762 the professorship of modern history became vacant, and, through a friend, Gray applied for it, but was refused; and "so I have made my fortune," he said, "like Sir Francis Wronghead." Three years afterwards, he made a journey into Scotland, where he became acquainted with Dr. Beattie, and, at his desire, authorized Foulis, of Glasgow, to publish an edition of his poems at the same time Dodsley was printing them in London. In both editions The Long Story was omitted, as the plates from Bentley's designs were worn out, and Gray said that "its only use, which was to explain the plates, was gone." The translations from the Welsh and Norwegian were substituted; and to his odes Gray now consented to add some notes, "partly," he says, "from justice to acknowledge the debt when I had borrowed anything: partly from ill temper, just to tell the gentle reader that Edward the First was not Oliver Cromwell, nor Queen Elizabeth the Witch of Endor."

In 1768 the professorship he had sought in vain six years previously became again vacant, and was bestowed on him, without solicitation, by the Duke of Grafton. When the duke was, the next year, elected to the chancellorship of the university, Gray wrote for his installation the celebrated Ode to Music, which, to the great disappointment of Dr. Burney, was composed, under the poet's direction, by Dr. Randall, then professor of music at Cambridge.

This ceremony over, Gray went on a tour to the lakes of Cumberland and Westmoreland, which is described in a series of letters to his friend Dr. Wharton, who was prevented, by sickness, from being the companion of his journey. In the winter of 1769, through the introduction of his intimate friend, Mr. Nicholls, of Blundeston, Gray made the acquaintance of Victor de Bonstetten, a young Swiss, then on his travels, and an affectionate intimacy soon grew up between them. They read the English poets together; but Bonstetten could never induce him to speak of his own works, or of his past history. On these points he maintained an uniform silence. He became more and more the victim of his inherited maladies. In the autumn of 1770 he made a tour into Wales, the outlines of which he sketched, in the May following, in a letter to Dr. Wharton. In this letter he complains of an incurable cough, and of spirits habitually depressed. He now became gloomy and miserable, sometimes without cause, and sometimes from anxiety with regard to the undischarged duties of his professorship. The hours grew longer and heavier to him, and he said that it was more than Herculean toil to push them along. He wished to "annihilate them." But the end was not far distant. While sitting at dinner in the college hall, he was seized with an attack of gout in the stomach, and, six days afterwards, on the night of the 30th of July, 1771, he died, in the fifty-fifth year of his age. He was buried, as he requested in his will, by the side of his mother, in the church-yard of Stoke Pogeis. A small stone, lately inserted in the wall of the church, alone marks the spot. Not far from the church-yard is a cenotaph erected by Mr. Penn to his memory. His monument in Westminster Abbey, erected in 1778, bears the following inscription, from the pen of Mr. Mason:

NO MORE THE GRECIAN MUSE UNRIVALLED REIGNS;
TO BRITAIN LET THE NATIONS HOMAGE PAY;
SHE FELT A HOMER'S FIRE IN MILTON'S STRAINS,
A PINDAR'S RAPTURE IN THE LYRE OF Gray.

His executors were Mr. Brown, the president of Pembroke College, and Mr. Mason. To the latter he bequeathed all his books and manuscripts, to be disposed of at his discretion. Mr. Mason placed such a liberal interpretation on his trust, that in the publication of the poet's letters he altered them to suit his own views of propriety. These books and manuscripts were bequeathed by Mr. Mason to his curate, Mr. Bright, and by him to his two sons. Through this channel they found their way to auction in London, in 1845, where the sale excited very great interest. His books were generally very ordinary copies, and pretty thoroughly used, but they brought large prices. The poet's Milton was one of Tonson's printing, in two volumes duodecimo, half-bound, interleaved, and in a very dingy state. It sold for thirty-three pounds. His "Linnæi Systema Naturæ," interleaved, with numerous MS. notes, and beautiful pen-and-ink drawings of birds and insects, brought forty guineas.

The most interesting of the manuscripts were purchased by Mr. Penn, of Stoke Pogeis, who, nine years afterwards, exposed them again for sale to the highest bidder. At this re-sale, to which we have already referred, a copy of the Strawberry Hill edition of the odes was sold for twenty-seven pounds and ten shillings. In this copy, Gray had marked in *The Bard* the musical time and the directions for the accompaniment. Gray's correspondence with Mason brought at the same sale thirty-one pounds, and a single letter to R. Stonhewer eleven pounds. The manuscript of *The Long Story* brought twenty-five pounds, and the poet's note-books of his tours twenty-six pounds and ten shillings. Mr. Penn's selection of the MSS. brought four hundred and eighteen pounds and seven shillings.

Neither Mr. Mason nor Lord Orford has given us any account of Gray's person. He is described by the reverend Mr. Cole, in manuscripts extant in the British Museum, as a man of small person, well put together, and, in his latter days, tending to plumpness. Jacob Bryant says that he was rather below the middle size, and that he had a pleasing countenance, in which there was no extraordinary expression, and therefore no indication of his internal power. Of his face there is no entirely authentic and satisfactory likeness; but a painting by Richardson, representing him at the age of fifteen years, is the most agreeable picture, and is esteemed the most valuable, from the reputation of the artist.

In his person and dress Gray was very nice and exact, even to a degree that was considered finical and effeminate. After his return from his travels, he commonly carried a muff, to the no small amusement of the Cambridge students. It is told that he once took it into his head to let his whiskers grow, to counteract the idea of his being less masculine than became the author of The Bard. A wag of the same college bribed one of the scouts to cultivate his whiskers, likewise; and, as he was a large, black-looking fellow, he soon left Gray quite in the back-ground, in this regard. This practical ridicule, with a rough joke, perhaps, from other quarters, soon put Gray out of the conceit of his whiskers, and he sacrificed them at the expense of the manly reputation he was seeking to establish. From the best information, we are inclined to believe that he was as much of a dandy, in his way, as Beau Brummel himself. It is said that a stanza in Beattie's Minstrel was revised in consequence of the undesigned resemblance which it bore to the poet:

" Fret not thyself, thou man of modern song,
Nor violate the plaster of thy hair,
Nor to that dainty coat do aught of wrong," &c.

Such was his dislike of appearing old, that nothing could induce him to wear spectacles; but, when his sight became impaired, he sometimes carried an eye-glass. His hand-writing was very delicate and elegant, the work of a crow-quill. In his rooms he was as neat and particular as in his person. His chamber-windows were always ornamented with mignonette, and other fragrant herbs and flowers, in elegant China vases.

In his manners he was polished, though shy and reserved; and, in his common intercourse with the world (particularly where he did not take a fancy to his company), fastidious and affected. If he went to a coffee-house, he would tell the waiter, in a lack-a-daisical tone, to hand him " that silly paper book," meaning the *Gentleman's Magazine*, or, sometimes, the *Monthly Review*. He was never on horseback. All his life he was remarkably sober and temperate. Horace Walpole said that he was the worst company in the world; and represents him as dining one day with Lady Ailesbury, when he never opened his lips but once, and then only to say, " Yes, my lady, I believe so." Dr. Beattie mentions that in general company he was much more silent than one could have wished; and Dr. Johnson did not hesitate to say that he was a "dull fellow, a very dull fellow." And yet, at times, Gray was not only instructing and fluent in conversation, but pointed and witty. Mr. Cradock, on reliable information, restores to Gray a *bon mot* that has been attributed to Johnson. A member of the college, particularly obnoxious to the poet, was standing by the fire "in Hall," and observed to him, "Mr. Gray, I have just rode from Newmarket, and was never so cut in my life; the north-west wind was full in my face." Whereupon Gray, turning to a friend, remarked, "I think in that face the north-west wind would have the worst of it." So, when asked what he thought of Garrick's Jubilee Ode, then just published, he replied, "I am easily pleased." He had more wit than humor. The "sportive effusions" which he extemporised in a post-chaise, for the amusement of his friend Dr. Wharton, are sufficiently "unexhilarating." *Par exemple:*

> "Here lies Dr. Keene, the good Bishop of Chester,
> Who eat a fat goose, and could not digest her."

He is said to have been perhaps the most learned man of his age, and certainly the most learned poet since Milton. When his friend Mr. Nicholls expressed astonishment at the extent of his reading, he replied, "Why should you be surprised? for I do nothing else." His acquaintance with the classics was minute and profound. We have seen that he was a laborious student of history, genealogy, antiquities, and natural history. He was versed, indeed, more or less, in every branch of knowledge, except mathematics and theology. His taste in prints and paintings was highly cultivated. He played on the harpsichord and pianoforte, and sometimes sang to his own accompaniments, with taste and feeling. His life was always that of a scholar, and only at intervals that of a poet; but for his fame he is indebted to half-a-dozen little poems, and not at all to the notes and fragments of criticism and commentary that he left in almost every department of human learning.

Though his works are so inconsiderable in number and extent, in spite of the cavils of his contemporaries and the damnatory judgment of Dr. Johnson, Gray now holds an undisputed position in the first rank of English poets. His few little pieces have furnished the text for whole volumes of criticism, commentary and annotation. In harmony and power of versification, in vigor and magnificence of diction, he is admitted to be without a superior. Where he deals with familiar sentiments, he makes them his own by his exquisite felicity of expression. Where he appropriates the happy epithets or thoughts of others, he so identifies them with the particular use to which he applies them, that they can never after be severed or successfully reclaimed. The compass of his thought is as remarkable as the condensation of his language; and, as his ideas were all distinct and definite, he exhibits them always in vivid and impressive pictures. Perhaps he only failed to become the first poet of his country by the necessity which his nature imposed upon him of becoming the most consummate artist.

ODES.

I. ON THE SPRING.

Lo! where the rosy-bosomed Hours,
  Fair Venus' train, appear,
Disclose the long-expecting flowers,
  And wake the purple year!
The Attic warbler pours her throat,
Responsive to the cuckoo's note,
  The untaught harmony of spring:
While, whispering pleasure as they fly,
Cool Zephyrs through the clear blue sky
  Their gathered fragrance fling.

Where'er the oak's thick branches stretch
  A broader, browner shade,
Where'er the rude and moss-grown beech
  O'er-canopies the glade,
Beside some water's rushy brink
With me the Muse shall sit, and think
  (At ease reclined in rustic state)
How vain the ardor of the crowd,
How low, how little are the proud,
  How indigent the great!

Still is the toiling hand of Care;
The panting herds repose:
Yet, hark, how through the peopled air
The busy murmur glows!
The insect-youth are on the wing,
Eager to taste the honeyed spring,
And float amid the liquid noon;
Some lightly o'er the current skim,
Some show their gayly-gilded trim
Quick-glancing to the sun.

To Contemplation's sober eye
Such is the race of Man:
And they that creep, and they that fly,
Shall end where they began.
Alike the Busy and the Gay
But flutter through life's little day,
In Fortune's varying colors drest:
Brushed by the hand of rough Mischance,
Or chilled by Age, their airy dance
They leave, in dust to rest.

Methinks I hear, in accents low,
The sportive, kind reply:
Poor moralist! and what art thou?
A solitary fly!
Thy joys no glittering female meets,
No hive hast thou of hoarded sweets,
No painted plumage to display:
On hasty wings thy youth is flown;
Thy sun is set, thy spring is gone—
We frolic while 't is May.

II. ON THE DEATH OF A FAVORITE CAT,

DROWNED IN A TUB OF GOLD FISHES.

'T WAS on a lofty vase's side,
Where China's gayest art had dyed
  The azure flowers, that blow;
Demurest of the tabby kind,
The pensive Selima, reclined,
  Gazed on the lake below.

Her conscious tail her joy declared;
The fair round face, the snowy beard,
  The velvet of her paws,
Her coat, that with the tortoise vies,
Her ears of jet and emerald eyes,
  She saw; and purred applause.

Still had she gazed; but 'midst the tide
Two angel forms were seen to glide,
  The Genii of the stream:
Their scaly armor's Tyrian hue
Through richest purple to the view
  Betrayed a golden gleam.

The hapless nymph with wonder saw:
A whisker first, and then a claw,
  With many an ardent wish,
She stretched, in vain, to reach the prize.
What female heart can gold despise,
  What Cat 's averse to fish?

Presumptuous maid! with looks intent
Again she stretched, again she bent,

Nor knew the gulf between:
(Malignant Fate sat by, and smiled)
The slippery verge her feet beguiled,
She tumbled headlong in.

Eight times emerging from the flood,
She mewed to every watery god,
Some speedy aid to send.
No Dolphin came, no Nereid stirred:
Nor cruel Tom nor Susan heard.
A favorite has no friend!

From hence, ye beauties, undeceived,
Know, one false step is ne'er retrieved,
And be with caution bold.
Not all that tempts your wandering eyes
And heedless hearts is lawful prize,
Nor all that glisters gold.

III. ON A DISTANT PROSPECT OF ETON COLLEGE

Ἄνθρωπος, ἱκανὴ πρόφασις εἰς τὸ δυστυχεῖν.

Menander. Incert. Fragm. ver. 382, ed. Cler. p 245.

Ye distant spires, ye antique towers,
That crown the watery glade,
Where grateful Science still adores
Her Henry's holy shade;
And ye, that from the stately brow
Of Windsor's heights the expanse below
Of grove, of lawn, of mead survey,
Whose turf, whose shade, whose flowers among
Wanders the hoary Thames along
His silver-winding way:

Ah, happy hills! ah, pleasing shade!
Ah, fields beloved in vain!
Where once my careless childhood strayed,
A stranger yet to pain!
I feel the gales that from ye blow
A momentary bliss bestow,
As, waving fresh their gladsome wing,
My weary soul they seem to soothe,
And, redolent of joy and youth.
To breathe a second spring.

Say, father Thames, for thou hast seen
Full many a sprightly race,
Disporting on thy margent green,
The paths of pleasure trace;
Who foremost now delight to cleave,
With pliant arm, thy glassy wave?
The captive linnet which enthrall?
What idle progeny succeed
To chase the rolling circle's speed,
Or urge the flying ball?

While some on earnest business bent
Their murmuring labors ply
'Gainst graver hours, that bring constraint
To sweeten liberty:
Some bold adventurers disdain
The limits of their little reign,
And unknown regions dare descry:
Still as they run they look behind,
They hear a voice in every wind,
And snatch a fearful joy.

Gay Hope is theirs, by Fancy fed,
  Less pleasing when possest;
The tear forgot as soon as shed,
  The sunshine of the breast:
Theirs buxom health of rosy hue,
Wild wit, invention ever new,
  And lively cheer, of vigor born;
The thoughtless day, the easy night,
The spirits pure, the slumbers light,
  That fly the approach of morn.

Alas! regardless of their doom,
  The little victims play;
No sense have they of ills to come,
  Nor care beyond to-day:
Yet see, how all around 'em wait
The ministers of human fate,
  And black Misfortune's baleful train!
Ah, show them where in ambush stand,
To seize their prey, the murtherous band!
  Ah, tell them they are men!

These shall the fury Passions tear,
  The vultures of the mind,
Disdainful Anger, pallid Fear,
  And Shame that skulks behind;
Or pining Love shall waste their youth,
Or Jealousy, with rankling tooth,
  That inly gnaws the secret heart;
And Envy wan, and faded Care,
Grim-visaged, comfortless Despair,
  And Sorrow's piercing dart.

Ambition this shall tempt to rise,
  Then whirl the wretch from high,
To bitter Scorn a sacrifice,
  And grinning Infamy.
The stings of Falsehood those shall try,
And hard Unkindness' altered eye,
  That mocks the tear it forced to flow;
And keen Remorse, with blood defiled,
And moody Madness laughing wild
  Amid severest woe.

Lo! in the vale of years beneath
  A grisly troop are seen,
The painful family of Death,
  More hideous than their queen:
This racks the joints, this fires the veins,
That every laboring sinew strains,
  Those in the deeper vitals rage:
Lo! Poverty, to fill the band,
That numbs the soul with icy hand,
  And slow-consuming Age.

To each his sufferings: all are men,
  Condemned alike to groan;
The tender for another's pain,
  The unfeeling for his own.
Yet, ah! why should they know their fate,
Since sorrow never comes too late,
  And happiness too swiftly flies?
Thought would destroy their paradise.
No more; — where ignorance is bliss,
  'T is folly to be wise.

HYMN TO ADVERSITY.

— Ζῆνα —

. . . .

Τὸν φρονεῖν βροτοὺς ὁδώ-
σαντα, τῷ πάθει μαθῶν
Θέντα κυρίως ἔχειν.

ÆSCH. AGAM. ver. 181.

DAUGHTER of Jove, relentless power,
Thou tamer of the human breast,
Whose iron scourge and torturing hour
The bad affright, afflict the best!
Bound in thy adamantine chain,
The proud are taught to taste of pain,
And purple tyrants vainly groan
With pangs unfelt before, unpitied and alone.

When first thy sire to send on earth
Virtue, his darling child, designed,
To thee he gave the heavenly birth,
And bade to form her infant mind.
Stern, rugged nurse! thy rigid lore
With patience many a year she bore:
What sorrow was, thou bad'st her know,
And from her own she learned to melt at others' woe.

Scared at thy frown terrific, fly
Self-pleasing Folly's idle brood,
Wild Laughter, Noise, and thoughtless Joy,
And leave us leisure to be good.
Light they disperse, and with them go
The summer friend, the flattering foe;
By vain Prosperity received,
To her they vow their truth, and are again believed.

Wisdom in sable garb arrayed,
  Immersed in rapturous thought profound,
And Melancholy, silent maid,
  With leaden eye that loves the ground,
Still on thy solemn steps attend:
Warm Charity, the general friend,
With Justice, to herself severe,
And Pity, dropping soft the sadly-pleasing tear.

O! gently on thy suppliant's head,
  Dread goddess, lay thy chastening hand!
Not in thy Gorgon terrors clad,
  Not circled with the vengeful band
(As by the impious thou art seen),
With thundering voice, and threatening mien,
With screaming Horror's funeral cry,
Despair, and fell Disease, and ghastly Poverty:

Thy form benign, O goddess, wear,
  Thy milder influence impart,
Thy philosophic train be there
  To soften, not to wound, my heart.
The generous spark extinct revive,
Teach me to love and to forgive,
Exact my own defects to scan,
What others are to feel, and know myself a Man.

THE PROGRESS OF POESY.

A PINDARIC ODE.

Φωνᾶντα συνετοῖσιν· ἐς
Δὲ τὸ πᾶν ἑρμηνέων
Χατίζει. PINDAR. OL. II. V. 152.

I. 1.

AWAKE, Æolian lyre, awake,
And give to rapture all thy trembling strings.
From Helicon's harmonious springs
A thousand rills their mazy progress take:
The laughing flowers, that round them blow,
Drink life and fragrance as they flow.
Now the rich stream of music winds along,
Deep, majestic, smooth, and strong,
Through verdant vales, and Ceres' golden reign:
Now rolling down the steep amain,
Headlong, impetuous, see it pour;
The rocks and nodding groves rebellow to the roar.

I. 2.

O! Sovereign of the willing soul,
Parent of sweet and solemn-breathing airs,
Enchanting shell! the sullen Cares
And frantic Passions hear thy soft control.
On Thracia's hills the Lord of War
Has curbed the fury of his car,
And dropt his thirsty lance at thy command.
Perching on the sceptred hand
Of Jove, thy magic lulls the feathered king
With ruffled plumes and flagging wing:
Quenched in dark clouds of slumber lie
The terror of his beak, and lightnings of his eye.

I. 3.

Thee the voice, the dance, obey,
Tempered to thy warbled lay.
O'er Idalia's velvet-green
The rosy-crownéd Loves are seen
On Cytherea's day;
With antic Sport, and blue-eyed Pleasures,
Frisking light in frolic measures;
Now pursuing, now retreating,
Now in circling troops they meet:
To brisk notes in cadence beating,
Glance their many-twinkling feet.
Slow melting strains their Queen's approach declare:
Where'er she turns, the Graces homage pay.
With arms sublime, that float upon the air,
In gliding state she wins her easy way:
O'er her warm cheek, and rising bosom, move
The bloom of young Desire and purple light of Love.

II. 1.

Man's feeble race what ills await!
Labor, and Penury, the racks of Pain,
Disease, and Sorrow's weeping train,
And Death, sad refuge from the storms of fate!
The fond complaint, my song, disprove,
And justify the laws of Jove.
Say, has he given in vain the heavenly Muse?
Night and all her sickly dews,
Her spectres wan, and birds of boding cry,
He gives to range the dreary sky;
Till down the eastern cliffs afar
Hyperion's march they spy, and glittering shafts of war.

II. 2.

In climes beyond the solar road,
Where shaggy forms o'er ice-built mountains roam,
The Muse has broke the twilight gloom
To cheer the shivering native's dull abode.
And oft, beneath the odorous shade
Of Chili's boundless forests laid,
She deigns to hear the savage youth repeat,
In loose numbers wildly sweet,
Their feather-cinctured chiefs and dusky loves.
Her track, where'er the goddess roves,
Glory pursue, and generous Shame,
The unconquerable Mind, and Freedom's holy flame.

II. 3.

Woods, that wave o'er Delphi's steep,
Isles that crown the Ægean deep,
Fields, that cool Ilissus laves,
Or where Mæander's amber waves
In lingering labyrinths creep,
How do your tuneful echoes languish,
Mute, but to the voice of anguish!
Where each old poetic mountain
Inspiration breathed around;
Every shade and hallowed fountain
Murmured deep a solemn sound:
Till the sad Nine, in Greece's evil hour,
Left their Parnassus for the Latian plains.
Alike they scorn the pomp of tyrant Power,
And coward Vice, that revels in her chains.
When Latium had her lofty spirit lost,
They sought, O Albion! next thy sea-encircled coast.

III. 1.

Far from the sun and summer-gale,
In thy green lap was Nature's darling laid,
What time, where lucid Avon strayed,
To him the mighty mother did unveil
Her awful face : the dauntless child
Stretched forth his little arms and smiled.
"This pencil take (she said), whose colors clear
Richly paint the vernal year :
Thine too these golden keys, immortal Boy!
This can unlock the gates of joy;
Of horror that, and thrilling fears,
Or ope the sacred source of sympathetic tears."

III. 2.

Nor second He, that rode sublime
Upon the seraph-wings of Ecstasy,
The secrets of the abyss to spy.
He passed the flaming bounds of place and time:
The living throne, the sapphire blaze,
Where angels tremble while they gaze,
He saw; but, blasted with excess of light,
Closed his eyes in endless night.
Behold, where Dryden's less presumptuous car
Wide o'er the fields of glory bear
Two coursers of ethereal race,
With necks in thunder clothed, and long-resounding pace.

III. 3.

Hark, his hands the lyre explore!
Bright-eyed Fancy, hovering o'er,
Scatters from her pictured urn
Thoughts that breathe, and words that burn.

But, ah! 't is heard no more——
  O! lyre divine, what daring spirit
  Wakes thee now? Though he inherit
Nor the pride nor ample pinion,
  That the Theban eagle bear,
Sailing with supreme dominion
  Through the azure deep of air:
Yet oft before his infant eyes would run
  Such forms as glitter in the Muse's ray,
With orient hues unborrowed of the sun:
  Yet shall he mount, and keep his distant way
Beyond the limits of a vulgar fate,
Beneath the Good how far — but far above the Great.

THE BARD.

A PINDARIC ODE.

I. 1.

"Ruin seize thee, ruthless king!
  Confusion on thy banners wait;
Though, fanned by Conquest's crimson wing,
  They mock the air with idle state.
Helm, nor hauberk's twisted mail,
Nor even thy virtues, Tyrant, shall avail
  To save thy secret soul from nightly fears,
  From Cambria's curse, from Cambria's tears!"
Such were the sounds that o'er the crested pride
  Of the first Edward scattered wild dismay,
As down the steep of Snowdon's shaggy side
  He wound with toilsome march his long array.

Stout Glo'ster stood aghast in speechless trance:
"To arms!" cried Mortimer, and couched his quivering
lance.

I. 2.

On a rock whose haughty brow
Frowns o'er old Conway's foaming flood,
Robed in the sable garb of woe,
With haggard eyes the poet stood
(Loose his beard, and hoary hair
Streamed, like a meteor, to the troubled air);
And with a master's hand, and prophet's fire,
Struck the deep sorrows of his lyre.
"Hark, how each giant-oak, and desert cave,
Sighs to the torrent's awful voice beneath!
O'er thee, O King! their hundred arms they wave,
Revenge on thee in hoarser murmurs breathe;
Vocal no more, since Cambria's fatal day,
To high-born Hoel's harp, or soft Llewellyn's lay.

I. 3.

"Cold is Cadwallo's tongue,
That hushed the stormy main:
Brave Urien sleeps upon his craggy bed:
Mountains, ye mourn in vain
Modred, whose magic song
Made huge Plinlimmon bow his cloud-topt head.
On dreary Arvon's shore they lie,
Smeared with gore, and ghastly pale:
Far, far aloof the affrighted ravens sail;
The famished eagle screams, and passes by.
Dear lost companions of my tuneful art,
Dear as the light that visits these sad eyes,

Dear as the ruddy drops that warm my heart,
  Ye died amidst your dying country's cries —
No more I weep. They do not sleep.
  On yonder cliffs, a grisly band,
I see them sit, they linger yet,
  Avengers of their native land:
With me in dreadful harmony they join,
And weave with bloody hands the tissue of thy line.

II. 1.

  "Weave the warp, and weave the woof,
The winding sheet of Edward's race.
  Give ample room, and verge enough
The characters of hell to trace.
Mark the year, and mark the night,
When Severn shall reëcho with affright
The shrieks of death, through Berkley's roof that ring,
Shrieks of an agonizing king!
  She-wolf of France, with unrelenting fangs,
That tear'st the bowels of thy mangled mate,
  From thee be born, who o'er thy country hangs
The scourge of Heaven. What terrors round him wait!
Amazement in his van, with Flight combined,
And Sorrow's faded form, and Solitude behind.

II. 2.

  "Mighty victor, mighty lord!
Low on his funeral couch he lies'
  No pitying heart, no eye, afford
A tear to grace his obsequies.
Is the sable warrior fled?
Thy son is gone. He rests among the dead.
The swarm, that in thy noontide beam were born?
Gone to salute the rising morn.

Fair laughs the morn, and soft the zephyr blows,
  While proudly riding o'er the azure realm
In gallant trim the gilded vessel goes;
  Youth on the prow, and Pleasure at the helm;
Regardless of the sweeping whirlwind's sway,
That, hushed in grim repose, expects his evening prey.

II. 3.

  "Fill high the sparkling bowl,
The rich repast prepare;
  Reft of a crown, he yet may share the feast:
Close by the regal chair
  Fell Thirst and Famine scowl
  A baleful smile upon their baffled guest.
Heard ye the din of battle bray,
  Lance to lance, and horse to horse?
  Long years of havoc urge their destined course,
And through the kindred squadrons mow their way
  Ye towers of Julius, London's lasting shame,
With many a foul and midnight murder fed,
  Revere his consort's faith, his father's fame,
And spare the meek usurper's holy head.
Above, below, the rose of snow,
  Twined with her blushing foe, we spread:
The bristled Boar in infant-gore
  Wallows beneath the thorny shade.
Now, brothers, bending o'er the accursed loom,
Stamp we our vengeance deep, and ratify his doom.

III. 1.

  "Edward, lo! to sudden fate
  (Weave we the woof. The thread is spun.)
    Half of thy heart we consecrate.
  (The web is wove. The work is done.)

Stay, O stay! nor thus forlorn
Leave me unblessed, unpitied, here to mourn:
In yon bright track, that fires the western skies,
They melt, they vanish from my eyes.
But, O! what solemn scenes on Snowdon's height
  Descending slow their glittering skirts unroll?
Visions of glory, spare my aching sight!
  Ye unborn ages, crowd not on my soul!
No more our long-lost Arthur we bewail.
All hail, ye genuine kings, Britannia's issue, hail!

III. 2.

  "Girt with many a baron bold
Sublime their starry fronts they rear;
  And gorgeous dames, and statesmen old
In bearded majesty appear.
In the midst a form divine!
Her eye proclaims her of the Briton-line;
Her lion-port, her awe-commanding face,
Attempered sweet to virgin-grace.
What strings symphonious tremble in the air!
  What strains of vocal transport round her play!
Hear from the grave, great Taliessin, hear;
  They breathe a soul to animate thy clay.
Bright Rapture calls, and, soaring as she sings,
Waves in the eye of heaven her many-colored wings

III. 3.

"The verse adorn again
  Fierce War and faithful Love,
And Truth severe, by fairy fiction drest.
  In buskined measures move
Pale Grief, and pleasing Pain,
With Horror, tyrant of the throbbing breast.

A voice, as of the cherub-choir,
Gales from blooming Eden bear;
And distant warblings lessen on my ear,
That lost in long futurity expire.
Fond impious man, think'st thou yon sanguine cloud,
Raised by thy breath, has quenched the orb of day?
To-morrow he repairs the golden flood,
And warms the nations with redoubled ray.
Enough for me; with joy I see
The different doom our fates assign.
Be thine despair, and sceptred care;
To triumph and to die, are mine."
He spoke, and headlong from the mountain's height
Deep in the roaring tide he plunged to endless night.

ODE FOR MUSIC.

(IRREGULAR.)

I. AIR.

"HENCE, avaunt, ('t is holy ground)
Comus and his midnight-crew,
And Ignorance with looks profound,
And dreaming Sloth of pallid hue,
Mad Sedition's cry profane,
Servitude that hugs her chain,
Nor in these consecrated bowers
Let painted Flattery hide her serpent train in flowers.

CHORUS.

Nor Envy base, nor creeping Gain,
Dare the Muse's walk to stain,
While bright-eyed Science watches round:
Hence, away, 't is holy ground!"

II. RECITATIVE.

From yonder realms of empyrean day
Bursts on my ear the indignant lay :
There sit the sainted sage, the bard divine,
The few, whom genius gave to shine
Through every unborn age, and undiscovered clime.
Rapt in celestial transport they :
Yet hither oft a glance from high,
They send of tender sympathy,
To bless the place, where on their opening soul
First the genuine ardor stole.
'T was Milton struck the deep-toned shell,
And, as the choral warblings round him swell,
Meek Newton's self bends from his state sublime,
And nods his hoary head, and listens to the rhyme.

III. AIR.

"Ye brown o'erarching groves,
That Contemplation loves,
Where willowy Camus lingers with delight!
Oft at the blush of dawn
I trod your level lawn,
Oft wooed the gleam of Cynthia silver-bright
In cloisters dim, far from the haunts of Folly,
With Freedom by my side, and soft-eyed Melancholy."

IV. RECITATIVE.

But, hark! the portals sound, and pacing forth
With solemn steps and slow,
High potentates, and dames of royal birth,
And mitred fathers in long order go :
Great Edward, with the lilies on his brow
From haughty Gallia torn,
And sad Chatillon, on her bridal morn

That wept her bleeding Love, and princely Clare,
And Anjou's heroine, and the paler rose,
The rival of her crown and of her woes,
And either Henry there,
The murdered saint, and the majestic lord,
That broke the bonds of Rome.
(Their tears, their little triumphs o'er,
Their human passions now no more,
Save Charity, that glows beyond the tomb.)

ACCOMPANIED.

All that on Granta's fruitful plain
Rich streams of regal bounty poured,
And bade these awful fanes and turrets rise,
To hail their Fitzroy's festal morning come;
And thus they speak in soft accord
The liquid language of the skies:

V. QUARTETTO.

"What is grandeur, what is power?
Heavier toil, superior pain.
What the bright reward we gain?
The grateful memory of the good.
Sweet is the breath of vernal shower,
The bee's collected treasures sweet,
Sweet music's melting fall, but sweeter yet
The still small voice of gratitude."

VI. RECITATIVE.

Foremost and leaning from her golden cloud
The venerable Margaret see!
"Welcome, my noble son, (she cries aloud)
To this, thy kindred train, and me:
Pleased in thy lineaments we trace
A Tudor's fire, a Beaufort's grace.

AIR.

Thy liberal heart, thy judging eye,
The flower unheeded shall descry,
And bid it round heaven's altars shed
The fragrance of its blushing head:
Shall raise from earth the latent gem
To glitter on the diadem.

VII. RECITATIVE.

"Lo! Granta waits to lead her blooming band,
  Not obvious, not obtrusive, she
No vulgar praise, no venal incense flings;
Nor dares with courtly tongue refined
Profane thy inborn royalty of mind:
  She reveres herself and thee.
With modest pride to grace thy youthful brow,
The laureate wreath, that Cecil wore, she brings,
  And to thy just, thy gentle hand,
  Submits the fasces of her sway,
While spirits blest above and men below
Join with glad voice the loud symphonious lay.

VIII. GRAND CHORUS.

"Through the wild waves as they roar,
  With watchful eye and dauntless mien,
    Thy steady course of honor keep,
Nor fear the rocks, nor seek the shore:
  The star of Brunswick smiles serene,
    And gilds the horrors of the deep."

THE FATAL SISTERS.

AN ODE. FROM THE NORSE TONGUE.

Now the storm begins to lower,
(Haste, the loom of hell prepare,)
Iron sleet of arrowy shower
Hurtles in the darkened air.

Glittering lances are the loom,
Where the dusky warp we strain,
Weaving many a soldier's doom,
Orkney's woe, and Randver's bane.

See the grisly texture grow!
('T is of human entrails made,)
And the weights, that play below,
Each a gasping warrior's head.

Shafts for shuttles, dipt in gore,
Shoot the trembling cords along.
Sword that once a monarch bore,
Keep the tissue close and strong.

Mista, black terrific maid,
Sangrida, and Hilda, see,
Join the wayward work to aid:
'T is the woof of victory.

Ere the ruddy sun be set,
Pikes must shiver, javelins sing,
Blade with clattering buckler meet,
Hauberk crash, and helmet ring.

(Weave the crimson web of war)
Let us go, and let us fly,

Where our friends the conflict share,
  Where they triumph, where they die.

As the paths of fate we tread,
  Wading through the ensanguined field,
Gondula, and Geira, spread
  O'er the youthful king your shield.

We the reins to slaughter give,
  Ours to kill, and ours to spare:
Spite of danger he shall live.
  (Weave the crimson web of war.)

They, whom once the desert-beach
  Pent within its bleak domain,
Soon their ample sway shall stretch
  O'er the plenty of the plain.

Low the dauntless earl is laid,
  Gored with many a gaping wound:
Fate demands a nobler head;
  Soon a king shall bite the ground.

Long his loss shall Eirin weep,
  Ne'er again his likeness see;
Long her strains in sorrow steep:
  Strains of immortality!

Horror covers all the heath,
  Clouds of carnage blot the sun.
Sisters, weave the web of death;
  Sisters, cease; the work is done.

Hail the task, and hail the hands!
  Songs of joy and triumph sing!

Joy to the victorious bands:
  Triumph to the younger king.

Mortal, thou that hear'st the tale,
  Learn the tenor of our song.
Scotland, through each winding vale
  Far and wide the notes prolong.

Sisters, hence with spurs of speed:
  Each her thundering falchion wield;
Each bestride her sable steed.
  Hurry, hurry to the field!

THE VEGTAM'S KIVITHA;

OR, THE DESCENT OF ODIN. AN ODE. FROM THE NORSE TONGUE.

UPROSE the king of men with speed,
And saddled straight his coal-black steed;
Down the yawning steep he rode,
That leads to Hela's drear abode.
Him the dog of darkness spied;
His shaggy throat he opened wide,
While from his jaws, with carnage filled,
Foam and human gore distilled:
Hoarse he bays with hideous din,
Eyes that glow, and fangs that grin;
And long pursues, with fruitless yell,
The father of the powerful spell.
Onward still his way he takes
(The groaning earth beneath him shakes),
Till full before his fearless eyes
The portals nine of hell arise.

Right against the eastern gate,
By the moss-grown pile he sate;
Where long of yore to sleep was laid
The dust of the prophetic maid.
Facing to the northern clime,
Thrice he traced the Runic rhyme;
Thrice pronounced, in accents dread,
The thrilling verse that wakes the dead:
Till from out the hollow ground
Slowly breathed a sullen sound.

PROPHETESS.

What call unknown, what charms presume
To break the quiet of the tomb?
Who thus afflicts my troubled sprite,
And drags me from the realms of night?
Long on these mouldering bones have beat
The winter's snow, the summer's heat,
The drenching dews, and driving rain!
Let me, let me sleep again.
Who is he, with voice unblest,
That calls me from the bed of rest?

ODIN.

A traveller, to thee unknown,
Is he that calls, a warrior's son.
Thou the deeds of light shalt know;
Tell me what is done below,
For whom yon glittering board is spread,
Dressed for whom yon golden bed?

PROPHETESS.

Mantling in the goblet see
The pure beverage of the bee:

O'er it hangs the shield of gold;
'T is the drink of Balder bold:
Balder's head to death is given.
Pain can reach the sons of heaven!
Unwilling I my lips unclose:
Leave me, leave me to repose.

ODIN.

Once again my call obey:
Prophetess, arise, and say,
What dangers Odin's child await,
Who the author of his fate?

PROPHETESS.

In Hoder's hand the hero's doom;
His brother sends him to the tomb.
Now my weary lips I close:
Leave me, leave me to repose.

ODIN.

Prophetess, my spell obey;
Once again arise, and say,
Who the avenger of his guilt,
By whom shall Hoder's blood be spilt?

PROPHETESS.

In the caverns of the west,
By Odin's fierce embrace comprest,
A wondrous boy shall Rinda bear,
Who ne'er shall comb his raven hair,
Nor wash his visage in the stream,
Nor see the sun's departing beam,
Till he on Hoder's corse shall smile
Flaming on the funeral pile.
Now my weary lips I close:
Leave me, leave me to repose.

ODIN.

Yet a while my call obey:
Prophetess, awake, and say,
What virgins these, in speechless woe,
That bend to earth their solemn brow,
That their flaxen tresses tear,
And snowy veils that float in air?
Tell me whence their sorrows rose:
Then I leave thee to repose.

PROPHETESS.

Ha! no traveller art thou,
King of men, I know thee now;
Mightiest of a mighty line ——

ODIN.

No boding maid of skill divine
Art thou, nor prophetess of good;
But mother of the giant brood!

PROPHETESS.

Hie thee hence, and boast at home,
That never shall inquirer come
To break my iron-sleep again;
Till Lok has burst his ten-fold chain;
Never, till substantial Night
Has reässumed her ancient right;
Till wrapt in flames, in ruin hurled,
Sinks the fabric of the world.

THE TRIUMPHS OF OWEN.

A FRAGMENT. FROM THE WELSH.

OWEN'S praise demands my song,
Owen swift, and Owen strong;
Fairest flower of Roderic's stem,
Gwyneth's shield, and Britain's gem.
He nor heaps his brooded stores,
Nor on all profusely pours;
Lord of every regal art,
Liberal hand, and open heart.

Big with hosts of mighty name,
Squadrons three against him came;
This the force of Eirin hiding,
Side by side as proudly riding,
On her shadow long and gay
Lochlin ploughs the watery way:
There the Norman sails afar
Catch the winds and join the war:
Black and huge along they sweep,
Burdens of the angry deep.

Dauntless on his native sands
The dragon-son of Mona stands;
In glittering arms and glory drest,
High he rears his ruby crest.
There the thundering strokes begin.
There the press, and there the din;
Talymalfra's rocky shore
Echoing to the battle's roar.
Checked by the torrent-tide of blood,
Backward Meinai rolls his flood;

While, heaped his master's feet around,
Prostrate warriors gnaw the ground.
Where his glowing eye-balls turn,
Thousand banners round him burn:
Where he points his purple spear,
Hasty, hasty Rout is there,
Marking with indignant eye
Fear to stop, and shame to fly.
There Confusion, Terror's child,
Conflict fierce, and Ruin wild,
Agony, that pants for breath,
Despair, and honorable death.
* * * * *

THE DEATH OF HOEL.

AN ODE. SELECTED FROM THE GODODIN.

Had I but the torrent's might,
With headlong rage and wild affright
Upon Deïra's squadrons hurled,
To rush, and sweep them from the world!

Too, too secure in youthful pride,
By them my friend, my Hoel, died,
Great Cian's son: of Madoc old
He asked no heaps of hoarded gold:
Alone in nature's wealth arrayed,
He asked and had the lovely maid.

To Cattraeth's vale in glittering row
Twice two hundred warriors go:

Every warrior's manly neck
Chains of regal honor deck,
Wreathed in many a golden link·
From the golden cup they drink
Nectar that the bees produce,
Or the grape's ecstatic juice.
Flushed with mirth and hope they burn:
But none from Cattraeth's vale return,
Save Aëron brave, and Conan strong,
(Bursting through the bloody throng,)
And I, the meanest of them all,
That live to weep and sing their fall.

HAVE ye seen the tusky boar,
Or the bull, with sullen roar,
On surrounding foes advance?
So Caràdoc bore his lance.

CONAN'S name, my lay, rehearse,
Build to him the lofty verse,
Sacred tribute of the bard,
Verse, the hero's sole reward.
As the flame's devouring force;
As the whirlwind in its course;
As the thunder's fiery stroke,
Glancing on the shivered oak;
Did the sword of Conan mow
The crimson harvest of the foe.

SONNET

ON THE DEATH OF MR. RICHARD WEST.

In vain to me the smiling mornings shine,
And reddening Phœbus lifts his golden fire:
The birds in vain their amorous descant join,
Or cheerful fields resume their green attire:
These ears, alas! for other notes repine,
A different object do these eyes require:
My lonely anguish melts no heart but mine,
And in my breast the imperfect joys expire.
Yet morning smiles the busy race to cheer,
And new-born pleasure brings to happier men:
The fields to all their wonted tribute bear;
To warm their little loves the birds complain;
I fruitless mourn to him that cannot hear,
And weep the more, because I weep in vain.

EPITAPH

ON MRS. JANE CLERKE.

Lo! where this silent marble weeps,
A friend, a wife, a mother sleeps:
A heart, within whose sacred cell
The peaceful virtues loved to dwell.
Affection warm, and faith sincere,
And soft humanity, were there.
In agony, in death resigned,
She felt the wound she left behind.

Her infant image here below
Sits smiling on a father's woe:
Whom what awaits, while yet he strays
Along the lonely vale of days?
A pang, to secret sorrow dear;
A sigh; an unavailing tear;
Till time shall every grief remove,
With life, with memory, and with love.

EPITAPH

ON SIR WILLIAM WILLIAMS.

Here, foremost in the dangerous paths of fame,
Young Williams fought for England's fair renown.
His mind each Muse, each Grace adorned his frame,
Nor Envy dared to view him with a frown.

At Aix his voluntary sword he drew,
There first in blood his infant honor sealed;
From fortune, pleasure, science, love, he flew,
And scorned repose when Britain took the field.

With eyes of flame, and cool undaunted breast,
Victor he stood on Belleisle's rocky steeps —
Ah, gallant youth! this marble tells the rest,
Where melancholy Friendship bends, and weeps.

ELEGY

WRITTEN IN A COUNTRY CHURCH-YARD.

THE curfew tolls the knell of parting day,
  The lowing herd wind slowly o'er the lea,
The ploughman homeward plods his weary way,
  And leaves the world to darkness and to me.

Now fades the glimmering landscape on the sight,
  And all the air a solemn stillness holds,
Save where the beetle wheels his droning flight,
  Or drowsy tinklings lull the distant folds:

Save that from yonder ivy-mantled tower
  The moping owl does to the moon complain
Of such as, wandering near her secret bower,
  Molest her ancient solitary reign.

Beneath those rugged elms, that yew-tree's shade,
  Where heaves the turf in many a mouldering heap,
Each in his narrow cell forever laid,
  The rude forefathers of the hamlet sleep.

The breezy call of incense-breathing morn,
  The swallow twittering from the straw-built shed,
The cock's shrill clarion, and the echoing horn,
  No more shall rouse them from their lowly bed.

For them no more the blazing hearth shall burn,
  Or busy housewife ply her evening care;
No children run to lisp their sire's return,
  Or climb his knees the envied kiss to share.

Oft did the harvest to their sickle yield,
Their furrow oft the stubborn glebe has broke :
How jocund did they drive their team afield !
How bowed the woods beneath their sturdy stroke !

Let not Ambition mock their useful toil,
Their homely joys, and destiny obscure ;
Nor Grandeur hear with a disdainful smile
The short and simple annals of the poor.

The boast of heraldry, the pomp of power,
And all that beauty, all that wealth e'er gave,
Await alike the inevitable hour.
The paths of glory lead but to the grave.

Nor you, ye proud, impute to these the fault,
If Memory o'er their tomb no trophies raise,
Where through the long-drawn aisle and fretted vault
The pealing anthem swells the note of praise.

Can storied urn, or animated bust,
Back to its mansion call the fleeting breath ?
Can Honor's voice provoke the silent dust,
Or Flattery soothe the dull, cold ear of Death ?

Perhaps in this neglected spot is laid
Some heart once pregnant with celestial fire ;
Hands that the rod of empire might have swayed,
Or waked to ecstasy the living lyre :

But Knowledge to their eyes her ample page,
Rich with the spoils of Time, did ne'er unroll,
Chill Penury repressed their noble rage,
And froze the genial current of the soul.

Full many a gem of purest ray serene
  The dark unfathomed caves of ocean bear :
Full many a flower is born to blush unseen,
  And waste its sweetness on the desert air.

Some village Hampden, that, with dauntless breast,
  The little tyrant of his fields withstood,
Some mute inglorious Milton here may rest,
  Some Cromwell, guiltless of his country's blood.

The applause of listening senates to command,
  The threats of pain and ruin to despise,
To scatter plenty o'er a smiling land,
  And read their history in a nation's eyes,

Their lot forbade : nor circumscribed alone
  Their growing virtues, but their crimes confined
Forbade to wade through slaughter to a throne,
  And shut the gates of mercy on mankind,

The struggling pangs of conscious truth to hide
  To quench the blushes of ingenuous shame,
Or heap the shrine of luxury and pride
  With incense kindled at the Muse's flame.

Far from the madding crowd's ignoble strife
  Their sober wishes never learned to stray ;
Along the cool sequestered vale of life
  They kept the noiseless tenor of their way.

Yet even these bones from insult to protect,
  Some frail memorial still erected nigh,
With uncouth rhymes and shapeless sculpture decked,
  Implores the passing tribute of a sigh.

Their name, their years, spelt by the unlettered Muse,
The place of fame and elegy supply:
And many a holy text around she strews,
That teach the rustic moralist to die.

For who, to dumb Forgetfulness a prey,
This pleasing anxious being e'er resigned,
Left the warm precincts of the cheerful day,
Nor cast one longing, lingering look behind:

On some fond breast the parting soul relies,
Some pious drops the closing eye requires:
Even from the tomb the voice of nature cries,
Even in our ashes live their wonted fires.

For thee, who, mindful of the unhonored dead,
Dost in these lines their artless tale relate,
If chance, by lonely Contemplation led,
Some kindred spirit shall inquire thy fate,—

Haply some hoary-headed swain may say,
"Oft have we seen him at the peep of dawn
Brushing with hasty steps the dews away,
To meet the sun upon the upland lawn;

"There, at the foot of yonder nodding beech,
That wreathes its old fantastic roots so high,
His listless length at noontide would he stretch,
And pore upon the brook that babbles by.

"Hard by yon wood, now smiling as in scorn,
Muttering his wayward fancies would he rove:
Now drooping, woful-wan, like one forlorn,
Or crazed with care, or crossed in hopeless love.

"One morn I missed him on the customed hill,
  Along the heath, and near his favorite tree;
Another came; nor yet beside the rill,
  Nor up the lawn, nor at the wood, was he:

"The next, with dirges due in sad array,
  Slow through the churchway path we saw him borne: —
Approach and read, for thou canst read, the lay
  Graved on the stone beneath yon aged thorn."

The Epitaph.

Here rests his head upon the lap of earth
  A youth, to fortune and to fame unknown:
Fair Science frowned not on his humble birth,
  And Melancholy marked him for her own.

Large was his bounty, and his soul sincere,
  Heaven did a recompense as largely send;
He gave to Misery all he had, a tear,
  He gained from Heaven ('t was all he wished) a friend.

No further seek his merits to disclose,
  Or draw his frailties from their dread abode,
(There they alike in trembling hope repose,)
  The bosom of his Father and his God.

A LONG STORY.

In Britain's isle, no matter where,
  An ancient pile of building stands:
The Huntingdons and Hattons there
  Employed the power of fairy hands

To raise the ceiling's fretted height,
  Each panel in achievements clothing,
Rich windows that exclude the light,
  And passages that lead to nothing.

Full oft within the spacious walls,
  When he had fifty winters o'er him,
My grave Lord-Keeper led the brawls;
  The seals and maces danced before him.

His bushy beard, and shoe-strings green,
  His high-crowned hat, and satin doublet,
Moved the stout heart of England's queen,
  Though Pope and Spaniard could not trouble it.

What, in the very first beginning!
  Shame of the versifying tribe!
Your history whither are you spinning?
  Can you do nothing but describe?

A house there is (and that 's enough)
  From whence one fatal morning issues
A brace of warriors, not in buff,
  But rustling in their silks and tissues.

The first came cap-a-pee from France,
  Her conquering destiny fulfilling,
Whom meaner beauties eye askance,
  And vainly ape her art of killing.

The other Amazon kind Heaven
  Had armed with spirit, wit, and satire;
But Cobham had the polish given,
  And tipped her arrows with good-nature.

To celebrate her eyes, her air —
  Coarse panegyrics would but tease her;
Melissa is her "nom de guerre."
  Alas, who would not wish to please her!

With bonnet blue and capuchine,
  And aprons long, they hid their armor:
And veiled their weapons, bright and keen,
  In pity to the country farmer.

Fame in the shape of Mr. P—t,
  (By this time all the parish know it)
Had told that thereabouts there lurked
  A wicked imp they call a poet:

Who prowled the country far and near,
  Bewitched the children of the peasants,
Dried up the cows, and lamed the deer,
  And sucked the eggs, and killed the pheasants.

My lady heard their joint petition,
  Swore, by her coronet and ermine,
She 'd issue out her high commission
  To rid the manor of such vermin.

The heroines undertook the task;
  Through lanes unknown, o'er stiles they ventured,
Rapped at the door, nor stayed to ask,
  But bounce into the parlor entered.

The trembling family they daunt,
  They flirt, they sing, they laugh, they tattle,
Rummage his mother, pinch his aunt,
  And up-stairs in a whirlwind rattle:

Each hole and cupboard they explore,
  Each creek and cranny of his chamber
Run hurry-skurry round the floor,
  And o'er the bed and tester clamber;

Into the drawers and china pry,
  Papers and books, a huge imbroglio!
Under a tea-cup he might lie,
  Or creased, like dog's-ears, in a folio.

On the first marching of the troops,
  The Muses, hopeless of his pardon,
Conveyed him underneath their hoops
  To a small closet in the garden.

So Rumor says. (Who will, believe.)
  But that they left the door ajar,
Where, safe and laughing in his sleeve,
  He heard the distant din of war.

Short was his joy. He little knew
  The power of magic was no fable;
Out of the window, whisk, they flew,
  But left a spell upon the table.

The words too eager to unriddle,
  The poet felt a strange disorder;
Transparent bird-lime formed the middle,
  And chains invisible the border.

So cunning was the apparatus,
  The powerful pot-hooks did so move him,
That, will he, nill he, to the Great-house
  He went, as if the devil drove him.

Yet on his way (no sign of grace,
For folks in fear are apt to pray)
To Phœbus he preferred his case,
And begged his aid that dreadful day.

The godhead would have backed his quarrel;
But with a blush, on recollection,
Owned that his quiver and his laurel
'Gainst four such eyes were no protection.

The court was sate, the culprit there;
Forth from their gloomy mansions creeping,
The lady Janes and Joans repair,
And from the gallery stand peeping:

Such as in silence of the night
Come (sweep) along some winding entry,
(Styack has often seen the sight)
Or at the chapel-door stand sentry:

In peakéd hoods and mantles tarnished,
Sour visages enough to scare ye,
High dames of honor once, that garnished
The drawing-room of fierce Queen Mary!

The peeress comes. The audience stare,
And doff their hats with due submission;
She curtseys, as she takes her chair,
To all the people of condition.

The bard, with many an artful fib,
Had in imagination fenced him,
Disproved the arguments of Squib,
And all that Groom could urge against him.

But soon his rhetoric forsook him,
  When he the solemn hall had seen;
A sudden fit of ague shook him,
  He stood as mute as poor Macleane.

Yet something he was heard to mutter,
  "How in the park beneath an old tree,
(Without design to hurt the butter,
  Or any malice to the poultry,)

"He once or twice had penned a sonnet;
  Yet hoped that he might save his bacon:
Numbers would give their oaths upon it,
  He ne'er was for a conjurer taken."

The ghostly prudes with hagged face
  Already had condemned the sinner.
My lady rose, and with a grace —
  She smiled, and bid him come to dinner.

"Jesu-Maria! Madam Bridget,
  Why, what can the Viscountess mean?"
(Cried the square-hoods in woful fidget)
  "The times are altered quite and clean!

"Decorum 's turned to mere civility;
  Her air and all her manners show it.
Commend me to her affability!
  Speak to a commoner and poet!"

[Here five hundred stanzas are lost.]

And so God save our noble king,
  And guard us from long-winded lubbers,
That to eternity would sing,
  And keep my Lady from her rubbers.

POSTHUMOUS POEMS AND FRAGMENTS.

ODE ON THE PLEASURE ARISING FROM VICISSITUDE.

Now the golden Morn aloft
  Waves her dew-bespangled wing,
With vermeil cheek and whisper soft
  She wooes the tardy Spring:
Till April starts, and calls around
The sleeping fragrance from the ground;
And lightly o'er the living scene
Scatters his freshest, tenderest green.

New-born flocks, in rustic dance,
  Frisking ply their feeble feet;
Forgetful of their wintry trance,
  The birds his presence greet:
But chief, the sky-lark warbles high
His trembling thrilling ecstasy;
And, lessening from the dazzled sight,
Melts into air and liquid light.

Rise, my soul! on wings of fire,
  Rise the rapturous choir among;

Hark! 't is Nature strikes the lyre,
And leads the general song:
'Warm let the lyric transport flow,
Warm as the ray that bids it glow;
And animates the vernal grove
With health, with harmony, and love.'

Yesterday the sullen year
Saw the snowy whirlwind fly;
Mute was the music of the air,
The herd stood drooping by;
Their raptures now that wildly flow,
No yesterday nor morrow know;
'T is Man alone that joy descries
With forward and reverted eyes.

Smiles on past Misfortune's brow
Soft Reflection's hand can trace;
And o'er the cheek of Sorrow throw
A melancholy grace;
While Hope prolongs our happier hour,
Or deepest shades, that dimly lower
And blacken round our weary way,
Gilds with a gleam of distant day.

Still, where rosy Pleasure leads,
See a kindred Grief pursue;
Behind the steps that Misery treads,
Approaching Comfort view:
The hues of bliss more brightly glow,
Chastised by sabler tints of woe;
And blended form, with artful strife,
The strength and harmony of life.

See the wretch, that long has tost
On the thorny bed of pain,
At length repair his vigor lost,
And breathe and walk again :
The meanest floweret of the vale,
The simplest note that swells the gale,
The common sun, the air, the skies,
To him are opening paradise.

Humble Quiet builds her cell,
Near the source whence pleasure flows ;
She eyes the clear crystalline well,
And tastes it as it goes.
'While' far below the 'madding' crowd
'Rush headlong to the dangerous flood,'
Where broad and turbulent it sweeps,
'And' perish in the boundless deeps.

Mark where Indolence and Pride,
'Soothed by Flattery's tinkling sound,'
Go, softly rolling, side by side,
Their dull but daily round :
'To these, if Hebe's self should bring
The purest cup from Pleasure's spring,
Say, can they taste the flavor high
Of sober, simple, genuine Joy ?

'Mark Ambition's march sublime
Up to Power's meridian height ;
While pale-eyed Envy sees him climb,
And sickens at the sight.
Phantoms of danger, death, and dread,
Float hourly round Ambition's head ;
While Spleen, within his rival's breast,
Sits brooding on her scorpion nest.

'Happier he, the peasant, far,
From the pangs of passion free,
That breathes the keen yet wholesome air
Of rugged penury.
He, when his morning task is done,
Can slumber in the noontide sun;
And hie him home, at evening's close,
To sweet repast, and calm repose.

'He, unconscious whence the bliss,
Feels, and owns in carols rude,
That all the circling joys are his,
Of dear Vicissitude.
From toil he wins his spirits light,
From busy day the peaceful night;
Rich, from the very want of wealth,
In Heaven's best treasures, peace and health.'

TRANSLATION OF A PASSAGE FROM STATIUS.

THEB. LIB. VI.

THEN thus the King: — Adrastus: —
Whoe'er the quoit can wield,
And furthest send its weight athwart the field,
Let him stand forth his brawny arm to boast.
Swift at the word, from out the gazing host,
Young Pterelas with strength unequal drew,
Laboring, the disc, and to small distance threw.
The band around admire the mighty mass,
A slippery weight, and formed of polished brass.

The love of honor bade two youths advance,
Achaians born, to try the glorious chance;
A third arose, of Acarnania he,
Of Pisa one, and three from Ephyre;
Nor more, for now Nesimachus's son,
By acclamations roused, came towering on.
Another orb upheaved his strong right hand,
Then thus: "Ye Argive flower, ye warlike band,
Who trust your arms shall raise the Tyrian towers
And batter Cadmus' walls with stony showers,
Receive a worthier load; yon puny ball
Let youngsters toss."
He said, and scornful flung the unheeded weight
Aloof; the champions, trembling at the sight,
Prevent disgrace, the palm despaired resign;
All but two youths the enormous orb decline,—
Those conscious shame withheld, and pride of noble line.
As bright and huge the spacious circle lay,
With double light it beamed against the day;
So glittering shows the Thracian's godhead's shield,
With such a gleam affrights Pangæa's field,
When blazing 'gainst the sun it shines from far,
And, clashed, re-bellows with the din of war.
Phlegyas the long-expected play began,
Summoned his strength, and called forth all the man.
All eyes were bent on his experienced hand,
For oft in Pisa's sports his native land
Admired that arm, oft on Alpheus' shore
The ponderous brass in exercise he bore;
Where flowed the wider stream he took his stand,
Nor stopped till it had cut the further strand.

And now in dust the polished ball he rolled,
Then grasped its weight, elusive of his hold;
Now fitting to his gripe and nervous arm,
Suspends the crowd with expectation warm;
Nor tempts he yet the plain, but hurled upright,
Emits the mass, a prelude of his might;
Firmly he plants each knee, and o'er his head,
Collecting all his force, the circle sped;
It towers to cut the clouds; now through the skies
Sings in its rapid way, and strengthens as it flies;
Anon, with slackened rage, comes quivering down,
Heavy and huge, and cleaves the solid ground.
So from the astonished stars, her nightly train,
The sun's pale sister, drawn by magic strain,
Deserts precipitant her darkened sphere;
In vain the nations with officious fear
Their cymbals toss, and sounding brass explore;
The Æmonian hag enjoys her dreadful hour,
And smiles malignant on the laboring power.
Third in the labors of the disc came on,
With sturdy step and slow, Hippomedon;
Artful and strong he poised the well-known weight,
By Phlegyas warned, and fired by Mnestheus' fate,
That to avoid, and this to emulate.
His vigorous arm he tried before he flung,
Braced all his nerves, and every sinew strung;
Then, with a tempest's whirl, and wary eye,
Pursued his cast, and hurled the orb on high,
The orb on high tenacious of its course,
True to the mighty arm that gave it force,
Far overleaps all bound, and joys to see
Its ancient lord secure of victory.

The theatre's green height and woody wall
Tremble ere it precipitates its fall;
The ponderous mass sinks in the cleaving ground,
While vales, and woods, and echoing hills rebound.
As when, from Ætna's smoking summit broke,
The eyeless Cyclops heaved the craggy rock;
Where Ocean frets beneath the dashing oar,
And parting surges round the vessel roar;
'T was there he aimed the meditated harm,
And scarce Ulysses scaped his giant arm.
A tiger's pride the victor bore away,
With native spots and artful labor gay,
A shining border round the margin rolled,
And calmed the terrors of his claws in gold.

Cambridge, May 8, 1736.

FRAGMENT OF THE TRAGEDY OF AGRIPPINA.

ACT I. Scene I.

AGRIPPINA. ACERONIA.

Agrip. 'T is well, begone! your errand is performed:
[*Speaks as to* Anicetus *entering*.
The message needs no comment. Tell your master,
His mother shall obey him. Say you saw her
Yielding due reverence to his high command:
Alone, unguarded and without a lictor,
As fits the daughter of Germanicus.
Say, she retired to Antium; there to tend
Her household cares, a woman's best employment.
What if you add, how she turned pale and trembled:

You think you spied a tear stand in her eye,
And would have dropped, but that her pride restrained it?
(Go! you can paint it well) 't will profit you,
And please the stripling. Yet 't would dash his joy
To hear the spirit of Britannicus
Yet walks on earth: at least there are who know
Without a spell to raise, and bid it fire
A thousand haughty hearts unused to shake
When a boy frowns, nor to be lured with smiles
To taste of hollow kindness, or partake
His hospitable board; they are aware
Of the unpledged bowl, they love not aconite.

ACER. He 's gone: and much I hope these walls alone
And the mute air are privy to your passion.
Forgive your servant's fears, who sees the danger
Which fierce resentment cannot fail to raise
In haughty youth, and irritated power.

AGRIP. And dost thou talk to me, to me of danger,
Of haughty youth and irritated power,
To her that gave it being, her that armed
This painted Jove, and taught his novice hand
To aim the forkéd bolt; while he stood trembling,
Scared at the sound, and dazzled with its brightness?
'T is like thou hast forgot, when yet a stranger
To adoration, to the grateful steam
Of flattery's incense, and obsequious vows
From voluntary realms, a puny boy,
Decked with no other lustre than the blood
Of Agrippina's race, he lived unknown
To fame or fortune; haply eyed at distance
Some edileship, ambitious of the power
To judge of weights and measures: scarcely dared

On expectation's strongest wing to soar
High as the consulate, that empty shade
Of long-forgotten liberty: when I
Oped his young eye to bear the blaze of greatness;
Showed him where empire towered, and bade him strike
The noble quarry. Gods! then was the time
To shrink from danger; Fear might then have worn
The mask of Prudence; but a heart like mine,
A heart that glows with the pure Julian fire,
If bright Ambition from her craggy seat
Display the radiant prize, will mount undaunted,
Gain the rough heights, and grasp the dangerous honor.
ACER. Through various life I have pursued your steps,
Have seen your soul and wondered at its daring:
Hence rise my fears. Nor am I yet to learn
How vast the debt of gratitude which Nero
To such a mother owes; the world, you gave him,
Suffices not to pay the obligation.
I well remember too (for I was present)
When in a secret and dead hour of night,
Due sacrifice performed with barbarous rites
Of muttered charms, and solemn invocation,
You bade the Magi call the dreadful powers,
That read futurity, to know the fate
Impending o'er your son: their answer was,
If the son reign, the mother perishes.
Perish (you cried) the mother! reign the son!
He reigns, the rest is Heaven's; who oft has bade,
Even when its will seemed wrote in lines of blood,
The unthought event disclose a whiter meaning.
Think too how oft in weak and sickly minds
The sweets of kindness lavishly indulged

Rankle to gall; and benefits too great
To be repaid sit heavy on the soul,
As unrequited wrongs. The willing homage
Of prostrate Rome, the senate's joint applause,
The riches of the earth, the train of pleasures
That wait on youth, and arbitrary sway:
These were your gift, and with them you bestowed
The very power he has to be ungrateful.

AGRIP. Thus ever grave and undisturbed reflection
Pours its cool dictates in the madding ear
Of rage, and thinks to quench the fire it feels not.
Say'st thou I must be cautious, must be silent,
And tremble at the phantom I have raised?
Carry to him thy timid counsels. He
Perchance may heed 'em: tell him too that one,
Who had such liberal power to give, may still
With equal power resume that gift, and raise
A tempest that shall shake her own creation
To its original atoms — tell me! say,
This mighty emperor, this dreaded hero,
Has he beheld the glittering front of war?
Knows his soft ear the trumpet's thrilling voice,
And outcry of the battle? Have his limbs
Sweat under iron harness? Is he not
The silken son of Dalliance, nursed in ease
And Pleasure's flowery lap? — Rubellius lives,
And Sylla has his friends, though schooled by fear
To bow the supple knee, and court the times
With shows of fair obeisance; and a call,
Like mine, might serve belike to wake pretensions
Drowsier than theirs, who boast the genuine blood
Of our imperial house.

ACER. Did I not wish to check this dangerous passion,
I might remind my mistress that her nod
Can rouse eight hardy legions, wont to stem
With stubborn nerves the tide, and face the rigor
Of bleak Germania's snows. Four, not less brave,
That in Armenia quell the Parthian force
Under the warlike Corbulo, by you
Marked for their leader: these, by ties confirmed,
Of old respect and gratitude, are yours.
Surely the Masians too, and those of Egypt,
Have not forgot your sire: the eye of Rome,
And the Prætorian camp, have long revered,
With customed awe, the daughter, sister, wife,
And mother of their Cæsars.
AGRIP. Ha! by Juno,
It bears a noble semblance. On this base
My great revenge shall rise; or say we sound
The trump of Liberty; there will not want,
Even in the servile senate, ears to own
Her spirit-stirring voice; Soranus there,
And Cassius; Vetus too, and Thrasea,
Minds of the antique cast, rough, stubborn souls,
That struggle with the yoke. How shall the spark
Unquenchable, that glows within their breasts,
Blaze into freedom, when the idle herd
(Slaves from the womb, created but to stare
And bellow in the Circus) yet will start,
And shake 'em at the name of Liberty,
Stung by a senseless word, a vain tradition,
As there were magic in it? Wrinkled beldams
Teach it their grandchildren, as somewhat rare
That anciently appeared, but when, extends

Beyond their chronicle — O! 't is a cause
To arm the hand of childhood, and rebrace
The slackened sinews of time-wearied age.
Yes, we may meet, ungrateful boy, we may!
Again the buried Genius of old Rome
Shall from the dust uprear his reverend head,
Roused by the shout of millions: there before
His high tribunal thou and I appear.
Let majesty sit on thy awful brow,
And lighten from thy eye: around thee call
The gilded swarm that wantons in the sunshine
Of thy full favor; Seneca be there
In gorgeous phrase of labored eloquence
To dress thy plea, and Burrhus strengthen it
With his plain soldier's oath, and honest seeming.
Against thee, Liberty and Agrippina:
The world, the prize; and fair befall the victors.
But soft! why do I waste the fruitless hours
In threats unexecuted? Haste thee, fly
These hated walls that seem to mock my shame,
And cast me forth in duty to their lord.
ACER. 'T is time to go; the sun is high advanced,
And, ere mid-day, Nero will come to Baiæ.
AGRIP. My thought aches at him; not the basilisk
More deadly to the sight, than is to me
The cool injurious eye of frozen kindness.
I will not meet its poison. Let him feel
Before he sees me.
ACER. Why then stays my sovereign,
Where he so soon may —
AGRIP. Yes, I will begone,
But not to Antium — all shall be confessed,

What'er the frivolous tongue of giddy fame
Has spread among the crowd; things, that but whispered
Have arched the hearer's brow, and riveted
His eyes in fearful ecstasy: no matter
What; so it be strange and dreadful. — Sorceries,
Assassinations, poisonings — the deeper
My guilt, the blacker his ingratitude.
And you, ye manes of Ambition's victims,
Enshrined Claudius, with the pitied ghosts
Of the Syllani, doomed to early death,
(Ye unavailing horrors, fruitless crimes!)
If from the realms of night my voice ye hear,
In lieu of penitence, and vain remorse,
Accept my vengeance. Though by me ye bled,
He was the cause. My love, my fears for him,
Dried the soft springs of pity in my heart,
And froze them up with deadly cruelty.
Yet if your injured shades demand my fate,
If murder cries for murder, blood for blood,
Let me not fall alone; but crush his pride,
And sink the traitor in his mother's ruin. [*Exeunt.*

SCENE II. — OTHO AND POPPÆA.

OTHO. Thus far we 're safe. Thanks to the rosy queen
Of amorous thefts: and had her wanton son
Lent us his wings, we could not have beguiled
With more elusive speed the dazzled sight
Of wakeful jealousy. Be gay securely;
Dispel, my fair, with smiles, the timorous cloud
That hangs on thy clear brow. So Helen looked,
So her white neck reclined, so was she borne
By the young Trojan to his gilded bark

With fond reluctance, yielding modesty,
And oft reverted eye, as if she knew not
Whether she feared, or wished to be pursued.
* * * * * * *

HYMN TO IGNORANCE.

A FRAGMENT.

Hail, Horrors, hail! ye ever gloomy bowers,
Ye Gothic fanes, and antiquated towers,
Where rushy Camus' slowly winding flood
Perpetual draws his humid train of mud:
Glad I revisit thy neglected reign,
O, take me to thy peaceful shade again.
But chiefly thee, whose influence breathed from high
Augments the native darkness of the sky;
Ah, Ignorance! soft, salutary power!
Prostrate with filial reverence I adore.
Thrice hath Hyperion rolled his annual race,
Since weeping I forsook thy fond embrace.
O say, successful dost thou still oppose
Thy leaden ægis 'gainst our ancient foes?
Still stretch, tenacious of thy right divine,
The massy sceptre o'er thy slumbering line?
And dews Lethean through the land dispense
To steep in slumbers each benighted sense?
If any spark of wit's delusive ray
Break out, and flash a momentary day,
With damp, cold touch forbid it to aspire,
And huddle up in fogs the dangerous fire.

O say she hears me not, but, careless grown,
Lethargic nods upon her ebon throne.
Goddess! awake, arise! alas, my fears!
Can powers immortal feel the force of years?
Not thus of old, with ensigns wide unfurled
She rode triumphant o'er the vanquished world;
Fierce nations owned her unresisted might,
And all was Ignorance, and all was Night.
O! sacred age! O! times forever lost!
(The schoolman's glory, and the churchman's boast.)
Forever gone — yet still to fancy new,
Her rapid wings the transient scene pursue,
And bring the buried ages back to view.
High on her car, behold the grandam ride
Like old Sesostris with barbaric pride;
* * * a team of harnessed monarchs bend
* * * * * *

THE ALLIANCE OF EDUCATION AND GOVERNMENT.

A FRAGMENT.

ESSAY I.

——— *Πόταγ', ὦ 'γαθέ· τὰν γὰρ ἀοιδὰν*
Οὔτι πω εἰς Ἀΐδαν γε τὸν ἐκλελάθοντα φυλαξεῖς.
Theocritus, Íd. I. 63.

As sickly plants betray a niggard earth,
Whose barren bosom starves her generous birth,
Nor genial warmth nor genial juice retains,
Their roots to feed, and fill their verdant veins;
And as in climes where Winter holds his reign
The soil, though fertile, will not teem in vain,

Forbids her germs to swell, her shades to rise,
Nor trusts her blossoms to the churlish skies :
So draw mankind in vain the vital airs,
Unformed, unfriended, by those kindly cares
That health and vigor to the soul impart,
Spread the young thought, and warm the opening heart :
So fond Instruction on the growing powers
Of nature idly lavishes her stores,
If equal Justice with unclouded face
Smile not indulgent on the rising race,
And scatter with a free, though frugal hand,
Light golden showers of plenty o'er the land :
But Tyranny has fixed her empire there,
To check their tender hopes with chilling fear,
And blast the blooming promise of the year.
This spacious animated scene survey,
From where the ruling orb, that gives the day,
His sable sons with nearer course surrounds
To either pole, and life's remotest bounds,
How rude soe'er the exterior form we find,
Howe'er opinion tinge the varied mind,
Alike to all, the kind, impartial Heaven
The sparks of truth and happiness has given :
With sense to feel, with memory to retain,
They follow pleasure, and they fly from pain ;
Their judgment mends the plan their fancy draws,
The event presages, and explores the cause ;
The soft returns of gratitude they know,
By fraud elude, by force repel the foe ;
While mutual wishes, mutual woes endear
The social smile, and sympathetic tear.

Say, then, through ages by what fate confined
To different climes seem different souls assigned?
Here measured laws and philosophic ease
Fix and improve the polished arts of peace;
There industry and gain their vigils keep,
Command the winds, and tame the unwilling deep:
Here force and hardy deeds of blood prevail;
There languid pleasure sighs in every gale.
Oft o'er the trembling nations from afar
Has Scythia breathed the living cloud of war;
And, where the deluge burst, with sweepy sway
Their arms, their kings, their gods, were rolled away:
As oft have issued, host impelling host,
The blue-eyed myriads from the Baltic coast.
The prostrate South to the destroyer yields
Her boasted titles, and her golden fields:
With grim delight the brood of winter view
A brighter day, and heavens of azure hue;
Scent the new fragrance of the breathing rose,
And quaff the pendent vintage as it grows.
Proud of the yoke, and pliant to the rod,
Why yet does Asia dread a monarch's nod,
While European freedom still withstands
The encroaching tide that drowns her lessening lands,
And sees far off, with an indignant groan,
Her native plains and empires once her own?
Can opener skies and suns of fiercer flame
O'erpower the fire that animates our frame;
As lamps, that shed at eve a cheerful ray,
Fade and expire beneath the eye of day?
Need we the influence of the northern star
To string our nerves and steel our hearts to war?

And, where the face of nature laughs around,
Must sickening virtue fly the tainted ground?
Unmanly thought! what seasons can control,
What fancied zone can circumscribe the soul,
Who, conscious of the source from whence she springs,
By Reason's light, on Resolution's wings,
Spite of her frail companion, dauntless goes
O'er Libya's deserts and through Zembla's snows?
She bids each slumbering energy awake,
Another touch, another temper take,
Suspends the inferior laws that rule our clay:
The stubborn elements confess her sway;
Their little wants, their low desires, refine,
And raise the mortal to a height divine.
  Not but the human fabric from the birth
Imbibes a flavor of its parent earth:
As various tracts enforce a various toil,
The manners speak the idiom of their soil.
An iron race the mountain-cliffs maintain,
Foes to the gentler genius of the plain:
For where unwearied sinews must be found
With side-long plough to quell the flinty ground,
To turn the torrent's swift-descending flood,
To brave the savage rushing from the wood,
What wonder if, to patient valor trained,
They guard with spirit what by strength they gained?
And while their rocky ramparts round they see,
The rough abode of want and liberty,
(As lawless force from confidence will grow)
Insult the plenty of the vales below?
What wonder in the sultry climes, that spread
Where Nile redundant o'er his summer-bed

From his broad bosom life and verdure flings,
And broods o'er Egypt with his watery wings.
If, with adventurous oar and ready sail,
The dusky people drive before the gale;
Or on frail floats to neighboring cities ride,
That rise and glitter o'er the ambient tide
* * * * *

[The following couplet, which was intended to have been introduced in the poem on the Alliance of Education and Government, is much too beautiful to be lost. — *Mason*, vol. iii., p. 114.]

When Love could teach a monarch to be wise,
And gospel-light first dawned from Bullen's eyes

STANZAS TO MR. BENTLEY.

A FRAGMENT.

In silent gaze the tuneful choir among,
  Half pleased, half blushing, let the Muse admire,
While Bentley leads her sister-art along,
  And bids the pencil answer to the lyre.

See, in their course, each transitory thought
  Fixed by his touch a lasting essence take;
Each dream, in Fancy's airy coloring wrought,
  To local symmetry and life awake!

The tardy rhymes that used to linger on,
  To censure cold, and negligent of fame,
In swifter measures animated run,
  And catch a lustre from his genuine flame.

Ah! could they catch his strength, his easy grace,
  His quick creation, his unerring line,
The energy of Pope they might efface,
  And Dryden's harmony submit to mine.

But not to one in this benighted age
  Is that diviner inspiration given,
That burns in Shakspeare's or in Milton's page,
  The pomp and prodigality of Heaven.

As when conspiring in the diamond's blaze,
  The meaner gems, that singly charm the sight,
Together dart their intermingled rays,
  And dazzle with a luxury of light.

Enough for me, if to some feeling breast
  My lines a secret sympathy 'impart;'
And as their pleasing influence 'flows confest,'
  A sigh of soft reflection 'heaves the heart.'

* * * * * *

SKETCH OF HIS OWN CHARACTER.

WRITTEN IN 1761, AND FOUND IN ONE OF HIS POCKET-BOOKS.

Too poor for a bribe, and too proud to importune,
He had not the method of making a fortune:
Could love, and could hate, so was thought somewhat odd;
No very great wit, he believed in a God:
A post or a pension he did not desire,
But left church and state to Charles Townshend ana Squire.

AMATORY LINES.

With beauty, with pleasure surrounded, to languish —
To weep without knowing the cause of my anguish:
To start from short slumbers, and wish for the morning —
To close my dull eyes when I see it returning;

Sighs sudden and frequent, looks ever dejected —
Words that steal from my tongue, by no meaning connected!
Ah! say, fellow-swains, how these symptoms befell me?
They smile, but reply not — Sure Delia will tell me!

SONG.

Thyrsis, when we parted, swore
   Ere the spring he would return —
Ah! what means yon violet flower,
   And the bud that decks the thorn?
'T was the lark that upward sprung!
'T was the nightingale that sung!

Idle notes! untimely green!
   Why this unavailing haste?
Western gales and skies serene
   Speak not always winter past.
Cease, my doubts, my fears to move,
Spare the honor of my love.

TOPHET.

AN EPIGRAM.

Thus Tophet looked; so grinned the brawling fiend,
Whilst frighted prelates bowed, and called him friend
Our mother-church, with half-averted sight,
Blushed as she blessed her grisly proselyte;
Hosannas rung through hell's tremendous borders,
And Satan's self had thoughts of taking orders.

IMPROMPTU,

SUGGESTED BY A VIEW, IN 1766, OF THE SEAT AND RUINS OF A DECEASED NOBLEMAN, AT KINGSGATE, KENT.

Old, and abandoned by each venal friend,
  Here Holland formed the pious resolution
To smuggle a few years, and strive to mend
  A broken character and constitution.

On this congenial spot he fixed his choice;
  Earl Goodwin trembled for his neighboring sand;
Here sea-gulls scream, and cormorants rejoice,
  And mariners, though shipwrecked, dread to land.

Here reign the blustering North and blighting East,
  No tree is heard to whisper, bird to sing;
Yet Nature could not furnish out the feast,
  Art he invokes new horrors still to bring.

Here mouldering fanes and battlements arise,
  Turrets and arches nodding to their fall,
Unpeopled monast'ries delude our eyes,
  And mimic desolation covers all.

"Ah!" said the sighing peer, "had Bute been true
  Nor Mungo's, Rigby's, Bradshaw's friendship vain,
Far better scenes than these had blest our view,
  And realized the beauties which we feign:

"Purged by the sword, and purified by fire,
  Then had we seen proud London's hated walls·
Owls would have hooted in St. Peter's choir,
  And foxes stunk and littered in St. Paul's."

THE CANDIDATE:

OR, THE CAMBRIDGE COURTSHIP.

When sly Jemmy Twitcher had smugged up his face,
With a lick of court whitewash and pious grimace,
A wooing he went, where three sisters of old
In harmless society guttle and scold.
  "Lord! sister," says Physic to Law, "I declare,
Such a sheep-biting look, such a pick-pocket air!
Not I for the Indies: — you know I 'm no prude, —
But his nose is a shame, — and his eyes are so lewd!
Then he shambles and straddles so oddly — I fear —
No — at our time of life 't would be silly, my dear."
  "I don't know," says Law, "but methinks for his look,
'T is just like the picture in Rochester's book;

Then his character, Phyzzy,— his morals — his life —
When she died I can't tell, but he once had a wife.
They say he 's no Christian, loves drinking and ——— ,
And all the town rings of his swearing and roaring!
His lying and filching, and Newgate-bird tricks; —
Not I — for a coronet, chariot and six."
   Divinity heard, between waking and dozing,
Her sisters denying, and Jemmy proposing:
From table she rose, and with bumper in hand,
She stroked up her belly, and stroked down her band —
"What a pother is here without wenching and roaring!
Why, David loved catches, and Solomon ——— :
Did not Israel filch from the Egyptians of old
Their jewels of silver and jewels of gold?
The prophet of Bethel, we read, told a lie:
He drinks — so did Noah; — he swears — so do I:
To reject him for such peccadillos, were odd;
Besides, he repents — for he talks about G** —
[*To* Jemmy.]
'Never hang down your head, you poor penitent elf,
Come buss me — I 'll be Mrs. Twitcher myself.'"
* * * * *

IMPROMPTU,

WHILE WALKING WITH MR. NICHOLLS, IN THE SPRING, IN THE NEIGHBORHOOD OF CAMBRIDGE.

THERE pipes the wood-lark, and the song-thrush there
Scatters his loose notes in the waste of air.

EXTRACTS.

PROPERTIUS, LIB. III. ELEG. V. v. 19.

IMITATED.

Long as of youth the joyous hours remain,
Me may Castalia's sweet recess detain,
Fast by the umbrageous vale lulled to repose,
Where Aganippe warbles as it flows :
Or roused by sprightly sounds from out the trance,
I 'd in the ring knit hands, and join the Muses' dance.
Give me to send the laughing bowl around,
My soul in Bacchus' pleasing fetters bound;
Let on this head unfading flowers reside,
There bloom the vernal rose's earliest pride;
And when, our flames commissioned to destroy,
Age step 'twixt Love and me, and intercept the joy;
When my changed head these locks no more shall know,
And all its jetty honors turn to snow;
Then let me rightly spell of Nature's ways;
To Providence, to Him my thoughts I 'd raise,
Who taught this vast machine its steadfast laws,
That first, eternal, universal Cause;
Search to what regions yonder star retires,
That monthly waning hides her paly fires,

And whence, anew revived, with silver light
Relumes her crescent orb to cheer the dreary night:
How rising winds the face of ocean sweep,
Where lie the eternal fountains of the deep,
And whence the cloudy magazines maintain
Their wintry war, or pour the autumnal rain;
How flames perhaps, with dire confusion hurled,
Shall sink this beauteous fabric of the world;
What colors paint the vivid arch of Jove;
What wondrous force the solid earth can move,
When Pindus' self approaching ruin dreads,
Shakes all his pines, and bows his hundred heads;
Why does yon orb, so exquisitely bright,
Obscure his radiance in a short-lived night;
Whence the Seven Sisters' congregated fires,
And what Boötes' lazy wagon tires;
How the rude surge its sandy bounds control;
Who measured out the year, and bade the seasons roll;
If realms beneath those fabled torments know,
Pangs without respite, fires that ever glow,
Earth's monster brood, stretched on their iron bed,
The hissing terrors round Alecto's head,
Scarce to nine acres Tityus' bulk confined,
The triple dog that scares the shadowy kind,
All angry heaven inflicts, or hell can feel,
The pendent rock, Ixion's whirling wheel,
Famine at feasts, or thirst amid the stream;
Or are our fears the enthusiast's empty dream,
And all the scenes, that hurt the grave's repose,
But pictured horror and poetic woes.
These soft inglorious joys my hours engage;
Be Love my youth's pursuit, and Science crown my age.

1738. Æt. 22.

PROPERTIUS, LIB. II. ELEG. I. v. 17.

"Quod mihi si tantum, Mæcenas, fata dedissent," &c.

YET would the tyrant Love permit me raise
My feeble voice, to sound the victor's praise,
To paint the hero's toil, the ranks of war,
The laurelled triumph, and the sculptured car;
No giant race, no tumult of the skies,
No mountain-structures in my verse should rise,
Nor tale of Thebes, nor Ilium there should be,
Nor how the Persian trod the indignant sea;
Not Marius' Cimbrian wreaths would I relate,
Nor lofty Carthage struggling with her fate.
Here should Augustus great in arms appear,
And thou, Mæcenas, be my second care;
Here Mutina from flames and famine free,
And there the ensanguined wave of Sicily,
And sceptred Alexandria's captive shore,
And sad Philippi, red with Roman gore:
Then, while the vaulted skies loud Ios rend,
In golden chains should loaded monarchs bend,
And hoary Nile with pensive aspect seem
To mourn the glories of his seven-fold stream,
While prows, that late in fierce encounter met,
Move through the sacred way and vainly threat.
Thee too the Muse should consecrate to fame,
And with her garlands weave thy ever-faithful name
  But nor Callimachus' enervate strain
May tell of Jove, and Phlegra's blasted plain,
Nor I with unaccustomed vigor trace
Back to its source divine the Julian race.

Sailors to tell of winds and seas delight,
The shepherd of his flocks, the soldier of the fight;
A milder warfare I in verse display;
Each in his proper art should waste the day:
Nor thou my gentle calling disapprove,
To die is glorious in the bed of Love.
  Happy the youth, and not unknown to fame.
Whose heart has never felt a second flame.
O, might that envied happiness be mine!
To Cynthia all my wishes I confine;
Or if, alas! it be my fate to try
Another love, the quicker let me die:
But she, the mistress of my faithful breast,
Has oft the charms of constancy confest,
Condemns her fickle sex's fond mistake,
And hates the tale of Troy for Helen's sake.
Me from myself the soft enchantress stole;
Ah! let her ever my desires control,
Or if I fall the victim of her scorn,
From her loved door may my pale corse be borne.
The power of herbs can other harms remove,
And find a cure for every ill, but Love.
The Lemnian's hurt Machaon could repair,
Heal the slow chief, and send again to war;
To Chiron Phœnix owed his long-lost sight,
And Phœbus' son recalled Androgeon to the light.
Here arts are vain, e'en magic here must fail,
The powerful mixture and the midnight spell;
The hand that can my captive heart release,
And to this bosom give its wonted peace,
May the long thirst of Tantalus allay,
Or drive the infernal vulture from his prey.

For ills unseen what remedy is found?
Or who can probe the undiscovered wound?
The bed avails not, nor the leech's care,
Nor changing skies can hurt, nor sultry air.
'T is hard the elusive symptoms to explore:
To-day the lover walks, to-morrow is no more;
A train of mourning friends attend his pall,
And wonder at the sudden funeral.
When then the Fates that breath they gave shall claim,
And the short marble but preserve a name,
A little verse my all that shall remain;
Thy passing courser's slackened speed restrain;
(Thou envied honor of thy poet's days,
Of all our youth the ambition and the praise!)
Then to my quiet urn a while draw near,
And say, while o'er that place you drop the tear,
Love and the fair were of his youth the pride;
He lived, while she was kind; and when she frowned, he died.

April, 1742. Æt. 26.

TASSO GERUS. LIB. CANT. XIV. ST. 32.

"Preser commiato, e sì 'l desio gli sprona," &c.

Dismissed at length, they break through all delay
To tempt the dangers of the doubtful way;
And first to Ascalon their steps they bend,
Whose walls along the neighboring sea extend,
Nor yet in prospect rose the distant shore;
Scarce the hoarse waves from far were heard to roar,

When thwart the road a river rolled its flood
Tempestuous, and all further course withstood;
The torrent stream his ancient bounds disdains,
Swollen with new force, and late-descending rains.
Irresolute they stand: when, lo! appears
The wondrous Sage: vigorous he seemed in years,
Awful his mien, low as his feet there flows
A vestment unadorned, though white as new-fallen snows;
Against the stream the waves secure he trod,
His head a chaplet bore, his hand a rod.
As on the Rhine, when Boreas' fury reigns,
And winter binds the floods in icy chains,
Swift shoots the village-maid in rustic play
Smooth, without step, adown the shining way,
Fearless in long excursion loves to glide,
And sports and wantons o'er the frozen tide.
So moved the Seer, but on no hardened plain;
The river boiled beneath, and rushed toward the main.
Where fixed in wonder stood the warlike pair,
His course he turned, and thus relieved their care:
"Vast, O my friends, and difficult the toil
To seek your hero in a distant soil!
No common helps, no common guide ye need,
Art it requires, and more than wingéd speed.
What length of sea remains, what various lands,
Oceans unknown, inhospitable sands!
For adverse fate the captive chief has hurled
Beyond the confines of our narrow world:
Great things and full of wonder in your ears
I shall unfold; but first dismiss your fears:
Nor doubt with me to tread the downward road
That to the grotto leads, my dark abode."

Scarce had he said, before the warriors' eyes
When mountain-high the waves disparted rise;
The flood on either hand its billows rears,
And in the midst a spacious arch appears.
Their hands he seized, and down the steep he led
Beneath the obedient river's inmost bed;
The watery glimmerings of a fainter day
Discovered half, and half concealed their way;
As when athwart the dusky woods by night
The uncertain crescent gleams a sickly light.
Through subterraneous passages they went,
Earth's inmost cells, and caves of deep descent;
Of many a flood they viewed the secret source,
The birth of rivers rising to their course,
Whate'er with copious train its channel fills,
Floats into lakes, and bubbles into rills;
The Po was there to see, Danubius' bed,
Euphrates' fount, and Nile's mysterious head.
Further they pass, where ripening minerals flow,
And embryon metals undigested glow,
Sulphureous veins and living silver shine,
Which soon the parent sun's warm powers refine,
In one rich mass unite the precious store,
The parts combine and harden into ore;
Here gems break through the night with glittering beam,
And paint the margin of the costly stream,
All stones of lustre shoot their vivid ray,
And mix attempered in a various day;
Here the soft emerald smiles of verdant hue,
And rubies flame, with sapphire's heavenly blue;
The diamond there attracts the wondrous sight,
Proud of its thousand dyes and luxury of light.

1738. Æt. 22.

POEMATA.

HYMENEAL

ON THE MARRIAGE OF HIS ROYAL HIGHNESS THE PRINCE OF WALES.

Ignaræ nostrûm mentes, et inertia corda,
Dum curas regum, et sortem miseramur iniquam,
Quæ solio affixit, vetuitque calescere flammâ
Dulci, quæ dono divûm, gratissima serpit
Viscera per, mollesque animis lene implicat æstus;
Nec teneros sensus, Veneris nec præmia nôrunt,
Eloquiumve oculi, aut facunda silentia linguæ:
  Scilicet ignorant lacrymas, sævosque dolores,
Dura rudimenta, et violentæ exordia flammæ;
Scilicet ignorant, quæ flumine tinxit amaro
Tela Venus, cæcique armamentaria Divi,
Irasque, insidias tacitum et sub pectore vulnus;
Namque sub ingressu, primoque in limine Amoris
Luctus et ultrices posuere cubilia Curæ;
Intus habent dulces Risus, et Gratia sedem,
Et roseis resupina toris, roseo ore Voluptas:
Regibus huc faciles aditus; communia spernunt
Ostia, jamque expers duris custodibus istis
Panditur accessus, penetraliaque intima Templi.

Tuque O! Angliacis, Princeps, spes optima regnis,
Ne tantum, ne finge metum: quid imagine captus
Hæres, et mentem pictura pascis inani?
Umbram miraris: nec longum tempus, et ipsa
Ibit in amplexus, thalamosque ornabit ovantes.
Ille tamen tabulis inhians longum haurit amorem,
Affatu fruitur tacito, auscultatque tacentem
Immemor artificis calami, risumque, ruboremque
Aspicit in fucis, pictæque in virginis ore:
Tanta Venus potuit; tantus tenet error amantes.

Nascere, magna Dies, qua sese AUGUSTA Britanno
Committat Pelago, patriamque relinquat amœnam;
Cujus in adventum jam nunc tria regna secundos
Attolli in plausus, dulcique accensa furore
Incipiunt agitare modos, et carmina dicunt:
Ipse animo sedenim juvenis comitatur euntem
Explorat ventos, atque auribus aëra captat,
Atque auras, atque astra vocat crudelia; pectus
Intentum exultat, surgitque arrecta cupido;
Incusat spes ægra fretum, solitoque videtur
Latior effundi pontus, fluctusque morantes.

Nascere, Lux major, qua sese AUGUSTA Britanno
Committat juveni totam, propriamque dicabit;
At citius (precor) O! cedas melioribus astris;
Nox finem pompæ, finemque imponere curis
Possit, et in thalamos furtim deducere nuptam;
Sufficiat requiemque viris, et amantibus umbras:
Adsit Hymen, et subridens cum matre Cupido
Accedant, sternantque toros, ignemque ministrent;
Ilicet haud pictæ incandescit imagine formæ
Ulterius juvenis, verumque agnoscit amorem.

Sculptile sicut ebur, faciemque arsisse venustam
Pygmaliona canunt : ante hanc suspiria ducit,
Alloquiturque amens, flammamque et vulnera narrat ;
Implorata Venus jussit cum vivere signum,
Fœmineam inspirans animam ; quæ gaudia surgunt,
Audiit ut primæ nascentia murmura linguæ,
Luctari in vitam, et paulatim volvere ocellos
Sedulus, aspexitque novâ splendescere flammâ ;
Corripit amplexu vivam, jamque oscula jungit
Acria confestim, recipitque rapitque ; prioris
Immemor ardoris, Nymphæque oblitus eburneæ.

T. GRAY, PET. COLL.

LUNA HABITABILIS.

Dum Nox rorantes, non incomitata per auras
Urget equos, tacitoque inducit sidera lapsu ;
Ultima sed nulli soror inficianda sororum,
Huc mihi, Musa ; tibi patet alti janua cœli,
Astra vides, nec te numeri, nec nomina fallunt.
Huc mihi, Diva, veni ; dulce est per aperta serena
Vere frui liquido, campoque errare silenti ;
Vere frui dulce est ; modo tu dignata petentem
Sis comes, et mecum gelidâ spatiere sub umbrâ.
Scilicèt hos orbes, cœli hæc decora alta putandum est,
Noctis opes, nobis tantum lucere ; virûmque
Ostentari oculis, nostræ laquearia terræ,
Ingentes scenas, vastique aulæa theatri ?
O ! quis me pennis æthræ super ardua sistet
Mirantem, propiusque dabit convexa tueri ;
Teque adeo, undè fluens reficit lux mollior arva
Pallidiorque dies, tristes solata tenebras ?

Sic ego, subridens Dea sic ingressa vicissim:
Non pennis opus hìc, supera ut simul illa petamus:
Disce, Puer, potiùs cœlo deducere Lunam;
Neu crede ad magicas te invitum accingier artes,
Thessalicosve modos; ipsam descendere Phœben
Conspicies novus Endymion; seque offeret ultrò
Visa tibi ante oculos, et notâ major imago.
Quin tete admoveas (tumuli super aggere spectas),
Compositum tubulo; simul imum invade canalem
Sic intentâ acie, cœli simul alta patescent
Atria; jamque, ausus Lunaria visere regna,
Ingrediêre solo, et caput inter nubila condes.
Ecce autem! vitri se in vertice sistere Phœben
Cernis, et Oceanum, et crebris Freta consita terris
Panditur *ille* atram faciem caligine condens
Sublustri; refugitque oculos, fallitque tuentem;
Integram Solis lucem quippè haurit aperto
Fluctu avidus radiorum, et longos imbibit ignes:
Verum *his*, quæ, maculis variata nitentibus, auro
Cœrula discernunt, celso sese insula dorso
Plurima protrudit, prætentaque littora saxis;
Liberior datur his quoniàm natura, minusque
Lumen depascunt liquidum; sed tela diei
Detorquent, retròque docent se vertere flammas.
Hinc longos videas tractus, terrasque jacentes
Ordine candenti, et claros se attollere montes;
Montes queîs Rhodope assurgat, quibus Ossa nivali
Vertice: tum scopulis infrà pendentibus antra
Nigrescunt clivorum umbrâ, nemorumque tenebris.
Non rores illi, aut desunt sua nubila mundo;
Non frigus gelidum, atque herbis gratissimus imber;
His quoque nota ardet picto Thaumantias arcu,
Os roseum Auroræ, propriique crepuscula cœli.

Et dubitas tantum certis cultoribus orbem
Destitui? exercent agros, sua mœnia condunt
Hi quoque, vel Martem invadunt, curantque triumphos
Victores: sunt hic etiam sua præmia laudi;
His metus, atque amor, et mentem mortalia tangunt.
Quin, uti nos oculis jam nunc juvat ire per arva,
Lucentesque plagas Lunæ, pontumque profundum;
Idem illos etiàm ardor agit, cum se aureus effert
Sub sudum globus, et terrarum ingentior orbis;
Scilicèt omne æquor tum lustrant, scilicèt omnem
Tellurem, gentesque polo sub utroque jacentes;
Et quidam æstivi indefessus ad ætheris ignes
Pervigilat, noctem exercens, cœlumque fatigat;
Jam Galli apparent, jam se Germania latè
Tollit, et albescens pater Apenninus ad auras;
Jam tandem in Borean, en! parvulus Anglia nævus
(Quanquam aliis longè fulgentior) extulit oras;
Formosum extemplò lumen, maculamque nitentem
Invisunt crebri Proceres, serùmque tuendo;
Hærent, certatimque suo cognomine signant:
Forsitan et Lunæ longinquus in orbe Tyrannus
Se dominum vocat, et nostrâ se jactat in aulâ.
Terras possim alias propiori sole calentes
Narrare, atque alias, jubaris queìs parcior usus,
Lunarum chorus, et tenuis penuria Phœbi;
Nì, meditans eadem hæc audaci evolvere cantu,
Jam pulset citharam soror, et præludia tentet.

Non tamen has proprias laudes, nec facta silebo
Jampridèm in fatis, patriæque oracula famæ.
Tempus erit, sursùm totos contendere cœtus
Quo cernes longo excursu, primosque colonos
Migrare in lunam, et notos mutare Penates:

Dum stupet obtutu tacito vetus incola, longèque
Insolitas explorat aves, classemque volantem.
Ut quondàm ignotum marmor, camposque natantes
Tranavit Zephyros visens, nova regna, Columbus;
Litora mirantur circùm, mirantur et undæ
Inclusas acies ferro, turmasque biformes,
Monstraque fœta armis, et non imitabile fulmen.
Fœdera mox icta, et gemini commercia mundi,
Agminaque assueto glomerata sub æthere cerno.
Anglia, quæ pelagi jamdudum torquet habenas,
Exercetque frequens ventos, atque imperat undæ;
Aëris attollet fasces, veteresque triumphos
Hùc etiam feret, et victis dominabitur auris.

SAPPHIC ODE: TO MR. WEST.

Barbaras ædes aditure mecum
Quas Eris semper fovet inquieta,
Lis ubi latè sonat, et togatum
Æstuat agmen;

Dulcius quanto, patulis sub ulmi
Hospitæ ramis temerè jacentem
Sic libris horas, tenuique inertes
Fallere Musâ?

Sæpe enim curis vagor expeditâ
Mente; dum, blandam meditans Camænam,
Vix malo rori, meminive seræ
Cedere nocti;

Et, pedes quò me rapiunt, in omni
Colle Parnassum videor videre
Fertilem sylvæ, gelidamque in omni
Fonte Aganippen.

Risit et Ver me, facilesque Nymphæ
Nare captantem, nec ineleganti,
Manè quicquid de violis eundo
Surripit aura:

Me reclinatum teneram per herbam;
Quà leves cursus aqua cunque ducit,
Et moras dulci strepitu lapillo
Nectit in omni.

Hæ novo nostrum ferè pectus anno
Simplices curæ tenuere, cœlum
Quamdiù sudum explicuit Favonì
Purior hora:

Otia et campos nec adhuc relinquo,
Nec magis Phœbo Clytie fidelis;
(Ingruant venti licet, et senescat
Mollior æstas;)

Namque, seu, lætos hominum labores
Prataque et montes recreante curru,
Purpurâ tractus oriens Eoos
Vestit, et auro;

Sedulus servo veneratus orbem
Prodigum splendoris; amœniori
Sive dilectam meditatur igne
Pingere Calpen;

Usque dum, fulgore magìs magìs jam
Languido circum, variata nubes
Labitur furtim, viridisque in umbras
Scena recessit.

O ego felix, vice si (nec unquam
Surgerem rursus) simili cadentem
Parca me lenis sineret quieto
Fallere Letho!

Multa flagranti radiisque cincto
Integris ah! quam nihil inviderem,
Cum Dei ardentes medius quadrigas
Sentit Olympus.

ALCAIC FRAGMENT.

O LACRYMARUM fons, tenero sacros
Ducentium ortus ex animo; quater
Felix! in imo qui scatentem
Pectore te, pia Nympha, sensit.

LATIN LINES

ADDRESSED TO MR. WEST, FROM GENOA.

HORRIDOS tractus, Boreæque linquens
Regna Taurini fera, molliorem
Advehor brumam, Genuæque amantes
Litora soles.

ELEGIAC VERSES,

OCCASIONED BY THE SIGHT OF THE PLAINS WHERE THE BATTLE OF TREBIA WAS FOUGHT.

QUA Trebie glaucas salices intersecat undâ,
Arvaque Romanis nobilitata malis;
Visus adhuc amnis veteri de clade rubere,
Et suspirantes ducere mœstus aquas;
Maurorumque ala, et nigræ increbescere turmae,
Et pulsa Ausonidum ripa sonare fugâ.

CARMEN AD C. FAVONIUM ZEPHYRINUM.

MATER rosarum, cui teneræ vigent
Auræ Favonì, cui Venus it comes
Lasciva, Nympharum choreis
Et volucrum celebrata cantu!
Dic, non inertem fallere quâ diem
Amat sub umbrâ, seu sinit aureum
Dormire plectrum, seu retentat
Pierio Zephyrinus antro
Furore dulci plenus, et immemor
Reptantis inter frigora Tusculi
Umbrosa, vel colles Amici
Palladiæ superantis Albæ.
Dilecta Fauno, et capripedum choris
Pineta, testor vos, Anio minax
Quæcunque per clivos volutus
Præcipiti tremefecit amne,

Illius altum Tibur, et Æsulæ
Audisse sylvas nomen amabiles,
Illius et gratas Latinis
Naïsin ingeminâsse rupes;
Nam me Latinæ Naïdes uvidâ
Vidêre ripâ, quâ niveas levi
Tam sæpe lavit rore plumas
Dulcè canens Venusinus ales;
Mirum! canenti conticuit nemus,
Sacrique fontes, et retinent adhuc
(Sic Musa jussit) saxa molles
Docta modos, veteresque lauri.
Mirare nec tu me citharæ rudem
Claudis laborantem numeris: loca
Amœna, jucundumque ver in-
compositum docuere carmen;
Hærent sub omni nam folio nigri
Phœbea lucì (credite) somnia,
Argutiusque et lympha et auræ
Nescio quid solito loquntur.

FRAGMENT OF A LATIN POEM ON THE GAURUS.

NEC procul infelix se tollit in æthera Gaurus,
Prospiciens vitreum lugenti vertice pontum:
Tristior ille diu, et veteri desuetus olivâ
Gaurus, pampineæque eheu! jam nescius umbræ;
Horrendi tam sæva premit vicinia montis,
Attonitumque urget latus, exuritque ferentem.
Nam fama est olim, mediâ dum rura silebant

Nocte, Deo victa, et molli perfusa quiete,
Infremuisse æquor ponti, auditamque per omnes
Latè tellurem surdùm immugire cavernas:
Quo sonitu nemora alta tremunt: tremit excita tuto
Parthenopæa sinu, flammantisque ora Vesevi.
At subitò se aperire solum, vastosque recessus
Pandere sub pedibus, nigrâque voragine fauces;
Tum piceas cinerum glomerare sub æthere nubes
Vorticibus rapidis, ardentique imbre procellam.
Præcipites fugere feræ, perque avia longè
Sylvarum fugit pastor, juga per deserta,
Ah, miser! increpitans sæpè altâ voce per umbram
Nequicquam natos, creditque audire sequentes.
Atque ille excelso rupis de vertice solus
Respectans notasque domos, et dulcia regna,
Nil usquàm videt infelix præter mare tristi
Lumine percussum, et pallentes sulphure campos
Fumumque, flammasque, rotataque turbine saxa.
  Quin ubi detonuit fragor, et lux reddita cœlo;
Mæstos confluere agricolas, passuque videres
Tandem iterum timido deserta requirere tecta:
Sperantes, si forte oculis, si forte darentur
Uxorum cineres, miserorumve ossa parentum
(Tenuia, sed tanti saltem solatia luctûs)
Unà colligere et justâ componere in urnâ.
Uxorum nusquam cineres, nusquam ossa parentum
(Spem miseram!) assuetosve Lares, aut rura videbunt.
Quippe ubi planities campi diffusa jacebat;
Mons novus: ille supercilium, frontemque favillâ
Incanum ostentans, ambustis cautibus, æquor
Subjectum, stragemque suam, mæsta arva, minaci
Despicit imperio, soloque in littore regnat.

Hinc infame loci nomen, multosque per annos
Immemor antiquæ laudis, nescire labores
Vomeris, et nullo tellus revirescere cultu.
Non avium colles, non carmine matutino
Pastorum resonare; adeò undique dirus habebat
Informes latè horror agros saltusque vacantes.
Sæpius et longè detorquens navita proram
Monstrabat digito littus, sævæque revolvens
Funera narrabat noctis, veteremque ruinam.
Montis adhuc facies manet hirta atque aspera saxis:
Sed furor extinctus jamdudum, et flamma quievit,
Quæ nascenti aderat; seu fortè bituminis atri
Defluxere olìm rivi, atque effœta lacuna
Pabula sufficere ardori, viresque recusat;
Sive in visceribus meditans incendia jam nunc
(Horrendùm) arcanis glomerat genti esse futuræ
Exitio, sparsos tacitusque recolligit ignes.
Raro per clivos haud secius ordine vidi
Canescentem oleam: longum post tempus amicti
Vite virent tumuli; patriamque revisere gaudens
Bacchus in assuetis tenerum caput exerit arvis
Vix tandem, infidoque audet se credere cœlo.

A FAREWELL TO FLORENCE.

* * O Fæsulæ amœna
Frigoribus juga, nec nimiùm spirantibus auris!
Alma quibus Tusci Pallas decus Apennini
Esse dedit, glaucâque suâ canescere sylvâ!
Non ego vos posthàc Arni de valle videbo

Porticibus circum, et candenti cincta coronâ
Villarum longè nitido consurgere dorso,
Antiquamve Ædem, et veteres præferre Cupressus
Mirabor, tectisque super pendentia tecta.

IMITATION OF AN ITALIAN SONNET

OF SIGNIOR ABBATE BUONDELMONTE.

Spesso Amor sotto la forma
D'amistà ride, e s'asconde:
Poi si mischia, e si confonde
Con lo sdegno, e col rancor.
In Pietade ei si trasforma;
Par trastullo, e par dispetto;
Mà nel suo diverso aspetto
Sempr' egli, è l' istesso Amor.

Lusit amicitiæ interdum velatus amictu,
Et benè compositâ veste fefellit Amor.
Mox iræ assumpsit cultus, faciemque minantem,
Inque odium versus, versus et in lacrymas:
Ludentem fuge, nec lacrymanti, aut crede furenti;
Idem est dissimili semper in ore Deus.

ALCAIC ODE,

WRITTEN IN THE ALBUM OF THE GRANDE CHARTREUSE, IN DAUPHINY, AUGUST 1741.

O Tu, severi Religio loci,
Quocunque gaudes nomine (non leve
Nativa nam certè fluenta
Numen habet, veteresque sylvas;

Præsentiorem et conspicimus Deum
Per invias rupes, fera per juga,
Clivosque præruptos, sonantes
Inter aquas, nemorumque noctem;
Quàm si repostus sub trabe citreâ
Fulgeret auro, et Phidiacâ manu;)
Salve vocanti ritè, fesso et
Da placidam juveni quietem.
Quod si invidendis sedibus, et frui
Fortuna sacrâ lege silentii
Vetat volentem, me resorbens
In medios violenta fluctus:
Saltem remoto des, Pater, angulo
Horas senectæ ducere liberas;
Tutumque vulgari tumultu
Surripias, hominumque curis.

PART OF AN HEROIC EPISTLE

FROM SOPHONISBA TO MASINISSA.

Egregium accipio promissi Munus amoris,
Inque manu mortem, jam fruitura, fero:
Atque utinam citius mandasses, luce vel unâ
Transieram Stygios non inhonesta lacus.
Victoris nec passa toros, nova nupta, mariti,
Nec fueram fastus, Roma superba, tuos.
Scilicet hæc partem tibi, Masinissa, triumphi
Detractam, hæc pompæ jura minora suæ
Imputat, atque uxor quòd non tua pressa catenis,
Objecta et sævæ plausibus orbis eo·

Quin tu pro tantis cepisti præmia factis,
  Magnum Romanæ pignus amicitiæ !
Scipiadæ excuses, oro, si, tardius utar
  Munere. Non nimiùm vivere, crede, velim.
Parva mora est, breve sed tempus mea fama requirit :
  Detinet hæc animam cura suprema meam.
Quæ patriæ prodesse meæ Regina ferebar,
  Inter Elisæas gloria prima nurus,
Ne videar flammæ nimis indulsisse secundæ,
  Vel nimis hostiles extimuisse manus.
Fortunam atque annos liceat revocare priores,
  Gaudiaque heu ! quantis nostra repensa malis.
Primitiasne tuas meministi atque arma Syphacis
  Fusa, et per Tyrias ducta trophæa vias ?
(Laudis at antiquæ forsan meminisse pigebit,
  Quodque decus quondam causa ruboris erit.)
Tempus ego certe memini, felicia Pœnis
  Quo te non puduit solvere vota deis ;
Mœniaque intrantem vidi : longo agmine duxit
  Turba salutantum, purpureique patres.
Fœminea ante omnes longe admiratur euntem,
  Hæret et aspectu tota caterva tuo.
Jam flexi, regale decus, per colla capilli,
  Jam decet ardenti fuscus in ore color !
Commendat frontis generosa modestia formam,
  Seque cupit laudi surripuisse suæ.
Prima genas tenui signat vix flore juventas,
  Et dextræ soli credimus esse virum.
Dum faciles gradiens oculos per singula jactas,
  (Seu rexit casus lumina, sive Venus)
In me (vel certè visum est) conversa morari
  Sensi ; virgineus perculit ora pudor.

Nescio quid vultum molle spirare tuendo,
  Credideramque tuos lentius ire pedes.
Quærebam, juxta æqualis si dignior esset,
  Quæ poterat visus detinuisse tuos:
Nulla fuit circum æqualis quæ dignior esset,
  Asseruitque decus conscia forma suum.
Pompæ finis erat. Totâ vix nocte quievi,
  Sin premat invitæ lumina victa sopor,
Somnus habet pompas, eademque recursat imago
  Atque iterum hesterno munere victor ades.
* * * * * *

DIDACTIC POEM, UNFINISHED, ENTITLED

DE PRINCIPIIS COGITANDI.

LIBER PRIMUS. AD FAVONIUM.

UNDE Animus scire incipiat; quibus inchoet orsa
Principiis seriem rerum, tenuemque catenam
Mnemosyne: Ratio unde rudi sub pectore tardum
Augeat imperium; et primum mortalibus ægris
Ira, Dolor, Metus, et Curæ nascantur inanes,
Hinc canere aggredior. Nec dedignare canentem,
O decus! Angliacæ certe O lux altera gentis!
Si quà primus iter monstras, vestigia conor
Signare incertâ, tremulâque insistere plantâ.
Quin potius duc ipse (potes namque omnia) sanctum
Ad limen (si ritè adeo, si pectore puro,)
Obscuræ reserans Naturæ ingentia claustra.
Tu cæcas rerum causas, fontemque severum

Pande, Pater; tibi enim, tibi, veri magne Sacerdos,
Corda patent hominum, atque altæ penetralia Mentis.
Tuque aures adhibe vacuas, facilesque, Favoni,
(Quod tibi crescit opus) simplex nec despice carmen,
Nec vatem: non illa leves primordia motus,
Quanquam parva, dabunt. Lætum vel amabile quicquid
Usquam oritur, trahit hinc ortum; nec surgit ad auras,
Quin ea conspirent simul, eventusque secundent.
Hinc variæ vitai artes, ac mollior usus,
Dulce et amicitiæ vinclum: Sapientia dia
Hinc roseum accendit lumen, vultuque sereno
Humanas aperit mentes, nova gaudia monstrans,
Deformesque fugat curas, vanosque timores:
Scilicet et rerum crescit pulcherrima Virtus.
Illa etiam, quæ te (mirùm!) noctesque diesque
Assiduè fovet inspirans, linguamque sequentem
Temperat in numeros, atque horas mulcet inertes
Aurea non aliâ se jactat origine Musa.
Principio, ut magnum fœdus Natura creatrix
Firmavit, tardis jussitque inolescere membris
Sublimes animas; tenebroso in carcere partem
Noluit æthereamlongo torpere veterno:
Nec per se proprium passa exercere vigorem est,
Ne sociæ molis conjunctos sperneret artus,
Ponderis oblita, et cœlestis conscia flammæ.
Idcircò innumero ductu tremere undique fibras
Nervorum instituit: tum toto corpore miscens
Implicuit latè ramos, et sensile textum,
Implevitque humore suo (seu lympha vocanda.
Sive aura est) tenuis certè, atque levissima quædam
Vis versatur agens, parvosque infusa canales
Perfluit; assiduè externis quæ concita plagis,

Mobilis, incussique fidelis nuntia motûs,
Hinc indè accensâ contage relabitur usque
Ad superas hominis sedes, arcemque cerebri.
Namque illìc posuit solium, et sua templa sacravit
Mens animi: hanc circum coëunt, densoque feruntur
Agmine notitiæ, simulacraque tenuia rerum:
Ecce autem naturæ ingens aperitur imago
Immensæ, variique patent commercia mundi.
Ac uti longinquis descendunt montibus amnes
Velivolus Tamisis, flaventisque Indus arenæ,
Euphratesque, Tagusque, et opimo flumine Ganges,
Undas quisque suas volvens, cursuque sonoro
In mare prorumpunt: hos magno acclinis in antro
Excipit Oceanus, natorumque ordine longo
Dona recognoscit venientûm, ultròque serenat
Cæruleam faciem, et diffuso marmore ridet.
Haud aliter species properant se inferre novellæ
Certatim menti, atque aditus quino agmine complent.
Primas tactus agit partes, primusque minutæ
Laxat iter cæcum turbæ, recipitque ruentem.
Non idem huic modus est, qui fratribus: amplius ille
Imperium affectat senior, penitusque medullis,
Visceribusque habitat totis, pellisque recentem
Funditur in telam, et latè per stamina vivit.
Necdum etiam matris puer eluctatus ab alvo
Multiplices solvit tunicas, et vincula rupit:
Sopitus molli somno, tepidoque liquore
Circumfusus adhuc: tactus tamen aura lacessit
Jamdudum levior sensus, animamque reclusit.
Idque magis simul, ac solitum blandumque calorem
Frigore mutavit cœli, quod verberat acri
Impete inassuetos artus: tum sævior adstat,

Humanæque comes vitæ Dolor excipit; ille
Cunctantem frustrà et tremulo multa ore querentem
Corripit invadens, ferreisque amplectitur ulnis.
Tum species primùm patefacta est candida Lucis
(Usque vices adeò Natura bonique, malique,
Exæquat, justâque manu sua damna rependit)
Tum primùm, ignotosque bibunt nova lumina soles.
  Carmine quo, Dea, te dicam, gratissima cœli
Progenies, ortumque tuum; gemmantia rore
Ut per prata levi lustras, et floribus halans
Purpureum Veris gremium, scenamque virentem
Pingis, et umbriferos colles, et cærula regna?
Gratia te, Venerisque Lepos, et mille Colorum,
Formarumque chorus sequitur, motusque decentes.
At caput invisum Stygiis Nox atra tenebris
Abdidit, horrendæque simul Formidinis ora,
Pervigilesque æstus Curarum, atque anxius Angor.
Undique lætitiâ florent mortalia corda,
Purus et arridet largis fulgoribus Æther.
  Omnia nec tu ideò invalidæ se pandere Menti
(Quippe nimis teneros posset vis tanta diei
Perturbare, et inexpertos confundere visus)
Nec capere infantes animos, neu cernere credas
Tam variam molem, et miræ spectacula lucis:
Nescio quâ tamen hæc oculos dulcedine parvos
Splendida percussit novitas, traxitque sequentes;
Nonne videmus enim, latis inserta fenestris
Sicubi se Phœbi dispergant aurea tela,
Sive lucernarum rutilus colluxerit ardor,
Extemplo hùc obverti aciem, quæ fixa repertos
Haurit inexpletum radios, fruiturque tuendo.

Altior huic verò sensu, majorque videtur
Addita, Judicioque arctè connexa potestas,
Quod simul atque ætas volventibus auxerit annis,
Hæc simul, assiduo depascens omnia visu,
Perspiciet, vis quanta loci, quid polleat ordo,
Juncturæ quis honos, ut res accendere rebus
Lumina conjurant inter se, et mutua fulgent.
Nec minor in geminis viget auribus insita virtus,
Nec tantum in curvis quæ pervigil excubet antris
Hinc atque hinc (ubi Vox tremefecerit ostia pulsu
Aëriis invecta rotis) longèque recurset:
Scilicet Eloquio hæc sonitus, hæc fulminis alas,
Et mulcere dedit dictis et tollere corda,
Verbaque metiri numeris, versuque ligare
Repperit, et quicquid discant Libethrides undæ,
Calliope quotiès, quotiès Pater ipse canendi
Evolvat liquidum carmen, calamove loquenti
Inspiret dulces animas, digitisque figuret.
At medias fauces, et linguæ humentia templa
Gustus habet, quà se insinuet jucunda saporum
Luxuries, dona Autumni, Bacchique voluptas.
Naribus interea consedit odora hominum vis,
Docta leves captare auras, Panchaïa quales
Vere novo exhalat, Floræve quod oscula fragrant,
Roscida, cum Zephyri furtìm sub vesperis horâ
Respondet votis, mollemque aspirat amorem.
Tot portas altæ capitis circumdedit arci
Alma Parens, sensûsque vias per membra reclusit;
Haud solas: namque intùs agit vivata facultas,
Quâ sese explorat, contemplatusque repentè
Ipse suas animus vires, momentaque cernit.
Quid velit, aut possit, cupiat, fugiatve, vicissìm

Percipit imperio gaudens; neque corpora fallunt
Morigera ad celeres actus, ac numina mentis.
Qualis Hamadryadum quondam si fortè sororum
Una, novos peragrans saltus, et devia rura:
(Atque illam in viridi suadet procumbere ripâ
Fontis pura quies, et opaci frigoris umbra)
Dum prona in latices speculi de margine pendet,
Mirata est subitam venienti occurrere Nympham:
Mox eosdem, quos ipsa, artus, eadem ora gerentem
Unà inferre gradus, unà succedere sylvæ
Aspicit alludens; seseque agnoscit in undis.
Sic sensu interno rerum simulacra suarum
Mens ciet, et proprios observat conscia vultus.
Nec verò simplex ratio, aut jus omnibus unum
Constat imaginibus. Sunt quæ bina ostia nôrunt;
Hæ privos servant aditus; sine legibus illæ
Passìm, quà data porta, ruunt, animoque propinquant.
Respice, cui à cunis tristes extinxit ocellos,
Sæva et in eternas mersit natura tenebras:
Illi ignota dies lucet, vernusque colorum
Offusus nitor est, et vivæ gratia formæ.
Corporis at filum, et motus, spatiumque, locique
Intervalla datur certo dignoscere tactu:
Quandoquidem his iter ambiguum est, et janua duplex,
Exclusæque oculis species irrumpere tendunt
Per digitos. Atqui solis concessa potestas
Luminibus blandæ est radios immittere lucis.
Undique proporrò sociis, quacunque patescit
Notitiæ campus, mistæ lasciva feruntur
Turba voluptatis comites, formæque dolorum
Terribiles visu, et portâ glomerantur in omni.
Nec vario minus introïtu magnum ingruit Illud,

Quo facere et fungi, quo res existere circùm
Quamque sibi proprio cum corpore scimus, et ire
Ordine, perpetuoque per ævum flumine labi.
  Nunc age quo valeat pacto, quâ sensilis arte
Affectare viam, atque animi tentare latebras
Materies (dictis aures adverte faventes)
Exsequar. Imprimìs spatii quam multa per æquor
Millia multigenis pandant se corpora seclis,
Expende. Haud unum invenies, quod mente licebit
Amplecti, nedum propriùs deprendere sensu,
Molis egens certæ, aut solido sine robore, cujus
Denique mobilitas linquit, texturave partes,
Ulla nec orarum circumcæsura coërcet.
Hæc conjuncta adeò totâ compage fatetur
Mundus, et extremo clamant in limine rerum,
(Si rebus datur extremum) primordia. Firmat
Hæc eadem tactus (tactum quis dicere falsum
Audeat ?) hæc oculi nec lucidus arguit orbis.
  Inde potestatum enasci densissima proles:
Nam quodcunque ferit visum, tangive laborat,
Quicquid nare bibis, vel concava concipit auris,
Quicquid lingua sapit, credas hoc omne, necesse est
Ponderibus, textu, discursu, mole, figurâ
Particulas præstare leves, et semina rerum.
Nunc oculos igitur pascunt, et luce ministrâ
Fulgere cuncta vides, spargique coloribus orbem,
Dum de sole trahunt alias, aliasque supernè
Detorquent, retròque docent se vertere flammas.
Nunc trepido inter se fervent corpuscula pulsu,
Ut tremor æthera per magnum, latèque natantes
Aurarum fluctus avidi vibrantia claustra
Auditûs queat allabi, sonitumque propaget.

Cominùs interdum non ullo interprete per se
Nervorum invadunt teneras quatientia fibras,
Sensiferumque urgent ultrò per viscera motum.

*   *   *   *   *   *   *

LIBER QUARTUS.

Hactenus haud segnis Naturæ arcana retexi
Musarum interpres, primusque Britanna per arva
Romano liquidum deduxi flumine rivum.
Cum Tu opere in medio, spes tanti et causa laboris,
Linquis, et æternam fati te condis in umbram!
Vidi egomet duro graviter concussa dolore
Pectora, in alterius non unquam lenta dolorem;
Et languere oculos vidi, et pallescere amantem
Vultum, quo nunquam Pietas nisi rara, Fidesque,
Altus amor Veri, et purum spirabat Honestum.
Visa tamen tardi demùm inclementia morbi
Cessare est, reducemque iterum roseo ore Salutem
Speravi, atque unà tecum, dilecte Favoni!
Credulus heu longos, ut quondàm, fallere Soles:
Heu spes nequicquam dulces, atque irrita vota!
Heu mæstos Soles, sine te quos ducere flendo
Per desideria, et questus jam cogor inanes!
At Tu, sancta anima, et nostri non indiga luctûs,
Stellanti templo, sincerique ætheris igne,
Unde orta es, fruere; atque ô si secura, nec ultra
Mortalis, notos olìm miserata labores
Respectes, tenuesque vacet cognoscere curas;
Humanam si fortè altâ de sede procellam
Contemplêre, metus, stimulosque cupidinis acres,

Gaudiaque et gemitus, parvoque in corde tumultum
Irarum ingentem, et sævos sub pectore fluctus;
Respice et has lacrymas, memori quas ictus amore
Fundo; quod possum, juxtà lugere sepulchrum
Dum juvat, et mutæ vana hæc jactare favillæ.
* * * * * * *

GREEK EPIGRAM.

Ἀζόμενος πολύθηρον ἑκηβόλου ἄλσος ἀνάσσας,
Τᾶς δεινᾶς τεμένη λεῖπε κυναγὲ θεᾶς,
Μοῦνοι ἄρ' ἔνθα κύνων ζαθέων κλαγγεῦσιν ὑλάγμοι,
Ἀνταχεῖς Νυμφᾶν ἀγροτερᾶν κελάδῳ.

TRANSLATIONS AND IMITATIONS.

PETRARCA PART I. SONETTO 170.

"Lasso ch' i' ardo, ed altri non mel crede ;" &c.

IMITATED.

Uror, io ; veros at nemo credidet ignes :
  Quin credunt omnes ; dura sed illa negat,
Illa negat, soli volumus cui posse probare ;
  Quin videt, et visos improba dissimulat.
Ah, durissima mì, sed et, ah, pulcherrima rerum !
  Nonne animam in miserâ, Cynthia, fronte vides ?
Omnibus illa pia est ; et, si non fata vetâssent,
  Tam longas mentem flecteret ad lacrymas.
Sed tamen has lacrymas, hunc tu, quem spreveris, ignem,
  Carminaque auctori non bene culta suo,
Turba futurorum non ignorabit amantûm :
  Nos duo, cumque erimus parvus uterque cinis.
Jamque faces, eheu ! oculorum, et frigida lingua,
  Hæ sine luce jacent, immemor illa loqui ;
Infelix musa æternos spirabit amores,
  Ardebitque urnâ multa favilla meâ.

FROM THE "ANTHOLOGIA GRÆCA."

IN BACCHÆ FURENTIS STATUAM.

Credite, non viva est Mænas; non spirat imago:
Artificis rabiem miscuit ære manus.

IN ALEXANDRUM, ÆRE EFFICTUM.

Quantum audet, Lysippe, manus tua! surgit in ære
Spiritus, atque oculis bellicus ignis adest:
Spectate hos vultus, miserisque ignoscite Persis:
Quid mirum, imbelles si leo sparsit oves?

IN MEDEÆ IMAGINEM, NOBILE TIMOMACHI OPUS.

En ubi Medeæ varius dolor æstuat ore,
Jamque animum nati, jamque maritus, habent!
Succenset, miseret, medio exardescit amore,
Dum furor inque oculo gutta minante tremit.
Cernis adhuc dubiam; quid enim? licet impia matris
Colchidos, at non sit dextera Timomachi.

IN NIOBES STATUAM.

Fecerat e vivâ lapidem me Jupiter; at me
Praxiteles vivam reddidit e lapide.

A NYMPH OFFERING A STATUE OF HERSELF TO VENUS.

Te tibi, sancta, fero nudam; formosius ipsa
Cum tibi, quod ferrem, te, Dea, nil habui.

IN AMOREM DORMIENTEM.

Docte puer vigiles mortalibus addere curas,
  Anne potest in te somnus habere locum?
Laxi juxta arcus, et fax suspensa quiescit,
  Dormit et in pharetrâ clausa sagitta suâ;
Longè mater abest; longè Cythereia turba:
  Verùm ausint alii te prope ferre pedem,
Non ego: nam metui valdè, mihi, perfide, quiddam
  Forsan et in somnis ne meditere mali.

FROM A FRAGMENT OF PLATO.

Itur in Idalios tractus, felicia regna,
  Fundit ubi densam myrtea sylva comam,
Intus Amor teneram visus spirare quietem,
  Dum roseo roseos imprimit ore toros;
Sublimem procul a ramis pendere pharetram,
  Et de languidulâ spicula lapsa manu,
Vidimus, et risu molli diducta labella
  Murmure quæ assiduo pervolitabat apis.

IN FONTEM AQUÆ CALIDÆ.

Sub platanis puer Idalius prope fluminis undam
  Dormiit, in ripâ deposuitque facem.
Tempus adest, sociæ, Nympharum audentior una,
  Tempus adest, ultra quid dubitamus? ait.
Ilicet incurrit, pestem ut divûmque hominumque
  Lampada collectis exanimaret aquis:
Demens! nam nequiit sævam restinguere flammam
  Nympha, sed ipsa ignes traxit, et inde calet.

IRREPSISSE suas murem videt Argus in ædes,
  Atque ait, heus, a me nunquid, amice, velis?
Ille autem ridens, metuas nihil, inquit; apud te,
  O bone, non epulas, hospitium petimus.

HANC tibi Rufinus mittit, Rodoclea, coronam,
  Has tibi decerpens texerat ipse rosas;
Est viola, est anemòne, est suave-rubens hyacinthus,
  Mistaque Narcisso lutea caltha suo:
Sume; sed aspiciens, ah, fidere desine formæ;
  Qui pinxit, brevis est, sertaque teque, color.

AD AMOREM.

PAULISPER vigiles, oro, compesce dolores,
  Respue nec musæ supplicis aure preces;
Oro brevem lacrymis veniam, requiemque furori:
  Ah, ego non possum vulnera tanta pati!
Intima flamma, vides, miseros depascitur artus,
  Surgit et extremis spiritus in labiis:
Quòd si tam tenuem cordi est exsolvere vitam,
  Stabit in opprobrium sculpta querela tuum.
Juro perque faces istas, arcumque sonantem,
  Spiculaque hoc unum figere docta jecur;
Heu fuge crudelem puerum, sævasque sagittas!
  Huic fuit exitii causa, viator, Amor.

APPENDIX.

THE following extracts from a Poem on the Letters of the Alphabet were transcribed from a manuscript of Gray, and are published in the fifth volume of Mr. Mitford's edition of his works. As they are not inserted among the Poems, which are contained in the first volume of that edition, we presume that they came into Mr. Mitford's possession after it was printed. They appear in what seems to be an imperfect or mutilated letter. Horace Walpole mentions that Gray would never allow this poem to be his, but the humor and versification were so much in Gray's style that he could not believe it to be written by any other hand. The manuscript says :

"To make my peace with the noble youth you mention, I send you a poem that I am sure they will read (as well as they can) — a masterpiece, it is said, being an admirable improvement on that beautiful piece called Pugna Porcorum, which begins —

'Plangite porcelli Porcorum pigra propago ;'

but that is in Latin, and not for their reading ; but indeed this is worth a thousand of it, and unfortunately it is not perfect, and it is not mine."

THE CHARACTERS OF THE CHRIST-CROSS ROW, BY A CRITIC, TO MRS. ——.

* * * * *

GREAT D *d*raws near — the *D*uchess sure is come,
Open the *d*oors of the withdrawing-room ;
Her daughters decked most daintily I see,
The Dowager grows a perfect double D.
E enters next, and with her Eve appears,
Not like yon Dowager deprest with years ;

What Ease and Elegance her person grace,
Bright beaming, as the Evening-star, her face;
Queen Esther next — how fair even after death,
Then one faint glimpse of Queen Elizabeth;
No more, our Esthers now are naught but Hetties,
Elizabeths all dwindled into Betties:
In vain you think to find them under E,
They 're all diverted into H and B.
F follows fast the fair — and in his rear
See Folly, Fashion, Foppery, straight appear,
All with fantastic clews, fantastic clothes,
With Fans and Flounces, Fringe and Furbelows.
Here Grub-street Geese presume to joke and jeer,
All, all, but Grannam Osborne's Gazetteer.
High heaves his hugeness H, methinks we see,
Henry the Eighth's most monstrous majesty;
But why on such *mock* grandeur should we dwell?
H mounts to Heaven, and H descends to Hell.

* * * * *

As H the Hebrew found, so I the Jew,
See Isaac, Joseph, Jacob, pass in view;
The walls of old Jerusalem appear,
See Israel, and all Judah thronging there.

* * * * *

P pokes his head out, yet has not a pain;
Like Punch, he peeps, but soon pops in again;
Pleased with his Pranks, the Pisgys call him Puck,
Mortals he loves to prick, and pinch, and pluck;
Now a pert Prig, he perks upon your face,
Now peers, pores, ponders with profound grimace,
Now a proud Prince, in pompous Purple drest,
And now a Player, a Peer, a Pimp, or Priest;

A Pea, a Pin, in a perpetual round,
Now seems a Penny, and now shows a Pound;
Like Perch or Pike, in Pond you see him come,
He in plantations hangs like Pear or Plum,
Pippin or Peach; then perches on the spray,
In form of Parrot, Pye, or Popinjay.
P, Proteus-like, all tricks, all shapes can show,
The Pleasantest Person in the Christ-Cross row.

* * * * *

As K a King, Q represents a Queen,
And seems small difference the sounds between;
K, as a man, with hoarser accent speaks,
In shriller notes Q like a female squeaks;
Behold K struts, as might a King become,
Q draws her train along the Drawing-room,
Slow follow all the quality of State,
Queer Queensbury only does refuse to wait.

* * * * *

Thus great R reigns in town, while, different far,
Rests in Retirement *little* Rural R;
Remote from cities lives in lone Retreat,
With Rooks and Rabbit burrows round his seat —
S, sails the Swan slow down the Silver stream.

* * * * *

So big with Weddings, waddles W,
And brings all Womankind before your view;
A Wench, a Wife, a Widow and a W——,
With Woe behind, and Wantonness before.

It would be unjust to Gray to insert the following extempore effusions among his Poems ; but they have been preserved and printed, and, that we may omit nothing in verse from his pen, we insert them in this place :

EPIGRAM ON DR. KEENE.

The Bishop of Chester,
Though wiser than Nestor,
And fairer than Esther,
If you scratch him will fester.

EPITAPH ON DR. KEENE.

Here lies Dr. Keene, the good Bishop of Chester,
Who eat a fat goose, and could not digest her.

EXTEMPORE EPITAPH

On Anne, Countess of Dorset, Pembroke and Montgomery, made by Mr. Gray on reading the Epitaph on her mother's tomb in the church at Appleby, composed by the Countess in the same manner.

Now clean, now hideous, mellow now, now gruff,
She swept, she hissed, she ripened and grew rough,
At Brougham, Pendragon, Appleby and Brough.

IMPROMPTU.

(From the Wharton Manuscript.)

When you rise from your dinner as light as before,
'T is a sign you have eat just enough and no more.

NOTES TO GRAY.

On the Spring.

Page 25. — Mason tells us that, in the original manuscript, Gray had given to this ode the title of *Noontide*.

Page 25, line 14.

" ——— a bank
O'er-canopied with luscious woodbine."
Mids. Night's Dream.

Page 26, line 7.

" Nare per æstatem liquidam." — Georg. iv. 59. — *Gray*.

Page 26, line 10.

" ——— sporting with *quick glance*,
Shew to the *sun* their waved coats dropt with gold."
Par. Lost, vii. 410. — *Gray*.

Page 26, line 23. — " While insects from the threshold preach." — Green, in the " Grotto." *Dodsley's Misc*. v. p. 161. — *Gray*.

On the Death of a Favorite Cat, drowned in a Tub of Gold Fishes.

Page 27. — The subject of this poem was a cat of Walpole's, which Gray said he was about to " immortalize for a week or a fortnight." After the poet's death, Walpole placed the china vase on a pedestal, inscribing on it the four first lines of the ode. From Strawberry Hill it was removed to the seat of Lord Derby, at Knowsley.

On a Distant Prospect of Eton College.

Page 28, line 20. — King Henry the Sixth, founder of the College. — *Gray*.

Page 29, line 9. — " And bees their honey *redolent of spring*." — Dryden's Fable on the Pythag. System. — *Gray*.

Page 31, line 9. — " Madness laughing in his ireful mood." — Dryden. — *Gray*.

The Progress of Poesy.

Page 34. — When the author first published this and the following Ode, he was advised, even by his friends, to subjoin some few explanatory notes ; but had too much respect for the understanding of his readers to take that liberty. — *Gray*.

Page 34, line 1.

" Awake, my glory : awake, lute and harp."
David's Psalms. — *Gray*.

" Awake, awake, my lyre,
And tell thy silent master's humble tale."
Cowley, " Ode of David."

Pindar styles his own poetry, with its musical accompaniments, *Αἰολὶς μολπὴ*, *Αἰολίδες χορδαὶ*, *Αἰολίδων πνοαὶ αὐλῶν*, Æolian song, Æolian strings, the breath of the Æolian flute.

The subject and simile, as usual with Pindar, are united. The various sources of poetry, which gives life and lustre to all it touches, are here described; its quiet majestic progress, enriching every subject (otherwise dry and barren) with a pomp of diction and luxuriant harmony of numbers; and its more rapid and irresistible course, when swollen and hurried away by the conflict of tumultuous passions.

Page 34, line 13. — Power of harmony to calm the turbulent sallies of the soul. The thoughts are borrowed from the first Pythian of Pindar. — *Gray.*

Page 34, line 20. — This is a weak imitation of some beautiful lines in the same Ode. — *Gray.*

Page 35, line 1. — Power of harmony to produce all the graces of motion in the body. — *Gray.*

Page 35, line 18. — To compensate the real and imaginary ills of life, the Muse was given to mankind by the same Providence that sends the day, by its cheerful presence to dispel the gloom and terrors of the night. — *Gray.*

Page 35, line 31.

"Or seen her [morning's] well-appointed star
Come marching up the eastern hills afar."

Cowley. — *Gray.*

Page 36, line 1. — Extensive influence of poetic genius over the remotest and most uncivilized nations: its connection with liberty, and the virtues that naturally attend on it.

"Extra anni solisque vias." — Virg. Æn. vi. 795.
"Tutta lontana dal camin del sole." — Petr. Canz. 2.

Gray.

Page 36, line 13. — Progress of poetry from Greece to Italy, and from Italy to England. Chaucer was not unacquainted with the writings of Dante or of Petrarch. The Earl of Surrey and Sir Thomas Wyatt had travelled in Italy, and formed their taste there. Spenser imitated the Italian writers; Milton improved on them; but this school expired soon after the Restoration, and a new one arose, on the French model, which has subsisted ever since. — *Gray.*

Page 37, line 1. — "Piu lontan del Ciel." — Dante, "Il Inferno," c. ix.

Page 37, line 12. — Shakspeare. — *Gray.*

"The flowery May, who from her *green lap* throws
The yellow cowslip, and the pale primrose."

Milton, Son. on May Morn. — *Gray.*

Page 37, line 13. — Milton, "Paradise Lost," vi. 771. — *Gray.*

Page 37, line 16. — "Flammantia mœnia mundi," Lucret. i. 74. — *Gray.*

Page 37, line 17. — "For the spirit of the living creature was in the wheels. And above the firmament that was over their heads was the likeness of a throne, as the appearance of a sapphire stone. This was the appearance of the glory of the Lord." — Ezek. 1: 20, 26, 28. — *Gray.*

Page 37, line 20. — *'Οφθαλμῶν μὲν ἄμερσε· δίδου δ' ἡδεῖαν ἀοιδήν.*
Hom. "Od. Θ." ver. 64. — *Gray.*

Page 37, line 24. — "Hast thou clothed his neck with thunder?" — Job. This verse and the foregoing are meant to express the stately march and sounding energy of Dryden's rhymes. — *Gray.*

Page 37, line 28. — "Words that weep and tears that speak." — Cowley. — *Gray.*

Page 38, line 1. — We have had in our language no other odes of the sublime kind than that of Dryden on St. Cecilia's Day; for Cowley, who had his merit, yet wanted judgment, style and harmony, for such a task. That of Pope is not worthy of so great a man. Mr. Mason, indeed, of late days, has touched the true chords, and with a masterly hand, in some of his choruses; above all in the last of Caractacus:

"Hark! heard ye not yon footstep dread?" &c. — *Gray.*

Gray was strangely insensible to the surpassing merits of Collins, who contests the lyric palm not only with himself, but with Dryden.

Page 38, line 5. — *Διὸς πρὸς ὄρνιχα Θεῖον,* "Olymp." Pindar compares himself to that bird, and his enemies to ravens that croak and clamor in vain below, while it pursues its flight regardless of their noise. — *Gray.*

Page 38, line 14.
"Mocking the air with colors idly spread."
"King John," Act v. sc. 1. — *Gray.*

Page 38, line 18. — The hauberk was a texture of steel ringlets, or rings interwoven, forming a coat of mail that sat close to the body, and adapted itself to every motion. — *Gray.*

Page 38, line 24. — Snowdon was a name given by the Saxons to that mountainous tract which the Welsh themselves call Craigian-eryri: it included all the highlands of Caernarvonshire and Merionethshire, as far east as the river Conway. R. Hygden, speaking of the castle of Conway, built by King Edward the First, says, "Ad ortum amnis Conway ad clivum montis Erery;" and Matthew of Westminster (ad ann. 1283), "Apud Aberconway ad pedes montis Snowdoniæ fecit erigi castrum forte." — *Gray.*

Page 39, line 1. — Gilbert de Clare, surnamed the Red, Earl of Gloucester and Hereford, son-in-law to King Edward. — *Gray.*

Page 39, line 21. — Edmond de Mortimer, Lord of Wigmore. — *Gray.*

They both were Lord Marchers, whose lands lay on the borders of Wales, and probably accompanied the king in this expedition. — *Gray.*

Page 39, line 7. — The image was taken from a well-known picture of Raphael, representing the Supreme Being in the vision of Ezekiel. There are two of these paintings, both believed to be originals, — one at Florence, the other in the Duke of Orleans' collection at Paris. — *Gray.*

Page 39, line 8. — "Shone like a meteor streaming to the wind." — Par. Lost. — *Gray.*

Page 39, line 23. — The shores of Caernarvonshire opposite the isle of Anglesey. — *Gray.*

Page 39, line 26. — Camden and others observe, that eagles used annually to build their eyrie among the rocks of Snowdon, which from thence (as some think) were named by the Welsh Craigian-eryri, or the crags of the eagles. At this day (I am told) the highest point of Snowdon is called the Eagle's nest. That bird is certainly no stranger to this island, as the Scots, and the people of Cumberland, Westmoreland, &c., can testify: it even has built its nest upon the peak of Derbyshire. (See Willoughby's "Ornithol.," by Ray.) — *Gray.*

Page 40, line 1.

"As dear to me as are the ruddy drops
That visit my sad heart."
"Jul. Cæsar," Act ii. sc. 1. — *Gray.*

Page 40, line 8. — See the Norwegian ode (the Fatal Sisters) that follows. — *Gray.*

Page 40, line 15. — Edward the Second, cruelly butchered in Berkley Castle. — *Gray.*

Page 40, line 17. — Isabel of France, Edward the Second's adulterous queen. — *Gray.*

Page 40, line 24. — Death of that king, abandoned by his children, and even robbed in his last moments by his courtiers and his mistress. — *Gray.*

Page 40, line 27. — Edward the Black Prince, dead some time before his father. — *Gray.*

Page 41, line 1. — Magnificence of Richard the Second's reign. See Froissart and other contemporary writers. — *Gray.*

Page 41, line 7. — Richard the Second, as we are told by Archbishop Scroop and the confederate Lords in their manifesto, by Thomas of Walsingham, and all the older writers, was starved to death. The story of his assassination by Sir Piers of Exton is of much later date. — *Gray.*

Page 41, line 13. — Ruinous wars of York and Lancaster. — *Gray.*

Page 41, line 17. — Henry the Sixth, George Duke of Clarence, Edward the Fifth, Richard Duke of York, &c., believed to be murdered secretly in the Tower of London. The oldest part of that structure is vulgarly attributed to Julius Cæsar. — *Gray.*

Page 41, line 19. — Margaret of Anjou, a woman of heroic spirit, who struggled hard to save her husband and her crown. Ibid. Henry the Fifth. — *Gray.*

Page 41, line 20. — Henry the Sixth, very near being canonized. The line of Lancaster had no right of inheritance to the crown. — *Gray.*

Page 41, line 21. — The white and red roses, devices of York and Lancaster. — *Gray.*

Page 41, line 23. — The silver boar was the badge of Richard the Third; whence he was usually known in his own time by the name of the Boar. — *Gray.*

Page 41, line 29. — Eleanor of Castile died a few years after the conquest of Wales. The heroic proof she gave of her affection for her lord is well known. The monuments of his regret and sorrow for the loss of her are still to be seen at Northampton, Gaddington, Waltham, and other places. — *Gray.*

Page 42, line 10. — Both Merlin and Taliessin had prophesied that the Welsh should regain their sovereignty over this island; which seemed to be accomplished in the house of Tudor. — *Gray.*

Page 42, line 17. — Speed, relating an audience given by Queen Elizabeth to Paul Dzialinski, ambassador of Poland, says, "And thus she, lion-like rising, daunted the malapert orator no less with her stately port and majestical deporture, than with the tartnesse of her princelie checkes." — *Gray.*

Page 42, line 21. — Taliessin, chief of the bards, flourished in the sixth century. His works are still preserved, and his memory held in high veneration among his countrymen. — *Gray.*

Page 43, line 26. — "Fierce wars and faithful loves shall moralize my song." Spenser's "Proeme to the F. Q." — *Gray.*

Page 41, line 28. — Shakspeare. — *Gray.*

Page 43, line 1. — Milton. — *Gray.*

Page 43, line 3. — The succession of poets after Milton's time. — *Gray.*

Page 43, line 4. — "Why you would alter 'lost in long futurity,' I do not see, unless because you think 'lost' and 'expire' are tautologies, or because it looks as if the end of the prophecy were disappointed by it, and that people may think that poetry in Britain was some time or other really to expire, whereas the meaning is only that it was lost to his ear from the immense distance. I cannot give up 'lost,' for it begins with an *l*." — *Gray* to *Mason*, June, 1757.

ODE TO MUSIC.

Page 43. — This ode was performed in the Senate House of Cambridge, July 1, 1769, at the installation of His Grace Augustus Henry Fitzroy, Duke of Grafton, Chancellor of the University.

Page 45, line 2. — Margaret of Anjou, wife of Henry VI., foundress of Queen's College. Elizabeth Widville, wife of Edward IV., hence called the paler rose, as being of the house of York. She added to the foundation of Margaret of Anjou.

Page 45, line 4. — Henry the Sixth and Eighth. The former the founder of King's, the latter the greatest benefactor to Trinity College. — *Gray.*

Page 45, line 25. — Countess of Richmond and Derby; the mother of Henry VII., founder of St. John's and Christ's Colleges. — *Gray.*

Page 46, line 14. — Lord Treasurer Burleigh was Chancellor of the University in the reign of Queen Elizabeth. — *Gray.*

THE FATAL SISTERS.

Page 47. — It was related to Walter Scott, that a clergyman, while some remains of the Norse were yet spoken in North Ronaldsha, carried this translation of Gray there when first published, and read it to some of the old people as referring to the ancient history of their islands. But as soon as he had proceeded a little way, they exclaimed they knew it very well in the original, and had often sang it to himself when he asked them for an old Norse song. They called it *The Enchantress.* Mason prints the Latin version, from which Gray composed his copies. The following is Gray's note of explanation:

"To be found in the Orcades of Thormodus Torfœus; Hafniæ, 1697, folio; and also in Bartholinus, p. 617, lib. iii., c. 1, 4to. (The song of the Weird Sisters, translated from the Norwegian, written about 1029. Wharton, MS.)

Page 47, line 3.

"How quick they wheeled, and, flying, behind them shot
Sharp *sleet of arrowy shower.*"
"Par. Reg." iii. 324. — *Gray.*

Page 47, line 4.

"The noise of battle hurtled in the air."
"Julius Cæsar," Act ii. sc. 2. — *Gray.*

The Vegtam's Kivitha.

Page 49, line 7. —"This ode is much more literally translated than the preceding. The original title I have restored from Gray's MS."—*Mitford.* The original is to be found in Sæmund's Edda, and in Bartholinus. Lord Orford thought the ode equal to any of Gray's.

Page 49, line 14. — Hela, in the Edda, is described with a dreadful countenance, and her body half flesh-color and half blue. — *Gray.*

Page 50, line 8. — The original word is *Valgalldr;* from *Valr*, mortuus, and *Galldr*, incantatio. — *Gray.*

Page 51, line 7. — Women were looked upon by the Gothic nations as having a peculiar insight into futurity; and some there were that made profession of magic arts and divination. These travelled round the country, and were received in every house with great respect and honor. Such a woman bore the name of Volva Seidkona or Spakona. The dress of Thorbiorga, one of these prophetesses, is described at large in Eirik's Rauda Sogu (apud Bartholin. lib. i. cap. iv. p. 688.) "She had on a blue vest spangled all over with stones, a necklace of glass beads, and a cap made of the skin of a black lamb lined with white cat-skin. She leaned on a staff adorned with brass, with a round head set with stones; and was girt with an Hunlandish belt, at which hung her pouch full of magical instruments. Her buskins were of rough calf-skin, bound on with thongs studded with knobs of brass, and her gloves of white cat-skin, the fur turned inward," &c. They were also called *Fiolkyngi*, or *Fiolkunnug*, that is, Multi-scia; and *Visindakona*, that is, Oraculorum Mulier; *Nornir*, that is, Parcæ. — *Gray.*

Page 52, line 18. — Lok is the evil being, who continues in chains till the *twilight of the gods* approaches: when he shall break his bonds, the human race, the stars and sun, shall disappear; the earth sink in the seas, and fire consume the skies: even Odin himself and his kindred deities shall perish. For a further explanation of this mythology, see "Introd. à l'Hist. de Dannemarc, par Mons. Mallet," 1755, quarto; or rather a translation of it published in 1770, and entitled "Northern Antiquities;" in which some mistakes in the original are judiciously corrected. — *Gray.*

The Triumphs of Owen.

Page 53, line 4. — *Gwyneth* — North Wales. — *Gray.*

Page 53, line 14. — *Lochlin* — Denmark. — *Gray.*

Page 53, line 20. — The red dragon is the device of Cadwalladar. — *Gray.*

Sonnet on the Death of West.

Page 56. — Mr. Wordsworth quotes this sonnet in support of his argument, that the language of good poetry does not for the most part differ from that of good prose. See his preface to his works.

Epitaph on Sir Wm. Williams.

Page 57. — Gray wrote this epitaph at the request of Mr. Frederick Montague, to place on a monument which he intended to erect at Belleisle. It was not a labor of love with Gray, as he was but slightly acquainted with the subject. Sir W. P. Williams was shot by one of the enemy's sentinels. Walpole calls him a gallant and ambitious young man, who had devoted himself to love and politics. The monument was never erected.

Elegy written in a Country Church-yard.

Page 58. — This poem is said to have been inspired by the church-yard of Stoke, and Jacob Bryant was convinced that much of it was actually composed there. Other churchyards have had their claims asserted, but its images and reflections were doubtless the suggestions of many scenes and places.

In Gray's first MS. of the elegy were the four following stanzas after the verse ending with the "Muse's flame:"

The thoughtless world to majesty may bow,
Exalt the brave, and idolize success;
But more to innocence their safety owe
Than power or genius e'er conspired to bless.

And thou, who, mindful of the unhonored dead,
Dost in these notes their artless tale relate,
By night and lonely contemplation led
To wander in the gloomy walks of fate:

Hark! how the sacred calm that breathes around
Bids every fierce, tumultuous passion cease;
In still small accents whispering from the ground
A grateful earnest of eternal peace.

No more with reason and thyself at strife,
Give anxious cares and endless wishes room;
But through the cool sequestered vale of life
Pursue the silent tenor of thy doom.

This was the original close of the poem. After the twenty-fifth stanza, ending with the word "lawn," was the following:

Him have we seen the greenwood-side along,
While o'er the heath we hied, our labor done,
What time the wood-lark piped her farewell song,
With wistful eyes pursue the setting sun.

In the MS. of Gray, a fac-simile of which is contained in Matthias' edition, the following stanza is added to the poem, and marked by asterisks immediately to precede the epitaph. This was printed in some of the early editions, but afterwards omitted as too long a paren thesis for the place:

There scattered oft, the earliest of the year,
By hands unseen, are showers of violets found;
The red-breast loves to build and warble there,
And little footsteps lightly print the ground.

Page 58, line 1.

"—— squilla di lontano
Che paia 'l giorno pianger, che si muore."
Dante, "Purgat." — *Gray.*

Page 61, line 4.

"Ch' io veggio nel pensier, dolce mio fuoco,
Fredda una lingua, e due begli occhi chiusi
Rimaner doppo noi pien di faville."
Petr. Son. clxix. — *Gray.*

A Long Story.

Page 62. — Lady Cobham resided in the old mansion at Stoke, and, having read the Elegy in manuscript, wished to know the author. To fulfil her desire, a relation, Miss Speed, and Lady Schaub, paid a visit to Gray, and left a note on the table. Not even a poetical hermit might disregard such an invitation. He returned the "call," and to divert Lady Cobham and her family the "Long Story" was written. Gray omitted this from his collected poems.

Page 62, line 19. — " —— paventosa speme."— Petr. Son. cxiv. — *Gray.*

Page 62, line 22. — Sir Edmond Coke's mansion, at Stoke-Pogeis, now the seat of Mr. Penn, was the scene of Gray's Long Story. The antique chimneys have been allowed to remain as vestiges of the poet's fancy, and a column with a statue of Coke marks the former abode of its illustrious inhabitant. — *D'Israeli.*

Page 63, line 7. — Sir Christopher Hatton, promoted by Queen Elizabeth for his graceful person and fine dancing. — *Gray.*

Page 66, line 15. — *Styack* — The housekeeper. — *Gray.*

Page 63, line 27. — *Squib* — Groom of the chamber. — *Gray.*

Page 63, line 28. — *Groom* — The steward. — *Gray.*

Page 67, line 4. — *Macleane* — A famous highwayman hanged the week before. — *Gray.*

ODE ON THE PLEASURE ARISING FROM VICISSITUDE.

Page 68. — Left unfinished by Gray. The additions, by Mason, are distinguished by inverted commas.

Page 77, line 9. — In Gray's MS. Agrippina's was one continued speech from this line to the end of the scene. Mr. Mason informs us that he has altered it to the state in which it now stands.

HYMN TO IGNORANCE.

Page 81. — This is supposed to have been written about the year 1742, when Gray returned to Cambridge. It received its title from Mason.

STANZAS TO MR. BENTLEY.

Page 86. — These lines were written in compliment to Bentley, who made the Designs with which the six poems were published, by way of illustration. The words within inverted commas in the last stanza were supplied by Mason, a corner of the MS. copy having been torn.

SKETCH OF HIS OWN CHARACTER.

Page 87. — "Charles Townshend,"— to whom Burke alludes as "another luminary," rising before the orb of Chatham was entirely set. "Squire," Bishop of St. David's, of whom Bishop Warburton said that he had made religion his trade, while Dean Tucker had made trade his religion.

SONG.

Page 88. — Written at the request of Miss Speed, to an old air of Geminiani: — the thought from the French. This and the Amatory Lines were presented by Miss Speed, then Countess de Viry, to the Rev. Mr. Leman, of Suffolk, while on a visit at her castle in Savoy, where she died in 1783.

TOPHET.

Page 89. — These verses were intended to illustrate a grotesque etching of Henry Etough, Rector of Therfield, Herts, said to be the ugliest person of that age. He was a Jew, but turned Christian for the sake of a good living.

IMPROMPTU.

Page 89. — One of the least known of Gray's friends was Mr. William Robinson, a Berkshire clergyman, who had a house — Denton Court — near Canterbury, where the poet twice visited him. On one of these occasions, this impromptu, written and left by the poet, was found in a drawer of his dressing-table. The cause of Gray's antipathy to Lord Holland is not stated; Scott calls him a "thorough-brèd statesman of that evil period."

THE CANDIDATE.

Page 90. — Not long before Lord Sandwich canvassed the electors for the High-stewardship of Cambridge, Gray wrote these bitter lines.

HYMENEAL.

Page 99. — Printed in the Cambridge collection, 1736, folio. In this collection also is a Latin copy of Hendecasyllables, by Horace Walpole.

LUNA HABITABILIS.

Page 101. — Written by desire of the college, in 1737, and printed without the author's name, in Musæ Etonenses, vol. ii., p. 107. It is referred to in Mason's Memoirs.

SAPPHIC ODE.

Page 104. — Mason considered this as the first original production of Gray's Muse ; the two former Latin poems being imposed as exercises, by the college.

CARMEN AD C. FAVONIUM ZEPHYRINUM.

Page 107. — To West, May, 1740, and written after the poet's visit to Frescati and the cascades of Tivoli.

FRAGMENT OF A LATIN POEM ON THE GAURUS.

Page 108. — Sent by Gray to his friend West, with a reference to Sandys' Travels, for the history of Monte Barbaro and Monte Nuovo. A translation of this poem may be seen in the *Gentleman's Magazine* for July, 1775.

ALCAIC ODE.

Page 111. — In 1789, a French visitor found the Album in the Chartreuse, and copied this ode from it. Not long afterwards, a mob of ruffians from Grenoble broke into the monastery and destroyed the books.

DE PRINCIPIIS COGITANDI.

Page 114. — When Gray was in Florence, in the April of 1741, West sent to him some fragments of a tragedy which he had begun to write on "Pausanias." Gray deferred his opinion of the piece until he had seen the whole, and, by way of letting West have his "revenge," he enclosed fifty-three lines of "De Principiis Cogitandi," which he called a metaphysic poem. Gray elsewhere alludes to it as Tommy Lucretius.

GREEK EPIGRAM.

Page 122. — "I send you an inscription for a wood adjoining to a park of mine (it is on the confines of Mount Cithæron, on the left hand, as you go to Thebes): you know I am no friend to hunters, and hate to be disturbed by their noise." — *Gray to West, May* 27, 1742.

FROM THE ANTHOLOGIA GRÆCA.

Page 124. — Mr. Gray enriched an interleaved edition of the "Anthologia Græca" (by Henry Stephens, 1566) with notes, parallel passages from various authors, and some conjectural emendations. He translated, or imitated, a few of the epigrams, of which the reader is presented with a specimen.

IN AMOREM DORMIENTEM.

Page 125. — "Anthol," p. 332. Catullianam illam spirat mollitiem. — *Gray.*

FROM A FRAGMENT OF PLATO.

Page 125. — Elegantissimum hercle fragmentum, quod sic Latinè nostro modo adumbravimus. — *Gray.*

THE
POETICAL WORKS
OF
OLIVER GOLDSMITH.

21*

CONTENTS.

LIFE OF GOLDSMITH.

Oliver Goldsmith was born in the remote village of Pallas, in Ireland, on the 10th of November, 1728. He was the son of the Rev. Charles Goldsmith, a Protestant clergyman, whose character is supposed to be delineated in The Vicar of Wakefield and the pastor of The Deserted Village. Two years after Oliver's birth, the fortunes of his father reached their zenith in a benefice of nearly two hundred pounds a year, to which he succeeded by the death of his wife's uncle, the rector of Kilkenny West. This called for the removal of the family to the pretty village of Lissoy. The children were at that time four in number: Catherine, Henry, Jane, and Oliver, then the youngest. In the next ten years the family was increased by Maurice, Charles, and John. The first-born, Margaret, and John, the youngest, died in childhood. Henry followed the calling of his father. The other boys seem to have led wandering and shiftless lives. Of the girls, Catherine married a wealthy husband, Mr. Hodson, and Jane a poor one; and both for some years survived their celebrated brother.

Oliver learned his letters from Elizabeth Delap, a dependant in his father's house, and afterwards schoolmistress of Lissoy. She lived to be ninety years old, and was fond of talking of the celebrated doctor, and telling how dull a boy he was. When six years of age, he was sent to the village school kept by Mr. Thomas Byrne, who had been a quarter-master in Marlborough's wars, and no doubt taught accordingly. Thence, he went to the Rev. Mr. Griffin's superior school of Elphin, where his school-fellows, we are told, " all considered him a stupid, heavy, block-head, little better than a fool, whom every one made fun of." He brightened up, however, before many years, and showed such lively talents that after some four years spent under the instruction of the Rev. Patrick Hughes at Edgeworthstown, it was resolved he should be sent to college. To Dublin college therefore he went as a sizar, or menial student, where his brother Henry had gone as a pensioner. But the poor clergyman's circumstances, humble as they were, had changed for the worse, by his effort to provide a portion for his daughter Catherine, who had privately married a young gentleman of fortune, Mr. Hodson, while pursuing his studies under the charge of her brother Henry. Oliver was a sensitive boy, reluctant to pursue liberal studies as a servant; but he was finally induced to submit to it by the kind persuasions of Thomas Contarine, a clergyman who had married the sister of Charles Goldsmith, and who alone of the poet's connections took an early and efficient interest in his education.

At college he seems to have had few acquaintances and no friends. His tutor was a brute; his position was humiliating, and the studies were little to his taste. In 1747, when he had been about eighteen months at college, he lost his father, and his situation became still more distressing. He saved himself from starvation by writing street-ballads, which he sold for five shillings apiece at the *Reindeer Repository*, and would steal out from college in the evening to hear them sung. This was the only gleam of sunshine in his college life — the consciousness of talents which could give pleasure to his fellow-men. He was engaged with some fellow-students in a riot, and was publicly admonished. Soon after, he sought to retrieve the disgrace by trying for a scholarship. This he lost; but he won a small college prize, and gave a dancing party on the strength of some thirty shillings thereby accruing. In the midst of the gayety, his tutor made his appearance, and without ceremony knocked down the hospitable sizar. Goldsmith forthwith ran away, and lived a few days on what he was able to raise by selling his books and clothes, when he turned his steps towards Lissoy. He was afterwards prevailed upon to return to college, and took his degree of bachelor of arts on the 27th of February, 1749. The two years following he passed at his mother's cottage at Ballymahon, where he assisted as usher in his brother Henry's school, fished and played the flute, and amused a club of jolly fellows at the old inn by his songs and stories.

It was now time to think of a profession : and, naturally enough, in view of his connections, he turned his thoughts to the church. To the Bishop of Elphin he applied for orders, and was rejected ; why, we are not fully informed. Some say that he offended his reverence by appearing in scarlet breeches ; others, that the bishop had been made acquainted with his juvenile irregularities. He tried private teaching a year, whereby he laid up thirty pounds, which he squandered ; and was again fitted out by uncle Contarine for London and the law. On his way, he fell in with a sharper at Dublin, was stripped of his last farthing at play, and returned, a penitent, to Ballymahon. Now he left his mother's house, and lived a while with his brother. Here, too, he seems to have worn out his welcome, and became an inmate of his uncle Contarine's household till with his ever ready aid he started for Edinburgh in the autumn of 1752, as a student of medicine. Eighteen months he passed here, not altogether unprofitably, though he gained more repute by his social qualities than in the schools. From Edinburgh he went to Leyden, where he is said to have attended the lectures on chemistry and anatomy, but again gave way to the seductions of gambling, till he was the owner again of only an empty purse. In this extremity he borrowed of a fellow-student, Mr. Ellis, a little money, to enable him to get away ; but spent it nearly all in the purchase of some rare and costly flower-roots for his uncle Contarine, and started on his travels with a guinea, one shirt, and a flute. It was in February, 1755.

He visited Louvain, where he took a degree as medical bachelor, and passed some little time at Brussels. He travelled chiefly on foot, and lived seemingly by his wits. It is as great a marvel how a poor medical student could get through Flanders, Italy and France, without money, as that a poet should manage to die two thousand pounds in debt. He, no doubt, was quick in making friends. At the establishments of learning and religion he recommended himself by his scholarship ; and he sometimes obtained a night's lodging among the peasants by playing "one of his most merry tunes." He visited Verona, Venice, Florence, remained six months at Padua, and passed some time at Geneva, where it was, probably, that he met Voltaire. In Switzerland he saw Schaffhausen frozen quite across, eat a savory dinner on the top of the Alps, flushed woodcocks on Mount Jura, and sent off to his brother eighty lines of the *Traveller*. In Paris he attended the lectures of Professor Rouelle, and admired the celebrated actress, Mademoiselle Clairon ; and thence he returned to England, poorer than when he left it, and found himself among a people where his music and his learning were less convertible than on the continent. He made a "shift to live," however, as assistant to a chemist, corrector of the press, medical practitioner, and usher in a classical academy kept by Dr. Milner. At the table of the doctor, one day, he met Griffiths the bookseller, proprietor of the most flourishing journal of the time. Griffiths was attracted by some remarks of the usher, and invited him to furnish a few specimens of criticism. The specimens were furnished, and led to an engagement by which Goldsmith bound himself, for a small money consideration, to board and lodge with Mr. and Mrs. Griffiths, and work on their *Monthly Review*.

In his twenty-ninth year, Goldsmith thus commenced the career of authorship, and wrote a number of critical articles in the *Review*, which are marked with Griffiths' hand-writing in a copy of the work now preserved at Oxford. These are printed in the collection of Goldsmith's works edited by Mr. Prior, and in that of Mr. Cunningham. The engagement with Mr. Griffiths terminated in its fifth month. As Goldsmith was merely a stipendiary, and the editorial charge of the work was in the hands of Mrs. Griffiths and her husband, the critic's labors were subjected, no doubt, to an annoying supervision ; and the worthy couple did not find their boarder and lodger quite so constant at his desk as he was expected to be ; and so, by mutual consent, they parted company. When, after the poet's death, it was stated that Goldsmith had at one time "superintended the *Monthly Review*," Griffiths contradicted it in very offensive style, and thus described the nature of their relations: "It is true, however, that he had for a while a seat at our board ; and that, so far as his knowledge of books extended, he was not an unuseful assistant."

In February, 1758, there appeared two duodecimo volumes, entitled 'Memoirs of a Protestant condemned to the Galleys of France for his Religion." This was a free translation from the autobiography of Jean Marteilhe, then recently published at the Hague. The name of the translator was given as James Willington ; but Mr. Forster says that the "writer could only write as Goldsmith." Any name was as good, no doubt, in the eyes of Mr. Griffiths, as that of his quondam "not unuseful assistant" in the *Review*.

Goldsmith now returned to London, from a temporary employment at Dr. Milner's, and took lodgings at No. 12 Green Arbor Court, Old Bailey. The doctor having promised his influence to obtain for him some medical appointment in the gift of the East India Company, to raise the necessary outfit he began the Inquiry into the Present State of Polite Learning in Europe, which was published by the Dodsleys in 1759. Meanwhile, he supplied his daily wants by writing for the *Critical Review*, and persuaded Griffiths to become his security for a suit of clothes, that he might present himself in a decent garb for examination before the college of surgeons. In consideration of this indispensable aid, he reviewed four books, which were furnished him, for the *Monthly*. The reviews written, the suit was provided, but the Court of Examiners found Goldsmith "not qualified for mate to an hospital." A few days after his rejection he pawned his clothes to raise money for his landlady, and obtained a small sum from a friend on a pledge of the four volumes sent him by Griffiths. A humiliating dispute with the brutal bibliopole ensued, which ended in a contract to write for him a Life of Voltaire for twenty pounds, from which the price of the clothes was to be deducted.

On Saturday, the 6th of October, 1759, there appeared "in crown octavo, and on good paper, containing two sheets, or thirty-two pages," the first number of *The Bee*. It was published by Wilkie, of the Bible, in St. Paul's church-yard. Pleasant and various as it was, the public would not buy; and with its eighth number it perished, on the 29th of November. Its author was immediately sought out by Dr. Smollett, and by Mr. John Newbery, the bookseller, who made him offers not to be declined. The Dodsleys soon after issued an edition of The Bee in an independent form; and Griffiths ordered it to be treated in the *Monthly* as the work "of an ingenious person." In a few weeks he was writing essays for Smollett's *British Magazine*, and the Chinese Letters for Newbery's new daily paper, *The Public Ledger*. The latter were collected and published under the title of *The Citizen of the World*.

His friend Mr. Percy visited Goldsmith in his lodgings in Green Arbor Court, and found him in a miserable, dirty-looking room, in which there was but one chair. In 1761, on the strength of his two guineas a week from Newbery, and his connection with *The British Magazine* and *The Lady's Magazine*, he went into chambers in Wine Office Court, where he was first visited by Dr. Johnson. Here he gave a supper to the great lexicographer, who honored the occasion by a new wig and a new suit of clothes. When Dr. Percy asked him the cause of such an unusual toilet, "Why, sir," he answered, "I hear that Goldsmith, who is a very great sloven, justifies his disregard of cleanliness and decency by quoting my practice; and I am desirous this night to show him a better example." Goldsmith's tailor's bill soon showed that he had improved upon it.

In 1762 his first undertaking was a pamphlet on the Cock Lane Ghost, which has perished. Sundry other jobs he executed for Mr Newbery, now for five guineas, now for ten pounds, and sometimes for twenty; but in money matters he went behind-hand, till he was glad to receive a guinea or two in advance from his bookseller, for incompleted task-work. This year he went, for his health, to Tunbridge and Bath. The recent death of Beau Nash suggested a topic for his pen; and he wrote the life of the king of fashion, for which he was paid fourteen guineas, in dribblets, by Mr. Newbery. It was published anonymously. While thus engaged, his social sphere was gradually enlarging. He made the acquaintance of Hogarth and Reynolds, the latter of whom, about this time, founded the club that has since become so famous in literary history, where Goldsmith soon found himself in intimate relations with Burke, Nugent, Langton, Chamier, Hawkins, Beauclerc, and Johnson — its original members.

While lodging at Islington, in 1764, Goldsmith wrote The Captivity, an oratorio, which remained in his desk unrepresented, and was not published during his lifetime. Here it was, no doubt, that Johnson rescued him from the hands of bailiffs, by the sale of The Vicar of Wakefield to Francis Newbery, the nephew, for sixty pounds. And here, too, Reynolds found him engaged in the completion of The Traveller, which was lying unpublished in the desk of the elder Newbery on the very day of Goldsmith's arrest. Shortly afterwards it was put to press. Johnson corrected the proof-sheets, added or amended a few lines, and wrote a hearty notice of it for the *Critical Review*, to appear simultaneously with the poem. When Boswell returned to London a year afterwards, he was amazed to hear the great doctor declare "that there had not been so fine a poem since Pope's time." Charles Fox pronounced it "one of the finest poems in the English language." Miss Reynolds, sister of the painter, after hearing Johnson read it aloud, protested that she never more should think Dr. Goldsmith ugly. Three months after its publication a second edition was issued; a third and fourth soon followed, and the ninth appeared in the year the poet died. It is doubtful if this large sale was of much advantage to Goldsmith, for he is supposed to have surrendered all his interest in the work for twenty guineas; and this at a time when Christopher Anstey commanded two hundred pounds for The New Bath Guide.

To this period is referred the authorship of The Hermit, a ballad, suggested in the course of his discussions with Percy, while the latter was engaged on his Reliques. It was first privately printed in 1764, with the following title-page: "Edwin and Angelina, a Ballad; by Mr. Goldsmith; printed for the amusement of the Countess of Northumberland." This edition is now rare, and is valuable from the light it throws on Goldsmith's habits of composition. His prose he wrote with great facility; "half a volume," as he told Mr. Cradock, "while you are nibbling about elegant phrases." But his poetry he elaborated with infinite care and pains-taking, changing the language, and trimming it of all superfluities. We have seen Gray rejecting one of the most beautiful stanzas in his Elegy because it made too long a parenthesis in the place where it was introduced. So Goldsmith, when he subsequently published his ballad, not only re-wrote four stanzas entirely, but removed the two concluding stanzas of the original copy, because the action of the piece was closed without them. Though thus rejected by the poet, they have been deemed well worthy of preservation:

"Here amidst sylvan bowers we 'll rove,
From lawn to woodland stray;
Blest as the songsters of the grove,
And innocent as they.

"To all that want, and all that wail,
Our pity shall be given;
And when this life of love shall fail,
We 'll love again in heaven."

This poem was first published in The Vicar of Wakefield, which was issued in 1766, in two volumes 12mo, by F. Newbery. Of this book, a celebrated and venerable poet, who was in his nursery when it appeared, and who still survives (August, 1854), remarked, several years ago, to Mr. Forster, that of all the books which, through the fitful changes of three generations, he had seen rise and fall, the charm of The Vicar of Wakefield had alone continued as at first; and, could he re-visit the world after an interval of many more generations, he should as surely look to find it undiminished. Little noise did it make, however, in its early days. Johnson took no interest in it after he had succeeded in selling it; and Burke was the only one of the Club who cared much about it. It made its way gradually into the universal favor which it has now maintained for nearly a century.

The Hermit was the favorite poem of the author. He was as entirely satisfied with it as Campbell is said to have been with the Farewell Stanzas to Kemble. In conversation with Mr. Cradock, a short time before his decease, he exclaimed, "As to my *Hermit*, that poem, Cradock, cannot be amended." When Mr. Burchell reads it, in the Vicar, he introduces it with the remark that "English poetry, like that in the latter empire of Rome, is nothing at present but a combination of luxurious images, without plot or connection; a string of epithets, that improve the sound without carrying on the sense," and offers this ballad as a production which, whatever be its other defects, is at least free from those he has mentioned.

In 1767, a communication appeared in the *St. James's Chronicle*, in which Goldsmith was charged with having taken the ballad from The Friar of Orders Gray, by Mr. Percy. He replied, in a letter to the printer of that paper, that if there was any resemblance between the two poems, his own was not the imitation, as it was written and read to Mr. Percy before the composition of his ballad. "Were it not," he adds, "for the busy disposition of some of your correspondents, the public should never have known that he owes me the hint of his ballad, or that I am obliged to his friendship and learning for communications of a much more important nature." In his next edition of the Reliques, Mr. Percy confirmed the statement in regard to the priority of composition, but suggests that, if there is any imitation in the case, both will be found indebted to the beautiful old ballad, The Gentle Herdsman, contained in the second volume of his work.

Mr. Mitford, in his edition of Goldsmith's poems, reprints a French ballad, entitled *Raimond et Angeline*, and, in the *Life* prefixed, alludes to the allegation that the English poet was a mere translator from "an old scarce French romance." Goldsmith's old enemy, Griffiths, had given countenance to the charge in the *Monthly Review;* and Mr. Mitford not only discusses the subject as if there were really some reason for believing it, but leaves the point unsettled. From the name of the volume — the Quiz — in which the charge originally appeared (in 1797, not 1767), the nature of it would seem obvious enough; but, by referring to the title "Goldsmith," in the *Biographie Universelle*, it will be found that there were *four* French translations of this ballad, one of which, by a poet of the name of Leonard, was published with the title of *Raimond et Angeline.* We presume there can be no doubt that this is the poem reprinted by Mr. Mitford as the *possible* original.

Goldsmith's increased reputation augmented his expenses, and brought new social demands upon his time, but added little to his income. This year he was glad to receive ten pounds from Payne, the bookseller, for compiling a duodecimo volume of Poems for Young Ladies; and especially was he pleased when, by the mere use of his judgment and a red-lead pencil, he could draw upon Griffin for fifty pounds, as the copy money of his Beauties of English Poetry. In this selection his "judgment" was so far at fault, that it admitted two exceptionable poems of Prior, which banished his volume from the parlor table even of circles so little squeamish as then composed English society. Such supplies, with two guineas, now and then, for writing a preface, and "five guineas for writing a short English grammar," did not prevent him from becoming a debtor, as per the memorandum still extant, in the sum of one pound one to Mr. Newbery, on the 6th of January, 1767.

In the midst of these petty and annoying labors, Goldsmith was aspiring to fame in another department of literature. He submitted to Garrick the manuscript of The Good-natured Man, a comedy not written after the prevailing sentimental taste, and which the great actor did not think likely to succeed. It was afterwards accepted by Colman, and first acted at Covent Garden on the 29th of January, 1768. The prologue was written by Johnson, and the character of Croaker was played with rich and peculiar humor by Shuter, — but the play was not very successful. It was performed ten consecutive nights; the author's three nights produced him four hundred pounds, and its publication by Griffin one hundred pounds more, which he soon wasted in his increased expenditures. At the close of this year, he had the honor to be appointed professor of ancient history in the Royal Academy of Arts; and early in 1769 he went to Oxford with Johnson, and received the degree of M. B. The same year he published, in two octavo volumes, his Roman History, a work for popular use, which met with a ready sale, and which Johnson pronounced a better abridgment than that of Lucius Florus or Eutropius. For this work he received two hundred and fifty guineas, and it led to a contract with Davies, its publisher, for a History of England, in four volumes, for five hundred guineas. Previous to this, however, he had entered into an engagement with Griffin for a Natural History, in eight volumes, at one hundred guineas each. His expenses kept more than even pace with his engagements, instead of his receipts. He lived on his prospective fortunes, and squandered his money, before he had earned it, in various forms of idle extravagance. His popularity was now at its height, and he levied upon it for the creation of new responsibilities and involvements, that led ultimately to pecuniary ruin and his premature death.

On the 26th of May, 1770, the *Public Advertiser* contained the following announcement: "This day, at 12, will be published, price two shillings, *The Deserted Village*, a Poem. By Dr. Goldsmith. Printed for W. Griffin, at Garrick's Head in Catherine-street, Strand." It was received with great favor. Four editions had appeared by the end of June. When Gray heard it read by his friend Nicholls at Malvern, he exclaimed, "*That man is a poet!*" Goethe was delighted with it, and immediately set to work to translate it into German. "What true and pretty pastoral images," exclaimed Burke, years afterwards, and when the poet was no longer living to enjoy the praise, "has Goldsmith in his Deserted Village! They beat all,—Pope, Phillips, and *Spenser*, too,—in my opinion."

Goldsmith is said to have been engaged four or five years in collecting materials for this work, and for two years in its construction. Lissoy, near Ballymahon, where his brother the clergyman had his living, has been claimed as the scene of the poem; and plates and descriptions of the local scenery supposed to be intended by the poet were published in 1811 in quarto by the Rev. R. H. Newell, fellow of St. John's College, Cork. Mr. Forster says, however, that the poem is too thoroughly English in the feelings, incidents, descriptions and allusions, to justify needless trouble in seeking to identify sweet Auburn with Lissoy. "It is quite natural," he adds, "that Irish enthusiasts should have found out the fence, the furze, the thorn, the decent church, the never-failing brook, the busy mill; it was to be expected that pilgrims should have borne away every vestige of the first hawthorn they could lay their hands on; it was perfectly reasonable, and in the way of business, to rebuild the village inn as Mr. Hogan did, and fix broken tea-cups in the wall that pilgrims might not carry *them* away, and to christen his speculation by the name of Auburn. All this, as Walter Scott has said, is a 'pleasing tribute to the poet in the land of his fathers,' but it is certainly no more."

What Goldsmith received for the poem is uncertain. The story runs that he had agreed with Griffin for one hundred pounds, but returned part of it on some one telling him that five shillings a couplet was more than any poetry was worth, and would only ruin the poor bookseller who gave it. It is so incredible that Goldsmith could have had the money to return, if he had been long enough in possession to spend it or give it away, that we are inclined to doubt the truth of this, though Bishop Percy says it would have been quite in character.

Soon after the publication of his poem, he accompanied Mrs. Horneck and her fair daughters on a journey to Paris, on his return from which he received letters informing him of his mother's death. During the summer, his Life of Parnell was published, the sale of which was so satisfactory that Davies immediately contracted with the author for another memoir, The Life of Bolingbroke. While engaged on this work he went into the country on a visit to Lord Clare, and Davies was plagued "to get the proofs from him." He continued with Lord Clare during the early months of 1771, and addressed to him during the year, it would seem for his special amusement, the verses entitled The Haunch of Venison. It was not till two years after the poet's death that they were made public, when they were printed from a copy given by his lordship to Mr. Bunbury.

Goldsmith returned to London for a short time, to see his English History through the press, and then again repaired to the country, to busy himself with another comedy. On the 15th of March, 1773, She Stoops to Conquer was performed at Covent Garden, and, in spite of the predictions of failure by Colman, the manager, with the most entire success. The account which Cumberland gives, in his Memoirs, of the efforts made by his friends to bring about this result, is now understood to be of very doubtful authority. Mr. Day, afterwards one of the Irish judges, then a student at the Temple, says that he and some of the author's friends, knowing the adverse expectations entertained of the comedy, had assembled in great force in the pit to protect it; but they found no difficulty to encounter, for it "was received throughout with the greatest acclamations." Goldsmith did not go to the theatre, but was found by a friend sauntering, between seven and eight o'clock, in the mall of St. James's Park. On his friend's earnestly representing to him that his presence might be very important, if any sudden alteration should be found necessary in any scene, he consented to go to the theatre. He entered the stage-door at the opening of the fifth act, and heard a solitary hiss. "What's that! what's that!" he cried out to the manager, not a little alarmed. "Psha! Doctor," replied Colman; "don't be afraid of a squib, when we have been sitting these two hours on a barrel of gunpowder." This joke Goldsmith never forgot or forgave, though he might well have done so, when his three nights yielded him between four and five hundred pounds, and the copyright settled an old debt of Newbery's, that had been a source of great annoyance to him.

A libel in the *London Packet* followed hard on this success, which led to an assault by Goldsmith on the publisher, a Welshman by the name of Evans. Goldsmith was no match for his stout antagonist, and a scuffle ensued, in which the poet is thought to have come off second best. At all events, he was indicted for his offence, and compromised it with Evans by paying fifty pounds to a Welsh charity. The papers abused the poet, and he defended himself in a well-written address to the public, which appeared in the *Daily Advertiser*. It was aimed at that abuse of the liberty of the press which had then become intolerable. Johnson said it was a foolish thing well done; and Boswell thought it so well done that he could not imagine it to have been written by any one but Johnson himself. This appears to have been the latest production of Goldsmith published in his lifetime.

His days were now made miserable by disputes with the bookseller to whom he owed money, and by the failure of his new schemes for raising it. The last work on which he was occupied we learn of from Cradock, the author of Zobeide, who was on a visit to London, and had taken lodgings in Goldsmith's neighborhood. He found his friend much altered, and at times very low; and devoted almost all his mornings to him. One morning Cradock called, and found him much better than he had expected, busied with his manuscripts. "Here," said Goldsmith, in an exulting tone, "are some of the best of my prose writings; I have been hard at work ever since midnight, and I desire you to examine them. They are intended as an introduction to a body of arts and sciences." The plan of this work was promising, and Burke, Johnson, Garrick and Reynolds, had agreed to assist him in it; but the booksellers declined to undertake it.

The end, however, was not to be without one more flash of his genius, even from the gloom of his despair. Several apocryphal statements are extant which give with great particularity the circumstances that led to the production of Retaliation. Cumberland's version of this matter is the most minute, but is said to be pure romance. The most reliable account has recently come to light in a manuscript of Garrick, first published in Mr. Peter Cunningham's edition of Goldsmith of 1854. From this it appears that Goldsmith was present at a company of intimate friends at the St. James Coffeehouse, and proposed to Garrick that they should try their epigrammatic powers by writing each other's epitaphs. Garrick says that he declared himself ready on the spot, and extemporized the following distich:

> "Here lies Nolly Goldsmith, for shortness called Noll,
> Who wrote like an angel, but talked like poor Poll."

The writer adds that the company was amused, and Goldsmith so much disconcerted that he could not or would not answer on the spot, but some weeks afterwards produced Retaliation. It was read at the Club, and gave rise to Burke's remark that "an epitaph was a *grave* epigram." The Club were averse to its publication; and Goldsmith said he would keep it as a rod in pickle for some future occasion. Portions of it, only, it is probable, were produced in the first instance, and were circulated in manuscript, for the poem was unfinished when the writer died. It is said that he was engaged with the lines on Reynolds when he was seized with his last illness. This was in the middle of March, 1774. On the 25th of that month he was anxious to attend the Club, but in the afternoon he took to his bed, and towards midnight sent for a skilful surgeon-apothecary named Hawes, whom he was in the habit of consulting. Contrary to all medical advice, he insisted upon dosing himself with James's fever powders, a fashionable medicine of the day, and thereby exasperated the nervous affection under which he was suffering. Some ten days passed, during which hopes were entertained of his recovery. But his malady was beyond the reach of medicine. Dr. Fordyce, who was then in attendance, called in another physician. Dr. Turton found that his patient could not sleep, and in his weak state feared that want of sleep alone would be fatal. It then occurred to him to ask a question. "Your pulse," he said, "is in greater disorder than it should be from the degree of fever which you have. *Is your mind at ease?*" "*No, it is not,*" was the melancholy answer. They were the last words he uttered. He soon after fell into a sound and calm sleep, but woke towards morning in strong convulsions, which continued without intermission till he died, a quarter before five o'clock, on Monday, the 4th of April, 1774.

The disclosure of the condition of his affairs rendered the ceremonies and expenses of a public funeral inappropriate, and his remains were privately interred in the Temple burying-ground. His debts amounted to two thousand pounds. His principal creditors were Griffin, the bookseller, and Mr. Botts, a barrister, his neighbor in the Temple. He owed Mr. Filby, his tailor, seventy-nine pounds; but we are told by the younger Filby that his father never blamed Goldsmith, — that he had been a good customer, and if he had lived would have paid every farthing. The suggestion of a monument in Westminster Abbey was made by Reynolds, who selected the spot where it was afterwards placed, over the south door in Poets' Corner. It consists of a large medallion likeness and tablet, sculptured by Nollekens. The inscription, written by Dr. Johnson two years after the poet's death, was the subject of the famous Round Robin of the Literary Club; but the doctor adhered to his original draft, and it thus stands on the monument (where the erroneous date of his birth remains uncorrected):

Olivarii Goldsmith,
Poetæ, Physici, Historici,
Qui nullum ferè scribendi genus
Non tetigit,
Nullum quod tetigit non ornavit:
Sive risus essent movendi,
Sive lacrymæ,
Affectuum potens, ut lenis dominator;
Ingenio sublimis, vividus, versatilis,
Oratione grandis, nitidus, venustus;
Hoc monumento memoriam coluit
Sodalium amor,
Amicorum fides,
Lectorum veneratio.
Natus in Hiberniâ Forneiæ Lonfordiensis,
In loco cui nomen Pallas,
Nov. XXIX. MDCCXXXI.
Eblanæ Literis institutus;
Objit Londini,
Apr. IV. MDCCLXXIV.

Goldsmith was rather below the middle stature; in his youth he was active and muscular, and fond of athletic sports. As he advanced in years, he grew stout and sturdy. Judge Day, of the Irish bench, describes him as about five feet six inches in height, strong but not heavy in make, rather fair in complexion, and with brown hair. His forehead was low and prominent; his face round, and pitted with the small-pox. All who knew him agree that his appearance was not prepossessing; and Boswell thought that Reynolds never gave a more striking proof of excellence in his art than in giving dignity to Goldsmith's countenance and yet preserving a strong likeness. Two portraits of him by Reynolds are said to be extant, — one at Knowle, the seat of the Duke of Dorset, and another in the possession of a descendant of Mrs. Hodson. A mezzotinto print from one of these figured in the print-shop windows in the latter years of Goldsmith's life. There is an etching by Bunbury which is said to be very like him.

Goldsmith always spoke with a decided Irish brogue, which he seems rather to have cultivated than studied to correct. In one of his criticisms for Griffiths, he objects to the rhyming of "key" with "be;" his ear was familiar with it as *kay*. His manners, in the opinion of his countryman, Judge Day, were simple and natural, but without the refinement and good breeding which the exquisite polish of his writings would lead us to expect. Reynolds told Northcote that by his boyish and social manners Goldsmith soon became the plaything and favorite of a company among whom his entrance had produced perhaps an "awful silence." His conversational powers were not of a high order. He said of himself, that he always argued best when alone. Horace Walpole styled him "an inspired idiot." Johnson remarked that "no man was more foolish when he had not a pen in his hand, nor more wise when he had." And yet he sometimes gave Johnson himself a hard hit. Reynolds told a story that shows *Ursa Major* had not always the best of it. Goldsmith was saying, one day, that he thought he could write a good fable, alluded to the simplicity which it requires, and observed that in most fables the animals introduced seldom talk in character. "For instance," said he, "the fable of the little fishes who saw birds fly over their heads, and, envying them, petitioned Jupiter to be changed into birds. The skill," he continued, "consists in making them talk like little fishes." At this, Johnson began to shake his sides and roll about with laughter. The comment of Goldsmith was inimitably apt and telling. "Why, Mr. Johnson, this is not so easy as you seem to think; for if *you* were to make little fishes talk, they would talk like WHALES."

He was excitable, and, when excited, destitute of self control. This temperament brought him into numerous scrapes. At one time he made proposals to Tonson for an edition of Pope. The bibliopole rejected his offer in somewhat disrespectful terms, and Goldsmith caned the messenger. At a party at Blackwall, a dispute arose about *Tristram Shandy*, that terminated in a fracas, in which the story is that Goldsmith was beaten. His assault on Evans we have already mentioned. He was easily duped. When his affairs were at the worst, he had about him a number of fellow-countrymen whose circumstances were even worse than his own, and who levied upon him for their support. He was eminently social in his disposition,—a "clubable man,"—and quite as fond of singing his songs and telling his stories to his jolly Irish comrades, at the Globe Tavern in Fleet-street, on Wednesday evening, as of taking part in the conversations of the Literary Club on Friday. With the same spirit he mingled in the pleasant circle of the Hornecks and Bunburys—dining, supping and playing cards with them, now joining in a minuet, and now figuring in a masquerade. A sloven in his early days, Goldsmith became somewhat eccentric in dress during his social career; and Boswell describes him as being "seriously vain" in this regard. His suit of "Tyrian bloom" has become historical, as Mr. William Filby, his tailor, has been immortalized for it, under the name of John. "Let me tell you," said Goldsmith to Garrick, one day, at a dinner of Boswell's, as the actor was quizzing him about his appearance, "when my tailor brought home my bloom-colored coat he said, 'Sir, I have a favor to beg of you. When anybody asks you who made your clothes, be pleased to mention John Filby, at the Harrow in Water-lane.'" "Why, sir," remarked Johnson, "that was because he knew the strange color would attract crowds to gaze at it, and thus they might hear of him, and see how well he could make a coat even of so absurd a color." Tyrian blooms, however, and Mr. Filby's bills, could not have ruined him. He spent large sums on his chambers and his entertainments, and never could resist temptation at a gaming-table. No experience could teach him the value of money, which he raised and squandered "by every artifice of acquisition and folly of expense."

To his habits of composition we have already alluded. Prose he would write "a volume a month," as he said. His manuscript was remarkably fair and clean, and for whole quires there was not an erasure or alteration. His thoughts flowed from him with perfect ease, in the best forms of expression. With his verse, his mode of composition was entirely different. Here he paused, erased, re-wrote, rejected, polished and refined, with almost as much labor as Gray. In writing The Deserted Village, as we are told by his friend Cooke, he first sketched a part of his design in prose, in which he expressed his ideas as they occurred to him. He then sat down to verify them, correct them, and add such other ideas as he thought better fitted to the subject; and if in this process he threw off any verses impromptu, those he would afterwards revise with great care, lest they should be found unconnected with his main design. Ten lines, from the tenth to the fifteenth, had been his second morning's work and when Cooke entered his chamber he read them to him aloud "Come," he added, "let me tell you this is no bad morning's work and now, my dear boy, if you are not better engaged, I should b glad to enjoy a *shoemaker's holiday* with you." This was a chea country excursion, terminated by a supper in town, at the Grecia Coffee-house or the Globe in Fleet-street.

It was by this patient elaboration, this toilsome devotion of the best hours of his best years, that he produced the two great poems on which his fame rests, and which, wherever the English language is spoken, and as long as it continues to be read, will carry and perpetuate the name of Goldsmith.

His blunders and his brogue, his vanity, and his habit of blurting out what was uppermost in his mind, — these defects made Goldsmith too often the butt of the circles in which he moved; and yet there seems to have been no one whose company was more liked. He was beloved by Burke and Reynolds. When the great statesman heard of his death he burst into tears. To Sir Joshua his loss is said to have been the severest blow he ever suffered. The stately and formal Bishop Percy, the earliest of his distinguished friends, was warmly attached to him. He says, not only that there never was a man more benevolent and friendly, but that whatever appeared of envy or jealousy in his conduct was a mere momentary sensation, that he knew not how, like other men, to conceal. Though coarse and rough with him as with all the world, Johnson admired Goldsmith, and permitted no one to abuse him with impunity. The simple, frolicsome, blundering, improvident, big-hearted, impulsive Irishman, was very dear to his sometime brother of Grub-street, the great sage and moralist, who appreciated his genius, and insisted always that whatever he undertook he did it better than anybody else.

Much that we know of Goldsmith we derive from writers who had no love for him. Neither Boswell, nor Beattie, nor Cumberland, can be entirely relied upon, when he is the subject. They had all private griefs, which distorted their judgment and gave a false color to their portraits. Boswell knew that he had spoken of him contemptuously, as a burr sticking to Johnson, and was jealous of his hold on the affections of their common friend. He rebuked Reynolds for flattering, in an allegorical picture, "so mean a writer as Beattie" at the expense of a genius like Voltaire; and Beattie thought that Goldsmith was envious of him! Cumberland was a coxcomb, and talks of Goldsmith's dining with "us," as if the poet was only a chance visitor, and himself an *habitué* of the brilliant circle in which they met. Not only, then, has he been represented as a mere fool by those who were really fools (as Northcote says), he was also disparaged by those who were more moved by malice than folly. But, in spite of all the cavils and caricatures of rivals, in spite of faults and foibles too well known and too severely punished in his lifetime, the praise cannot be denied him of being a perfectly pure writer; and one to whom Dr. Johnson consented to award the title could not have been otherwise than a very great man.

"Goldsmith's poetry," says Mr. Campbell, who was no less a critic than poet, "enjoys a calm and steady popularity. It inspires us, indeed, with no admiration of daring design or of fertile invention; but it presents, within its narrow limits, a distinct and unbroken view of poetical delightfulness. His descriptions and sentiments have the pure zest of nature. He is refined without false delicacy, and correct without insipidity. Perhaps there is an intellectual composure in his manner, which may, in some passages, be said to approach to the reserved and prosaic; but he unbends from this graver strain of reflection to tenderness, and even to playfulness, with an ease and grace almost exclusively his own; and connects extensive views of the happiness and interests of society with pictures of life that touch the heart by their familiarity. His language is certainly simple, though it is not cast in a rugged or careless mould. He is no disciple of the gaunt and famished school of simplicity. Deliberately as he wrote, he cannot be accused of wanting natural and idiomatic expression. He uses the ornaments which must always distinguish true poetry from prose; and when he adopts colloquial plainness, it is with the utmost care and skill, to avoid a vulgar humility. There is more of this sustained simplicity, of this chaste economy and choice of words, in Goldsmith, than in any modern poet."

THE TRAVELLER.

DEDICATION.

TO THE REV. HENRY GOLDSMITH.

Dear Sir: I am sensible that the friendship between us can acquire no new force from the ceremonies of a dedication; and perhaps it demands an excuse thus to prefix your name to my attempts, which you decline giving with your own. But as a part of this poem was formerly written to you from Switzerland, the whole can now, with propriety, be only inscribed to you. It will also throw a light upon many parts of it, when the reader understands that it is addressed to a man who, despising fame and fortune, has retired early to happiness and obscurity with an income of forty pounds a year.

I now perceive, my dear brother, the wisdom of your humble choice. You have entered upon a sacred office, where the harvest is great, and the laborers are but few; while you have left the field of ambition, where the laborers are many, and the harvest not worth carrying away. But of all kinds of ambition — what from the refinement of the times, from different systems of criticism, and from the divisions of party — that which pursues poetical fame is the wildest.

Poetry makes a principal amusement among unpolished nations; but in a country verging to the extremes of refinement, Painting and Music come in for a share. As these offer the feeble mind a less laborious entertainment, they at first rival Poetry, and at length supplant her; they engross all that favor once shown to her, and though but younger sisters, seize upon the elder's birthright.

Yet, however this art may be neglected by the powerful, it is still in greater danger from the mistaken efforts of the learned to improve it. What criticisms have we not heard of late in favor of blank verse and Pindaric odes, choruses, anapests, and iambics, alliterative care and happy negligence! Every absurdity has now a champion to defend it: and as he is generally much in the wrong, so he has always much to say; for error is ever talkative.

But there is an enemy to this art still more dangerous — I mean party. Party entirely distorts the judgment, and destroys the taste. When the mind is once infected with this disease, it can only find pleasure in what contributes to increase the distemper. Like the tiger, that seldom desists from pursuing man after having once preyed upon human flesh, the reader who has once gratified his appetite with calumny makes ever after the most agreeable feast upon murdered reputation. Such readers generally admire some half-witted thing, who wants to be thought a bold man, having lost the character of a wise one. Him they dignify with the name of poet: his tawdry lampoons are called satires; his turbulence is said to be force, and his frenzy fire.

What reception a Poem may find, which has neither abuse, party, nor blank verse, to support it, I cannot tell, nor am I solicitous to know. My aims are right. Without espousing the cause of any party, I have attempted to moderate the rage of all. I have endeavored to show that there may be equal happiness in states that are differently governed from our own; that every state has a particular principle of happiness; and that this principle in each may be carried to a mischievous excess. There are few can judge better than yourself how far these positions are illustrated in this poem.

I am, dear sir,
Your most affectionate brother,
Oliver Goldsmith.

THE TRAVELLER;

OR, A PROSPECT OF SOCIETY.

REMOTE, unfriended, melancholy, slow,
Or by the lazy Scheldt or wandering Po;
Or onward, where the rude Carinthian boor
Against the houseless stranger shuts the door;
Or where Campania's plain forsaken lies,
A weary waste expanding to the skies —
Where'er I roam, whatever realms to see,
My heart untravelled fondly turns to thee;
Still to my Brother turns, with ceaseless pain,
And drags at each remove a lengthening chain.
  Eternal blessings crown my earliest friend,
And round his dwelling guardian saints attend.
Blest be that spot, where cheerful guests retire
To pause from toil, and trim their evening fire;
Blest that abode, where want and pain repair,
And every stranger finds a ready chair;
Blest be those feasts with simple plenty crowned,
Where all the ruddy family around
Laugh at the jests or pranks that never fail,
Or sigh with pity at some mournful tale;
Or press the bashful stranger to his food,
And learn the luxury of doing good.
  But me, not destined such delights to share,
My prime of life in wandering spent and care;

Impelled with steps unceasing to pursue
Some fleeting good, that mocks me with the view;
That, like the circle bounding earth and skies,
Allures from far, yet, as I follow, flies;
My fortune leads to traverse realms alone,
And find no spot of all the world my own.
  Even now, where Alpine solitudes ascend,
I sit me down a pensive hour to spend;
And placed on high, above the storm's career,
Look downward where an hundred realms appear;
Lakes, forests, cities, plains extending wide,
The pomp of kings, the shepherd's humbler pride.
  When thus Creation's charms around combine,
Amidst the store, should thankless pride repine?
Say, should the philosophic mind disdain
That good which makes each humbler bosom vain?
Let school-taught pride dissemble all it can,
These little things are great to little man;
And wiser he whose sympathetic mind
Exults in all the good of all mankind.
Ye glittering towns, with wealth and splendor crowned,
Ye fields where summer spreads profusion round,
Ye lakes whose vessels catch the busy gale,
Ye bending swains that dress the flowery vale;
For me your tributary stores combine;
Creation's heir, the world, the world is mine!
  As some lone miser, visiting his store,
Bends at his treasure, counts, recounts it o'er:
Hoards after hoards his rising raptures fill,
Yet still he sighs, for hoards are wanting still:
Thus to my breast alternate passions rise,
Pleased with each good that Heaven to man supplies:

Yet oft a sigh prevails, and sorrows fall,
To see the hoard of human bliss so small;
And oft I wish, amidst the scene, to find
Some spot to real happiness consigned,
Where my worn soul, each wandering hope at rest,
May gather bliss, to see my fellows blest.
But where to find that happiest spot below,
Who can direct, when all pretend to know?
The shuddering tenant of the frigid zone
Boldly proclaims that happiest spot his own;
Extols the treasures of his stormy seas,
And his long nights of revelry and ease:
The naked negro, panting at the line,
Boasts of his golden sands and palmy wine,
Basks in the glare, or stems the tepid wave,
And thanks his gods for all the good they gave.
Such is the patriot's boast, where'er we roam,
His first, best country ever is at home.
And yet, perhaps, if countries we compare,
And estimate the blessings which they share,
Though patriots flatter, still shall wisdom find
An equal portion dealt to all mankind;
As different good, by Art or Nature given
To different nations, makes their blessings even.
Nature, a mother kind alike to all,
Still grants her bliss at Labor's earnest call:
With food as well the peasant is supplied
On Idra's cliffs as Arno's shelvy side:
And, though the rocky-crested summits frown,
These rocks, by custom, turn to beds of down.
From Art more various are the blessings sent;
Wealth, commerce, honor, liberty, content.

Yet these each other's power so strong contest,
That either seems destructive of the rest.
Where wealth and freedom reign contentment fails,
And honor sinks where commerce long prevails.
Hence every state, to one loved blessing prone,
Conforms and models life to that alone.
Each to the favorite happiness attends,
And spurns the plan that aims at other ends;
Till, carried to excess in each domain,
This favorite good begets peculiar pain.
 But let us try these truths with closer eyes,
And trace them through the prospect as it lies:
Here for a while my proper cares resigned,
Here let me sit in sorrow for mankind;
Like yon neglected shrub, at random cast,
That shades the steep, and sighs at every blast.
 Far to the right, where Apennine ascends,
Bright as the summer, Italy extends:
Its uplands sloping deck the mountain's side,
Woods over woods in gay theatric pride,
While oft some temple's mouldering tops between
With venerable grandeur mark the scene.
 Could Nature's bounty satisfy the breast
The sons of Italy were surely blest.
Whatever fruits in different climes are found,
That proudly rise, or humbly court the ground;
Whatever blooms in torrid tracts appear,
Whose bright succession decks the varied year;
Whatever sweets salute the northern sky
With vernal lives, that blossom but to die;
These here disporting own the kindred soil,
Nor ask luxuriance from the planter's toil;

While sea-born gales their gelid wings expand
To winnow fragrance round the smiling land.
  But small the bliss that sense alone bestows,
And sensual bliss is all the nation knows;
In florid beauty groves and fields appear,
Man seems the only growth that dwindles here.
Contrasted faults through all his manners reign;
Though poor, luxurious; though submissive, vain;
Though grave, yet trifling; zealous, yet untrue;
And even in penance planning sins anew.
All evils here contaminate the mind,
That opulence departed leaves behind;
For wealth was theirs — nor far removed the date
When commerce proudly flourished through the state.
At her command the palace learned to rise,
Again the long-fallen column sought the skies;
The canvas glowed, beyond even Nature warm,
The pregnant quarry teemed with human form:
Till, more unsteady than the southern gale,
Commerce on other shores displayed her sail;
While naught remained of all that riches gave,
But towns unmanned, and lords without a slave:
And late the nation found, with fruitless skill,
Its former strength was but plethoric ill.
  Yet, still the loss of wealth is here supplied
By arts, the splendid wrecks of former pride:
From these the feeble heart and long-fallen mind
An easy compensation seem to find.
Here may be seen, in bloodless pomp arrayed,
The pasteboard triumph and the cavalcade;
Processions formed for piety and love,
A mistress or a saint in every grove.

By sports like these are all their cares beguiled,
The sports of children satisfy the child.
Each nobler aim, repressed by long control,
Now sinks at last, or feebly mans the soul;
While low delights, succeeding fast behind,
In happier meanness occupy the mind.
As in those domes, where Cæsars once bore sway,
Defaced by time and tottering in decay,
There in the ruin, heedless of the dead,
The shelter-seeking peasant builds his shed;
And, wondering man could want the larger pile,
Exults, and owns his cottage with a smile.
  My soul, turn from them; turn we to survey
Where rougher climes a nobler race display,
Where the bleak Swiss their stormy mansions tread,
And force a churlish soil for scanty bread.
No product here the barren hills afford
But man and steel, the soldier and his sword;
No vernal blooms their torpid rocks array,
But winter lingering chills the lap of May;
No Zephyr fondly sues the mountain's breast,
But meteors glare, and stormy glooms invest.
  Yet still, even here, content can spread a charm,
Redress the clime, and all its rage disarm.
Though poor the peasant's hut, his feast though small,
He sees his little lot the lot of all;
Sees no contiguous palace rear its head,
To shame the meanness of his humble shed;
No costly lord the sumptuous banquet deal,
To make him loathe his vegetable meal;
But calm, and bred in ignorance and toil,
Each wish contracting, fits him to the soil.

Cheerful at morn, he wakes from short repose,
Breasts the keen air, and carols as he goes;
With patient angle trolls the finny deep,
Or drives his venturous ploughshare to the steep;
Or seeks the den where snow-tracks mark the way
And drags the struggling savage into day.
At night returning, every labor sped,
He sits him down, the monarch of a shed;
Smiles by his cheerful fire, and round surveys
His children's looks, that brighten at the blaze;
While his loved partner, boastful of her hoard,
Displays her cleanly platter on the board:
And haply too some pilgrim, thither led,
With many a tale repays the nightly bed.
Thus every good his native wilds impart
Imprints the patriot passion on his heart;
And even those ills, that round his mansion rise,
Enhance the bliss his scanty fund supplies.
Dear is that shed to which his soul conforms,
And dear that hill which lifts him to the storms;
And as a child, when scaring sounds molest,
Clings close and closer to the mother's breast,
So the loud torrent and the whirlwind's roar
But bind him to his native mountains more.
Such are the charms to barren states assigned
Their wants but few, their wishes all confined.
Yet let them only share the praises due;
If few their wants, their pleasures are but few;
For every want that stimulates the breast
Becomes a source of pleasure when redrest.
Whence from such lands each pleasing science flies,
That first excites desire, and then supplies;

Unknown to them, when sensual pleasures cloy,
To fill the languid pause with finer joy;
Unknown those powers that raise the soul to flame,
Catch every nerve, and vibrate through the frame.
Their level life is but a smouldering fire,
Unquenched by want, unfanned by strong desire;
Unfit for raptures, or, if raptures cheer
On some high festival of once a year,
In wild excess the vulgar breast takes fire,
Till, buried in debauch, the bliss expire.
But not their joys alone thus coarsely flow;
Their morals, like their pleasures, are but low:
For, as refinement stops, from sire to son
Unaltered, unimproved, the manners run;
And love's and friendship's finely-pointed dart
Fall blunted from each indurated heart.
Some sterner virtues o'er the mountain's breast
May sit, like falcons cowering on the nest;
But all the gentler morals, such as play
Through life's more cultured walks, and charm the way,—
These, far dispersed, on timorous pinions fly,
To sport and flutter in a kinder sky.
To kinder skies, where gentler manners reign,
I turn; and France displays her bright domain.
Gay, sprightly land of mirth and social ease,
Pleased with thyself, whom all the world can please,
How often have I led thy sportive choir,
With tuneless pipe, beside the murmuring Loire,
Where shading elms along the margin grew,
And freshened from the wave the zephyr flew!
And haply, though my harsh touch, faltering still,
But mocked all tune, and marred the dancer's skill,

Yet would the village praise my wondrous power,
And dance, forgetful of the noontide hour.
Alike all ages: dames of ancient days
Have led their children through the mirthful maze;
And the gay grandsire, skilled in gestic lore,
Has frisked beneath the burthen of threescore.
So blest a life these thoughtless realms display;
Thus idly busy rolls their world away:
Theirs are those arts that mind to mind endear,
For honor forms the social temper here:
Honor, that praise which real merit gains,
Or even imaginary worth obtains,
Here passes current; paid from hand to hand,
It shifts, in splendid traffic, round the land;
From courts to camps, to cottages it strays,
And all are taught an avarice of praise;
They please, are pleased; they give to get esteem,
Till, seeming blest, they grow to what they seem.
But while this softer art their bliss supplies,
It gives their follies also room to rise;
For praise too dearly loved, or warmly sought,
Enfeebles all internal strength of thought;
And the weak soul, within itself unblest,
Leans for all pleasure on another's breast.
Hence ostentation here, with tawdry art,
Pants for the vulgar praise which fools impart:
Here vanity assumes her pert grimace,
And trims her robes of frieze with copper-lace;
Here beggar pride defrauds her daily cheer,
To boast one splendid banquet once a year:
The mind still turns where shifting fashion draws,
Nor weighs the solid worth of self-applause.

To men of other minds my fancy flies,
Embosomed in the deep where Holland lies.
Methinks her patient sons before me stand,
Where the broad ocean leans against the land,
And, sedulous to stop the coming tide,
Lift the tall rampire's artificial pride.
Onward, methinks, and diligently slow,
The firm connected bulwark seems to grow;
Spreads its long arms amidst the watery roar,
Scoops out an empire, and usurps the shore:
While the pent ocean, rising o'er the pile,
Sees an amphibious world beneath him smile;
The slow canal, the yellow-blossomed vale,
The willow-tufted bank, the gliding sail,
The crowded mart, the cultivated plain,
A new creation rescued from his reign.
Thus, while around the wave-subjected soil
Impels the native to repeated toil,
Industrious habits in each bosom reign,
And industry begets a love of gain.
Hence all the good from opulence that springs,
With all those ills superfluous treasure brings,
Are here displayed. Their much-loved wealth imparts
Convenience, plenty, elegance and arts;
But view them closer, craft and fraud appear,
Even liberty itself is bartered here.
At gold's superior charms all freedom flies;
The needy sell it, and the rich man buys:
A land of tyrants, and a den of slaves,
Here wretches seek dishonorable graves,
And, calmly bent, to servitude conform,
Dull as their lakes that slumber in the storm.

Heavens! how unlike their Belgic sires of old!
Rough, poor, content, ungovernably bold;
War in each breast, and freedom on each brow; —
How much unlike the sons of Britain now!
Fired at the sound, my genius spreads her wing,
And flies where Britain courts the western spring;
Where lawns extend that scorn Arcadian pride,
And brighter streams than famed Hydaspes glide.
There all around the gentlest breezes stray;
There gentle music melts on every spray;
Creation's mildest charms are there combined,
Extremes are only in the master's mind!
Stern o'er each bosom reason holds her state,
With daring aims irregularly great;
Pride in their port, defiance in their eye,
I see the lords of human kind pass by,
Intent on high designs — a thoughtful band,
By forms unfashioned, fresh from Nature's hand,
Fierce in their native hardiness of soul,
True to imagined right, above control;
While even the peasant boasts these rights to scan,
And learns to venerate himself as man.
Thine, Freedom, thine the blessings pictured here,
Thine are those charms that dazzle and endear;
Too blest indeed were such without alloy,
But fostered even by Freedom ills annoy;
That independence Britons prize too high
Keeps man from man, and breaks the social tie:
The self-dependent lordlings stand alone,
All claims that bind and sweeten life unknown;
Here, by the bonds of Nature feebly held,
Minds combat minds, repelling and repelled;

Ferments arise, imprisoned factions roar,
Repressed Ambition struggles round her shore,
Till, over-wrought, the general system feels
Its motion stop, or frenzy fire the wheels.
Nor this the worst. As Nature's ties decay,
As duty, love, and honor fail to sway,
Fictitious bonds, the bonds of wealth and law,
Still gather strength, and force unwilling awe.
Hence all obedience bows to these alone,
And talent sinks, and merit weeps unknown:
Till time may come, when, stript of all her charms,
The land of scholars, and the nurse of arms,
Where noble stems transmit the patriot flame,
Where kings have toiled, and poets wrote for fame,
One sink of level avarice shall lie,
And scholars, soldiers, kings, unhonored die.
Yet think not, thus when Freedom's ills I state,
I mean to flatter kings, or court the great:
Ye powers of truth, that bid my soul aspire,
Far from my bosom drive the low desire!
And thou, fair Freedom, taught alike to feel
The rabble's rage, and tyrant's angry steel;
Thou transitory flower, alike undone
By proud contempt or favor's fostering sun,
Still may thy blooms the changeful clime endure,
I only would repress them to secure;
For just experience tells, in every soil,
That those who think must govern those that toil;
And all that Freedom's highest aims can reach
Is but to lay proportioned loads on each.
Hence, should one order disproportioned grow,
Its double weight must ruin all below.

O, then, how blind to all that truth requires,
Who think it freedom when a part aspires!
Calm is my soul, nor apt to rise in arms,
Except when fast-approaching danger warms;
But when contending chiefs blockade the throne,
Contracting regal power to stretch their own;
When I behold a factious band agree
To call it freedom when themselves are free;
Each wanton judge new penal statutes draw,
Laws grind the poor, and rich men rule the law;
The wealth of climes, where savage nations roam,
Pillaged from slaves to purchase slaves at home;
Fear, pity, justice, indignation start,
Tear off reserve, and bare my swelling heart;
Till half a patriot, half a coward grown,
I fly from petty tyrants to the throne.
Yes, Brother, curse with me that baleful hour,
When first Ambition struck at regal power;
And thus, polluting honor in its source,
Gave wealth to sway the mind with double force.
Have we not seen, round Britain's peopled shore,
Her useful sons exchanged for useless ore?
Seen all her triumphs but destruction haste,
Like flaring tapers brightening as they waste;
Seen Opulence, her grandeur to maintain,
Lead stern Depopulation in her train,
And over fields where scattered hamlets rose,
In barren solitary pomp repose?
Have we not seen, at Pleasure's lordly call,
The smiling long-frequented village fall?
Beheld the duteous son, the sire decayed,
The modest matron, and the blushing maid.

Forced from their homes, a melancholy train,
To traverse climes beyond the western main;
Where wild Oswego spreads her swamps around,
And Niagàra stuns with thundering sound?
  Even now, perhaps, as there some pilgrim strays
Through tangled forests, and through dangerous ways
Where beasts with man divided empire claim,
And the brown Indian marks with murderous aim;
There, while above the giddy tempest flies,
And all around distressful yells arise,
The pensive exile, bending with his woe,
To stop too fearful, and too faint to go,
Casts a long look where England's glories shine,
And bids his bosom sympathize with mine.
  Vain, very vain, my weary search to find
That bliss which only centres in the mind.
Why have I strayed from pleasure and repose,
To seek a good each government bestows?
In every government, though terrors reign,
Though tyrant-kings or tyrant-laws restrain,
How small, of all that human hearts endure,
That part which laws or kings can cause or cure!
Still to ourselves in every place consigned,
Our own felicity we make or find:
With secret course, which no loud storms annoy
Glides the smooth current of domestic joy.
The lifted axe, the agonizing wheel,
Luke's iron crown, and Damiens' bed of steel,
To men remote from power but rarely known—
Leave reason, faith, and conscience, all our own.

THE DESERTED VILLAGE.

DEDICATION.

TO SIR JOSHUA REYNOLDS.

DEAR SIR, I can have no expectations, in an address of this kind, either to add to your reputation or to establish my own. You can gain nothing from my admiration, as I am ignorant of that art in which you are said to excel; and I may lose much by the severity of your judgment, as few have a juster taste in poetry than you. Setting interest therefore aside, to which I never paid much attention, I must be indulged at present in following my affections. The only dedication I ever made was to my brother, because I loved him better than most other men. He is since dead. Permit me to inscribe this poem to you.

How far you may be pleased with the versification and mere mechanical parts of this attempt, I do not pretend to inquire: but I know you will object — and, indeed, several of our best and wisest friends concur in the opinion — that the depopulation it deplores is nowhere to be seen, and the disorders it laments are only to be found in the poet's own imagination. To this I can scarce make any other answer, than that I sincerely believe what I have written; that I have taken all possible pains, in my country excursions, for these four or five years past, to be certain of what I allege; and that all my views and inquiries have led me to believe those miseries real which I here attempt to display. But this is not the place to enter into an inquiry whether the country be depopulating or not; the discussion would take up much room, and I should prove myself, at best, an indifferent politician, to tire the reader with a long preface, when I want his unfatigued attention to a long poem.

In regretting the depopulation of the country, I inveigh against the increase of our luxuries; and here also I expect the shout of modern politicians against me. For twenty or thirty years past, it has been the fashion to consider luxury as one of the greatest national advantages; and all the wisdom of antiquity, in that particular, as erroneous. Still, however, I must remain a professed ancient on that head, and continue to think those luxuries prejudicial to states by which so many vices are introduced, and so many kingdoms have been undone. Indeed, so much has been poured out of late on the other side of the question, that, merely for the sake of novelty and variety, one would sometimes wish to be in the right. I am, dear sir,

Your sincere friend, and ardent admirer,

OLIVER GOLDSMITH.

THE DESERTED VILLAGE

SWEET AUBURN ! loveliest village of the plain,
Where health and plenty cheered the laboring swain,
Where smiling Spring its earliest visit paid,
And parting Summer's lingering blooms delayed:
Dear lovely bowers of innocence and ease,
Seats of my youth, when every sport could please,
How often have I loitered o'er thy green,
Where humble happiness endeared each scene!
How often have I paused on every charm,—
The sheltered cot, the cultivated farm,
The never-failing brook, the busy mill,
The decent church that topped the neighboring hill,
The hawthorn bush, with seats beneath the shade,
For talking age and whispering lovers made!
How often have I blessed the coming day
When toil remitting lent its turn to play,
And all the village train, from labor free,
Led up their sports beneath the spreading tree;
While many a pastime circled in the shade,
The young contending as the old surveyed,
And many a gambol frolicked o'er the ground,
And sleights of art and feats of strength went round:
And still, as each repeated pleasure tired,
Succeeding sports the mirthful band inspired;
The dancing pair that simply sought renown
By holding out to tire each other down;

The swain mistrustless of his smutted face,
While secret laughter tittered round the place;
The bashful virgin's sidelong looks of love,
The matron's glance that would those looks reprove.
These were thy charms, sweet village! sports like these,
With sweet succession taught even toil to please;
These round thy bowers their cheerful influence shed;
These were thy charms — but all these charms are fled.
Sweet smiling village, loveliest of the lawn,
Thy sports are fled, and all thy charms withdrawn;
Amidst thy bowers the tyrant's hand is seen,
And desolation saddens all thy green:
One only master grasps the whole domain,
And half a tillage stints thy smiling plain.
No more thy glassy brook reflects the day,
But choked with sedges works its weedy way;
Along thy glades, a solitary guest,
The hollow-sounding bittern guards its nest;
Amidst thy desert walks the lapwing flies,
And tires their echoes with unvaried cries.
Sunk are thy bowers in shapeless ruin all,
And the long grass o'ertops the mouldering wall;
And, trembling, shrinking from the spoiler's hand,
Far, far away thy children leave the land.
Ill fares the land, to hastening ills a prey,
Where wealth accumulates and men decay:
Princes and lords may flourish, or may fade;
A breath can make them, as a breath has made;
But a bold peasantry, their country's pride,
When once destroyed, can never be supplied.
A time there was, ere England's griefs began,
When every rood of ground maintained its man:

For him light labor spread her wholesome store,
Just gave what life required, but gave no more;
His best companions, Innocence and Health;
And his best riches, ignorance of wealth.
  But times are altered; trade's unfeeling train
Usurp the land, and dispossess the swain:
Along the lawn where scattered hamlets rose,
Unwieldy wealth and cumbrous pomp repose;
And every want to opulence allied,
And every pang that folly pays to pride.
Those gentle hours that plenty bade to bloom,
Those calm desires that asked but little room,
Those healthful sports that graced the peaceful scene,
Lived in each look, and brightened all the green,
These, far departing, seek a kinder shore,
And rural mirth and manners are no more.
  Sweet AUBURN! parent of the blissful hour,
Thy glades forlorn confess the tyrant's power.
Here, as I take my solitary rounds
Amidst thy tangling walks and ruined grounds,
And, many a year elapsed, return to view
Where once the cottage stood, the hawthorn grew,
Remembrance wakes with all her busy train,
Swells at my breast, and turns the past to pain.
  In all my wanderings round this world of care,
In all my griefs — and God has given my share —
I still had hopes my latest hours to crown,
Amidst these humble bowers to lay me down;
To husband out life's taper at the close,
And keep the flame from wasting, by repose.
I still had hopes, for pride attends us still,
Amidst the swains to show my book-learned skill,

Around my fire an evening group to draw,
And tell of all I felt, and all I saw;
And, as an hare, whom hounds and horns pursue,
Pants to the place from whence at first he flew,
I still had hopes, my long vexations past,
Here to return, and die at home at last.
  O blest retirement, friend to life's decline,
Retreats from care, that never must be mine!
How happy he who crowns, in shades like these,
A youth of labor with an age of ease:
Who quits a world where strong temptations try,
And, since 't is hard to combat, learns to fly!
For him no wretches, born to work and weep,
Explore the mine, or tempt the dangerous deep;
No surly porter stands, in guilty state,
To spurn imploring Famine from the gate;
But on he moves, to meet his latter end,
Angels around befriending Virtue's friend —
Bends to the grave with unperceived decay,
While Resignation gently slopes the way —
And, all his prospects brightening to the last,
His heaven commences ere the world be past.
  Sweet was the sound, when oft at evening's close
Up yonder hill the village murmur rose;
There, as I passed with careless steps and slow,
The mingling notes came softened from below;
The swain responsive as the milk-maid sung,
The sober herd that lowed to meet their young,
The noisy geese that gabbled o'er the pool,
The playful children just let loose from school,
The watch-dog's voice that bayed the whispering wind,
And the loud laugh that spoke the vacant mind;

These all in sweet confusion sought the shade,
And filled each pause the nightingale had made.
But now the sounds of population fail,
No cheerful murmurs fluctuate in the gale,
No busy steps the grass-grown footway tread,
For all the bloomy flush of life is fled:
All but yon widowed, solitary thing,
That feebly bends beside the plashy spring;
She, wretched matron, forced in age, for bread,
To strip the brook with mantling cresses spread,
To pick her wintry fagot from the thorn,
To seek her nightly shed, and weep till morn;
She only left of all the harmless train,
The sad historian of the pensive plain!
  Near yonder copse, where once the garden smiled,
And still where many a garden flower grows wild,
There, where a few torn shrubs the place disclose,
The village preacher's modest mansion rose.
A man he was to all the country dear,
And passing rich with forty pounds a year.
Remote from towns he ran his godly race,
Nor e'er had changed, nor wished to change, his place;
Unpractised he to fawn, or seek for power
By doctrines fashioned to the varying hour,
Far other aims his heart had learned to prize,
More skilled to raise the wretched than to rise.
His house was known to all the vagrant train;
He chid their wanderings, but relieved their pain;
The long-remembered beggar was his guest,
Whose beard descending swept his aged breast;
The ruined spendthrift, now no longer proud,
Claimed kindred there, and had his claim allowed;

The broken soldier, kindly bade to stay,
Sat by his fire, and talked the night away;
Wept o'er his wounds, or, tales of sorrow done,
Shouldered his crutch, and showed how fields were won.
Pleased with his guests, the good man learned to glow,
And quite forgot their vices in their woe;
Careless their merits or their faults to scan,
His pity gave ere charity began.
  Thus to relieve the wretched was his pride,
And even his failings leaned to virtue's side;
But in his duty prompt, at every call,
He watched and wept, he prayed and felt for all;
And, as a bird each fond endearment tries
To tempt its new-fledged offspring to the skies,
He tried each art, reproved each dull delay,
Allured to brighter worlds, and led the way.
  Beside the bed where parting life was laid,
And sorrow, guilt, and pain, by turns dismayed,
The reverend champion stood: at his control
Despair and anguish fled the struggling soul;
Comfort came down the trembling wretch to raise,
And his last faltering accents whispered praise.
  At church, with meek and unaffected grace,
His looks adorned the venerable place;
Truth from his lips prevailed with double sway,
And fools who came to scoff remained to pray.
The service passed, around the pious man,
With steady zeal, each honest rustic ran;
Even children followed, with endearing wile,
And plucked his gown, to share the good man's smile.
His ready smile a parent's warmth expressed,
Their welfare pleased him, and their cares distressed.

To them his heart, his love, his griefs were given,
But all his serious thoughts had rest in heaven.
As some tall cliff, that lifts its awful form,
Swells from the vale, and midway leaves the storm,
Though round its breast the rolling clouds are spread,
Eternal sunshine settles on its head.
  Beside yon straggling fence that skirts the way,
With blossomed furze unprofitably gay,
There, in his noisy mansion, skilled to rule,
The village master taught his little school.
A man severe he was, and stern to view;
I knew him well, and every truant knew:
Well had the boding tremblers learned to trace
The day's disasters in his morning face;
Full well they laughed with counterfeited glee
At all his jokes, for many a joke had he;
Full well the busy whisper, circling round,
Conveyed the dismal tidings when he frowned:
Yet he was kind, or if severe in aught,
The love he bore to learning was in fault.
The village all declared how much he knew;
'T was certain he could write, and cipher too,
Lands he could measure, terms and tides presage —
And even the story ran — that he could gauge.
In arguing, too, the parson owned his skill,
For even though vanquished he could argue still;
While words of learned length and thundering sound
Amazed the gazing rustics ranged around;
And still they gazed, and still the wonder grew
That one small head could carry all he knew.
  But passed is all his fame. The very spot,
Where many a time he triumphed, is forgot.

Near yonder thorn, that lifts its head on high,
Where once the sign-post caught the passing eye,
Low lies that house where nut-brown draughts inspired,
Where gray-beard mirth and smiling toil retired,
Where village statesmen talked with looks profound,
And news much older than their ale went round.
Imagination fondly stoops to trace
The parlor splendors of that festive place;
The whitewashed wall, the nicely-sanded floor,
The varnished clock that clicked behind the door;
The chest contrived a double debt to pay,
A bed by night, a chest of drawers by day;
The pictures placed for ornament and use,
The twelve good rules, the royal game of goose;
The hearth, except when winter chilled the day,
With aspen boughs, and flowers, and fennel gay,
While broken tea-cups, wisely kept for show,
Ranged o'er the chimney, glistened in a row.
Vain transitory splendors! could not all
Reprieve the tottering mansion from its fall?
Obscure it sinks, nor shall it more impart
An hour's importance to the poor man's heart;
Thither no more the peasant shall repair
To sweet oblivion of his daily care;
No more the farmer's news, the barber's tale,
No more the woodman's ballad shall prevail;
No more the smith his dusky brow shall clear,
Relax his ponderous strength, and lean to hear
The host himself no longer shall be found
Careful to see the mantling bliss go round;
Nor the coy maid, half-willing to be prest,
Shall kiss the cup to pass it to the rest.

Yes ! let the rich deride, the proud disdain,
These simple blessings of the lowly train —
To me more dear, congenial to my heart,
One native charm, than all the gloss of art :
Spontaneous joys, where Nature has its play,
The soul adopts, and owns their first-born sway ;
Lightly they frolic o'er the vacant mind,
Unenvied, unmolested, unconfined;
But the long pomp, the midnight masquerade,
With all the freaks of wanton wealth arrayed,
In these, ere triflers half their wish obtain,
The toiling pleasure sickens into pain :
And, even while fashion's brightest arts decoy,
The heart distrusting asks, if this be joy ?
Ye friends to truth, ye statesmen, who survey
The rich man's joys increase, the poor's decay,
'T is yours to judge, how wide the limits stand
Between a splendid and a happy land.
Proud swells the tide with loads of freighted ore,
And shouting Folly hails them from her shore ;
Hoards even beyond the miser's wish abound,
And rich men flock from all the world around.
Yet count our gains. This wealth is but a name
That leaves our useful products still the same.
Not so the loss. The man of wealth and pride
Takes up a space that many poor supplied ;
Space for his lake, his park's extended bounds,
Space for his horse, his equipage, and hounds :
The robe that wraps his limbs in silken sloth
Has robbed the neighboring fields of half their growth ;
His seat, where solitary sports are seen,
Indignant spurns the cottage from the green ;

Around the world each needful product flies,
For all the luxuries the world supplies.
While thus the land, adorned for pleasure — all
In barren splendor feebly waits the fall.
  As some fair female, unadorned and plain,
Secure to please while youth confirms her reign,
Slights every borrowed charm that dress supplies,
Nor shares with art the triumph of her eyes :
But when those charms are past, for charms are frail,
When time advances, and when lovers fail —
She then shines forth, solicitous to bless,
In all the glaring impotence of dress.
Thus fares the land, by luxury betrayed :
In nature's simplest charms at first arrayed,
But verging to decline, its splendors rise,
Its vistas strike, its palaces surprise ;
While, scourged by famine, from the smiling land
The mournful peasant leads his humble band ;
And while he sinks, without one arm to save,
The country blooms — a garden, and a grave.
  Where, then, ah ! where shall poverty reside,
To 'scape the pressure of contiguous pride ?
If to some common's fenceless limits strayed
He drives his flock to pick the scanty blade,
Those fenceless fields the sons of wealth divide,
And even the bare-worn common is denied.
  If to the city sped — what waits him there ?
To see profusion that he must not share ;
To see ten thousand baneful arts combined
To pamper luxury, and thin mankind ;
To see each joy the sons of pleasure know
Extorted from his fellow-creature's woe.

Here, while the courtier glitters in brocade,
There the pale artist plies the sickly trade;
Here, while the proud their long-drawn pomps display,
There the black gibbet glooms beside the way.
The dome where Pleasure holds her midnight reign,
Here, richly decked, admits the gorgeous train;
Tumultuous grandeur crowds the blazing square,
The rattling chariots clash, the torches glare.
Sure scenes like these no troubles e'er annoy!
Sure these denote one universal joy!
Are these thy serious thoughts? — Ah, turn thine eyes
Where the poor houseless shivering female lies.
She once, perhaps, in village plenty blessed,
Has wept at tales of innocence distressed —
Her modest looks the cottage might adorn,
Sweet as the primrose peeps beneath the thorn;
Now lost to all — her friends, her virtue fled,
Near her betrayer's door she lays her head,
And, pinched with cold, and shrinking from the shower,
With heavy heart deplores that luckless hour,
When idly first, ambitious of the town,
She left her wheel, and robes of country brown.
Do thine, sweet AUBURN! thine, the loveliest train,
Do thy fair tribes participate her pain?
Even now, perhaps, by cold and hunger led,
At proud men's doors they ask a little bread!
Ah, no! To distant climes, a dreary scene,
Where half the convex world intrudes between,
Through torrid tracts with fainting steps they go,
Where wild Altama murmurs to their woe.
Far different there from all that charmed before,
The various terrors of that horrid shore;

Those blazing suns that dart a downward ray,
And fiercely shed intolerable day;
Those matted woods where birds forget to sing,
But silent bats in drowsy clusters cling;
Those poisonous fields with rank luxuriance crowned,
Where the dark scorpion gathers death around;
Where at each step the stranger fears to wake
The rattling terrors of the vengeful snake;
Where crouching tigers wait their hapless prey,
And savage men more murderous still than they;
While oft in whirls the mad tornado flies,
Mingling the ravaged landscape with the skies.
Far different these from every former scene,
The cooling brook, the grassy-vested green.
The breezy covert of the warbling grove,
That only sheltered thefts of harmless love.
  Good Heaven! what sorrows gloomed that parting day,
That called them from their native walks away.
When the poor exiles, every pleasure past,
Hung round their bowers, and fondly looked their last,
And took a long farewell, and wished in vain
For seats like these beyond the western main;
And shuddering still to face the distant deep,
Returned and wept, and still returned to weep.
The good old sire the first prepared to go
To new-found worlds, and wept for others' woe;
But for himself, in conscious virtue brave,
He only wished for worlds beyond the grave.
His lovely daughter, lovelier in her tears,
The fond companion of his helpless years,
Silent went next, neglectful of her charms,
And left a lover's for a father's arms.

With louder plaints the mother spoke her woes,
And blessed the cot where every pleasure rose,
And kissed her thoughtless babes with many a tear,
And clasped them close, in sorrow doubly dear;
Whilst her fond husband strove to lend relief
In all the silent manliness of grief.
O Luxury! thou cursed by Heaven's decree,
How ill exchanged are things like these for thee!
How do thy potions, with insidious joy,
Diffuse their pleasures only to destroy!
Kingdoms by thee, to sickly greatness grown,
Boast of a florid vigor not their own;
At every draught more large and large they grow,
A bloated mass of rank, unwieldy woe;
Till, sapped their strength, and every part unsound,
Down, down they sink, and spread a ruin round.
Even now the devastation is begun,
And half the business of destruction done;
Even now, methinks, as pondering here I stand,
I see the rural Virtues leave the land.
Down where yon anchoring vessel spreads the sail,
That idly waiting flaps with every gale,
Downward they move, a melancholy band,
Pass from the shore, and darken all the strand.
Contented toil, and hospitable care,
And kind connubial tenderness are there;
And piety with wishes placed above,
And steady loyalty, and faithful love.
And thou, sweet Poetry, thou loveliest maid,
Still first to fly where sensual joys invade,
Unfit in these degenerate times of shame
To catch the heart, or strike for honest fame;

Dear charming nymph, neglected and decried,
My shame in crowds, my solitary pride;
Thou source of all my bliss, and all my woe,
That found'st me poor at first, and keep'st me so;
Thou guide by which the nobler arts excel,
Thou nurse of every virtue — fare thee well!
Farewell! and O! where'er thy voice be tried,
On Torno's cliffs, or Pambamarca's side,
Whether where equinoctial fervors glow,
Or winter wraps the polar world in snow,
Still let thy voice, prevailing over time,
Redress the rigors of the inclement clime;
Aid slighted truth: with thy persuasive strain
Teach erring man to spurn the rage of gain;
Teach him, that states of native strength possessed,
Though very poor, may still be very blessed;
That trade's proud empire hastes to swift decay,
As ocean sweeps the labored mole away —
While self-dependent power can time defy,
As rocks resist the billows and the sky.

RETALIATION.

26

ADVERTISEMENT.

THE following account by Garrick of the origin of *Retaliation*, and the notes annexed, by Mr. Peter Cunningham, are extracted from the very complete edition of Goldsmith's works just issued by Mr. Murray.

"As the cause of writing the following printed poem, called *Retaliation*, has not yet been fully explained, a person concerned in the business begs leave to give the following just and minute account of the whole affair.

"At a meeting of a company of gentlemen,* who were well known to each other, and diverting themselves, among many other things, with the peculiar oddities of Dr. Goldsmith, who never would allow a superior in any art, from writing poetry down to dancing a hornpipe, the doctor, with great eagerness, insisted on trying his epigrammatic powers with Mr. Garrick, and each of them was to write the other's epitaph. Mr. Garrick immediately said that his epitaph was finished, and spoke the following distich extempore:

'Here lies Nolly Goldsmith, for shortness called Noll,
Who wrote like an angel, but talked like poor Poll.'

Goldsmith, upon the company's laughing very heartily, grew very thoughtful, and either would not or could not write anything at that time; however, he went to work, and some weeks after produced the following printed poem, called *Retaliation*, which has been much admired, and gone through several editions. The public in general have been mistaken in imagining that this poem was written in anger by the doctor; it was just the contrary; the whole on all sides was done with the greatest good humor; and the following poems in manuscript were written by several of the gentlemen on purpose to provoke the doctor to an answer, which came forth at length with great credit to him in *Retaliation*." — D. GARRICK, [MS.]

"To this highly interesting account (now first printed, or even referred to, by any biographer or editor of Goldsmith) I am indebted to my friend Mr. George Daniel, of Islington, who allowed me to transcribe it from the original in Garrick's own handwriting, discovered among the Garrick papers, and evidently designed as a preface to a collected edition of the poems which grew out of Goldsmith's trying his epigrammatic powers with Garrick. I may observe also that Garrick's epitaph or distich on Goldsmith is (through this very paper) the first time printed as it was spoken by its author.

"*Retaliation* was the last work of Goldsmith, and a posthumous publication — appearing for the first time on the 18th of April, 1774." — PETER CUNNINGHAM.

* At the St. James's Coffee House in St. James's-street.

RETALIATION.

Of old when Scarron his companions invited,
Each guest brought his dish, and the feast was united;
If our landlord supplies us with beef and with fish,
Let each guest bring himself,— and he brings the best dish;
Our Dean shall be venison, just fresh from the plains;
Our Burke shall be tongue, with the garnish of brains;
Our Will shall be wild-fowl, of excellent flavor;
And Dick with his pepper shall heighten their savor;
Our Cumberland's sweet-bread its place shall obtain;
And Douglas is pudding, substantial and plain;
Our Garrick 's a salad,— for in him we see
Oil, vinegar, sugar, and saltness agree;
To make out the dinner, full certain I am
That Ridge is anchovy, and Reynolds is lamb;
That Hickey 's a capon, and, by the same rule,
Magnanimous Goldsmith a gooseberry fool.
At a dinner so various, at such a repast,
Who 'd not be a glutton, and stick to the last?
Here, waiter, more wine! let me sit while I 'm able,
Till all my companions sink under the table;
Then, with chaos and blunders encircling my head,
Let me ponder, and tell what I think of the dead.
   Here lies the good Dean, reünited to earth,
Who mixed reason with pleasure, and wisdom with mirth;
If he had any faults, he has left us in doubt,
At least, in six weeks, I could not find them out;

Yet some have declared, and it can't be denied 'em,
That sly-boots was cursedly cunning to hide 'em.
Here lies our good Edmund, whose genius was such,
We scarcely can praise it, or blame it too much;
Who, born for the universe, narrowed his mind,
And to party gave up what was meant for mankind:
Though fraught with all learning, yet straining his throat
To persuade Tommy Townshend to lend him a vote;
Who, too deep for his hearers, still went on refining,
And thought of convincing, while they thought of dining:
Though equal to all things, for all things unfit;
Too nice for a statesman, too proud for a wit;
For a patriot too cool; for a drudge disobedient;
And too fond of the right to pursue the expedient.
In short, 't was his fate, unemployed, or in place, sir—
To eat mutton cold, and cut blocks with a razor.
Here lies honest William, whose heart was a mint,
While the owner ne'er knew half the good that was in 't;
The pupil of impulse, it forced him along,
His conduct still right, with his argument wrong;
Still aiming at honor, yet fearing to roam,
The coachman was tipsy, the chariot drove home;
Would you ask for his merits? alas! he had none;
What was good was spontaneous, his faults were his own.
Here lies honest Richard, whose fate I must sigh at;
Alas! that such frolic should now be so quiet!
What spirits were his! what wit and what whim!
Now breaking a jest, and now breaking a limb;
Now wrangling and grumbling to keep up the ball;
Now teasing and vexing—yet laughing at all!
In short, so provoking a devil was Dick,
That we wished him full ten times a day at Old Nick;

But, missing his mirth and agreeable vein,
As often we wished to have Dick back again.
  Here Cumberland lies, having acted his parts,
The Terence of England, the mender of hearts;
A flattering painter, who made it his care
To draw men as they ought to be, not as they are.
His gallants are all faultless, his women divine,
And comedy wonders at being so fine!
Like a tragedy queen he has dizened her out,—
Or rather like tragedy giving a rout.
His fools have their follies so lost in a crowd
Of virtues and feelings that folly grows proud;
And coxcombs, alike in their failings alone,
Adopting his portraits, are pleased with their own.
Say, where has our poet this malady caught?
Or wherefore his characters thus without fault?
Say, was it that vainly directing his view
To find out men's virtues, and finding them few,
Quite sick of pursuing each troublesome elf,
He grew lazy at last — and drew from himself?
  Here Douglas retires from his toils to relax,
The scourge of impostors, the terror of quacks;
Come, all ye quack bards, and ye quacking divines,
Come, and dance on the spot where your tyrant reclines!
When satire and censure encircled his throne,
I feared for your safety,— I feared for my own:
But now he is gone, and we want a detector,
Our Dodds shall be pious, our Kenricks shall lecture;
Macpherson write bombast, and call it a style;
Our Townshend make speeches, and I shall compile;
New Lauders and Bowers the Tweed shall cross over,
No countryman living their tricks to discover;

Detection her taper shall quench to a spark,
And Scotchman meet Scotchman, and cheat in the dark
Here lies David Garrick,—describe me, who can,
An abridgment of all that was pleasant in man:
As an actor, confessed without rival to shine;
As a wit, if not first, in the very first line;
Yet, with talents like these, and an excellent heart,
The man had his failings,—a dupe to his art.
Like an ill-judging beauty, his colors he spread,
And beplastered with rouge his own natural red.
On the stage he was natural, simple, affecting;
'T was only that when he was off he was acting.
With no reason on earth to go out of his way,
He turned and he varied full ten times a day.
Though secure of our hearts, yet confoundedly sick
If they were not his own by finessing and trick;
He cast off his friends, as a huntsman his pack,
For he knew when he pleased he could whistle them back.
Of praise a mere glutton, he swallowed what came,
And the puff of a dunce, he mistook it for fame;
Till his relish grown callous, almost to disease,
Who peppered the highest was surest to please.
But let us be candid, and speak out our mind,—
If dunces applauded, he paid them in kind.
Ye Kenricks, ye Kellys, and Woodfalls so grave,
What a commerce was yours, while you got and you gave!
How did Grub-street reëcho the shouts that you raised,
While he was be-Rosciused, and you were be-praised!
But peace to his spirit, wherever it flies,
To act as an angel, and mix with the skies;
Those poets, who owe their best fame to his skill,
Shall still be his flatterers, go where he will;

Old Shakspeare receive him with praise and with love,
And Beaumonts and Bens be his Kellys above.
Here Hickey reclines, a most blunt pleasant creature,
And slander itself must allow him good-nature;
He cherished his friend, and he relished a bumper;
Yet one fault he had, and that one was a thumper.
Perhaps you may ask if the man was a miser?
I answer, no, no,—for he always was wiser;
Too courteous, perhaps, or obligingly flat?
His very worst foe can't accuse him of that;
Perhaps he confided in men as they go,
And so was too foolishly honest? Ah, no!
Then what was his failing? come, tell it, and burn ye—
He was—could he help it?—a special attorney.
Here Reynolds is laid, and, to tell you my mind,
He has not left a better or wiser behind;
His pencil was striking, resistless, and grand;
His manners were gentle, complying, and bland;
Still born to improve us in every part,—
His pencil our faces, his manners our heart.
To coxcombs averse, yet most civilly steering,
When they judged without skill, he was still hard of hearing;
When they talked of their Raphaels, Correggios, and stuff,
He shifted his trumpet, and only took snuff.

POSTSCRIPT.

HERE Whitefoord reclines, and, deny it who can,
Though he merrily lived, he is now a grave man;
Rare compound of oddity, frolic, and fun,—
Who relished a joke, and rejoiced in a pun;

Whose temper was generous, open, sincere —
A stranger to flattery, a stranger to fear;
Who scattered around wit and humor at will;
Whose daily *bons mots* half a column might fill;
A Scotchman, from pride and from prejudice free;
A scholar, yet surely no pedant was he.
  What pity, alas! that so liberal a mind
Should so long be to newspaper essays confined;
Who perhaps to the summit of science could soar,
Yet content "if the table he set on a roar,"—
Whose talents to fill any station were fit,
Yet happy if Woodfall confessed him a wit.
  Ye newspaper witlings! ye pert scribbling folks!
Who copied his squibs, and reëchoed his jokes:
Ye tame imitators, ye servile herd, come,
Still follow your master, and visit his tomb;
To deck it bring with you festoons of the vine,
And copious libations bestow on his shrine;
Then strew all around it — you can do no less —
Cross-readings, *ship-news*, and *mistakes of the press.*
  Merry Whitefoord, farewell! for thy sake I admit
That a Scot may have humor — I had almost said wit:
This debt to thy memory I cannot refuse —
"Thou best-humored man with the worst-humored Muse."

LYRICAL AND MISCELLANEOUS.

LYRICAL AND MISCELLANEOUS.

TO AN IMPERTINENT MUSICIAN.

EXTEMPORE.

Our herald hath proclaimed this saying:
"See Æsop dancing," — and his monkey playing.

THE CLOWN'S REPLY.

John Trott was desired by two witty peers
To tell them the reason why asses had ears:
"An't please you," quoth John, "I'm not given to letters,
Nor dare I pretend to know more than my betters;
Howe'er, from this time I shall ne'er see your graces,
As I hope to be saved! without thinking on asses."

EPIGRAM

ON A BEAUTIFUL YOUTH STRUCK BLIND BY LIGHTNING.

Sure 't was by Providence designed,
Rather in pity than in hate,
That he should be, like Cupid, blind,
To save him from Narcissus' fate.

THE GIFT.

TO IRIS, IN BOW-STREET, COVENT-GARDEN.

SAY, cruel Iris, pretty rake,
  Dear mercenary beauty,
What annual offering shall I make
  Expressive of my duty?

My heart, a victim to thine eyes,
  Should I at once deliver —
Say, would the angry fair-one prize
  The gift, who slights the giver?

A bill, a jewel, watch, or toy,
  My rivals give — and let them:
If gems or gold impart a joy,
  I'll give them — when I get them.

I'll give — but not the full-blown rose,
  Or rosebud more in fashion;
Such short-lived offerings but disclose
  A transitory passion.

I'll give thee something yet unpaid,
  Not less sincere than civil:
I'll give thee — ah! too charming maid,
  I'll give thee — to the devil!

THE LOGICIANS REFUTED.

IN IMITATION OF DEAN SWIFT.

LOGICIANS have but ill-defined
As rational the human mind;

Reason, they say, belongs to man —
But let them prove it if they can.
Wise Aristotle and Smiglecius,
By ratiocinations specious,
Have strove to prove with great precision,
With definition and division,
Homo est ratione prœditum —
But for my soul I cannot credit 'em:
And must in spite of them maintain
That man and all his ways are vain,
And that this boasted lord of nature
Is both a weak and erring creature;
That instinct is a surer guide
Than reason, boasting mortals' pride,
And that brute beasts are far before 'em:
Deus est anima brutorum.
Who ever knew an honest brute
At law his neighbor prosecute;
Bring action for assault and battery,
Or friend beguile with lies and flattery?
O'er plains they ramble unconfined,
No politics disturb their mind;
They eat their meals, and take their sport,
Nor know who's in or out at court;
They never to the levee go
To treat as dearest friend a foe;
They never importune his grace,
Nor ever cringe to men in place;
Nor undertake a dirty job.
Nor draw the quill to write for Bob.
Fraught with invective they ne'er go
To folks at Paternoster-row:

No judges, fiddlers, dancing-masters,
No pickpockets, or poetasters,
Are known to honest quadrupeds;
No single brute his fellow leads.
Brutes never meet in bloody fray,
Nor cut each other's throats for pay.
Of beasts, it is confessed, the ape
Comes nearest us in human shape:
Like man, he imitates each fashion,
And malice is his ruling passion,
But both in malice and grimaces
A courtier any ape surpasses.
Behold him, humbly cringing, wait
Upon the minister of state:
View him soon after to inferiors
Aping the conduct of superiors;
He promises with equal air,
And to perform takes equal care.
He in his turn finds imitators;
At court, the porters, lackeys, waiters,
Their masters' manners still contract —
And footmen lords and dukes can act.
Thus, at the court, both great and small
Behave alike — for all ape all.

A MADRIGAL.

IMITATED FROM THE FRENCH OF SAINT PAVIN.

WEEPING, murmuring, complaining,
  Lost to every gay delight —
Myra, too sincere for feigning,
  Fears the approaching bridal night.

Yet why impair thy bright perfection,
  Or dim thy beauty with a tear?
Had Myra followed my direction,
  She long had wanted cause of fear.

STANZAS

ON THE TAKING OF QUEBEC.

Amidst the clamor of exulting joys,
  Which triumph forces from the patriot heart,
Grief dares to mingle her soul-piercing voice,
  And quells the raptures which from pleasure start.

O Wolfe, to thee a streaming flood of woe
  Sighing we pay, and think even conquest dear;
Quebec in vain shall teach our breast to glow,
  Whilst thy sad fate extorts the heart-wrung tear.

Alive, the foe thy dreadful vigor fled,
  And saw thee fall with joy-pronouncing eyes;
Yet they shall know thou conquerest, though dead —
  Since from thy tomb a thousand heroes rise.

AN ELEGY

ON THAT GLORY OF HER SEX, MRS. MARY BLAIZE.

Good people all, with one accord,
  Lament for Madam Blaize,
Who never wanted a good word —
  From those who spoke her praise.

The needy seldom passed her door,
  And always found her kind;
She freely lent to all the poor —
  Who left a pledge behind.

She strove the neighborhood to please
  With manners wondrous winning,
And never followed wicked ways —
  Unless when she was sinning.

At church, in silks and satins new,
  With hoop of monstrous size,
She never slumbered in her pew —
  But when she shut her eyes.

Her love was sought, I do aver,
  By twenty beaux and more;
The king himself has followed her —
  When she has walked before.

But now her wealth and finery fled,
  Her hangers-on cut short all;
The doctors found, when she was dead —
  Her last disorder mortal.

Let us lament, in sorrow sore,
  For Kent-street well may say,
That, had she lived a twelvemonth more —
  She had not died to-day.

DESCRIPTION OF AN AUTHOR'S BED-CHAMBER.

Where the Red Lion, flaring o'er the way,
Invites each passing stranger that can pay —

Where Calvert's butt, and Parson's *black champagne*,
Regale the drabs and bloods of Drury-lane —
There in a lonely room, from bailiffs snug,
The Muse found Scroggen, stretched beneath a rug.
A window, patched with paper, lent a ray
That dimly showed the state in which he lay:
The sanded floor that grits beneath the tread;
The humid wall with paltry pictures spread;
The royal game of goose was there in view,
And the twelve rules the royal martyr drew;
The seasons, framed with listing, found a place,
And brave prince William showed his lamp-black face.
The morn was cold — he views with keen desire
The rusty grate, unconscious of a fire;
With beer and milk arrears the frieze was scored,
And five cracked tea-cups dressed the chimney-board;
A night-cap decked his brows instead of bay,
A cap by night — a stocking all the day!

LINES,

ON SEEING MRS. * * PERFORM IN THE CHARACTER OF * * *.

To you, bright fair, the Nine address their lays,
And tune my feeble voice to sing thy praise;
The heartfelt power of every charm divine,
Who can withstand their all-commanding shine?
See how she moves along with every grace,
While soul-brought tears steal down each shining face.
She speaks! 't is rapture all, and nameless bliss;
Ye gods! what transport e'er compared to this?
As when in Paphian groves the Queen of Love
With fond complaint addressed the listening Jove —

'T was joy and endless blisses all around,
And rocks forgot their hardness at the sound.
Then first, at last, even Jove was taken in;
And felt her charms, without disguise, within.

ELEGY

ON THE DEATH OF THE RIGHT HON. * * *

Ye Muses, pour the pitying tear
  For Pollio snatched away;
O! had he lived another year —
  He had not died to-day.

O! were he born to bless mankind
  In virtuous times of yore,
Heroes themselves had fallen behind —
  Whene'er he went before.

How sad the groves and plains appear,
  And sympathetic sheep;
Even pitying hills would drop a tear —
  If hills could learn to weep.

His bounty in exalted strain
  Each bard might well display,
Since none implored relief in vain —
  That went relieved away.

And hark! I hear the tuneful throng
  His obsequies forbid;
He still shall live, shall live as long —
  As ever dead man did.

TRANSLATION

OF A SOUTH AMERICAN ODE.

In all my Enna's beauties blest,
Amidst profusion still I pine;
For though she gives me up her breast,
Its panting tenant is not mine.

THE CAPTIVITY.

AN ORATORIO.

THE PERSONS.

First Israelitish Prophet. *First Chaldean Priest.*
Second Israelitish Prophet. *Second Chaldean Priest.*
Israelitish Woman. *Chaldean Woman.*

Chorus of Youths and Virgins.

Scene — *The Banks of the River Euphrates, near Babylon.*

ACT I.

FIRST PROPHET. — RECITATIVE.

Ye captive tribes, that hourly work and weep,
Where flows Euphrates, murmuring to the deep —
Suspend a while the task, the tear suspend,
And turn to God, your father and your friend:
Insulted, chained, and all the world a foe,
Our God alone is all we boast below.

CHORUS OF ISRAELITES.

Our God is all we boast below,
To Him we turn our eyes;
And every added weight of woe
Shall make our homage rise ·

And though no temple richly drest,
Nor sacrifice, is here,
We 'll make His temple in our breast,
And offer up a tear.

SECOND PROPHET. — RECITATIVE.

That strain once more ! it bids remembrance rise,
And brings my long-lost country to mine eyes.
Ye fields of Sharon, dressed in flowery pride;
Ye plains where Jordan rolls its glassy tide;
Ye hills of Lebanon, with cedars crowned;
Ye Gilead groves, that fling perfumes around:
Those hills how sweet! those plains how wondrous fair!
But sweeter still, when Heaven was with us there.

Air.

O Memory, thou fond deceiver!
Still importunate and vain;
To former joys recurring ever,
And turning all the past to pain.

Thou, like the world, the oppressed oppressing,
Thy smiles increase the wretch's woe ·
And he who wants each other blessing
In thee must ever find a foe.

FIRST PROPHET. — RECITATIVE.

Yet, why repine? What though by bonds confined,
Should bonds enslave the vigor of the mind?
Have we not cause for triumph, when we see
Ourselves alone from idol worship free?
Are not, this very day, those feasts begun
Where prostrate folly hails the rising sun?

Do not our tyrant lords this day ordain
For superstitious rites and mirth profane?
And should we mourn? Should coward Virtue fly,
When impious Folly rears her front on high?
No! rather let us triumph still the more —
And as our fortune sinks, our wishes soar.

Air.

The triumphs that on vice attend
Shall ever in confusion end;
The good man suffers but to gain,
And every virtue springs from pain:

As aromatic plants bestow
No spicy fragrance while they grow;
But crushed, or trodden to the ground,
Diffuse their balmy sweets around.

SECOND PROPHET. — RECITATIVE.

But hush, my sons! our tyrant lords are near —
The sound of barbarous mirth offends mine ear;
Triumphant music floats along the vale —
Near, nearer still, it gathers on the gale:
The growing note their near approach declares; —
Desist, my sons, nor mix the strain with theirs.

Enter CHALDEAN PRIESTS, *attended.*

FIRST PRIEST.

Air.

Come on, my companions, the triumph display;
Let rapture the minutes employ;
The sun calls us out on this festival day,
And our monarch partakes of our joy.

SECOND PRIEST.

Like the sun, our great monarch all pleasure supplies;
  Both similar blessings bestow :
The sun with his splendor illumines the skies ;
  And our monarch enlivens below.

Air.

CHALDEAN WOMAN.

Haste, ye sprightly sons of pleasure;
Love presents its brightest treasure,
  Leave all other sports for me.

CHALDEAN ATTENDANT.

Or, rather, love's delights despising,
Haste to raptures ever rising ;
  Wine shall bless the brave and free.

SECOND PRIEST.

Wine and beauty thus inviting,
Each to different joys exciting,
  Whither shall my choice incline?

FIRST PRIEST.

I 'll waste no longer thought in choosing ;
But, neither love nor wine refusing,
  I 'll make them both together mine.

RECITATIVE.

But whence, when joy should brighten o'er the land,
This sullen gloom in Judah's captive band?
Ye sons of Judah, why the lute unstrung?
Or why those harps on yonder willows hung?
Come, take the lyre, and pour the strain along,
The day demands it: sing us Sion's song.

Dismiss your griefs, and join our tuneful choir;
For who like you can wake the sleeping lyre!

SECOND PROPHET.

Bowed down with chains, the scorn of all mankind
To want, to toil, and every ill consigned —
Is this a time to bid us raise the strain,
And mix in rites that Heaven regards with pain?
No, never! May this hand forget each art
That speeds the power of music to the heart,
Ere I forget the land that gave me birth,
Or join with sounds profane its sacred mirth!

FIRST PRIEST.

Insulting slaves! if gentler methods fail,
The whip and angry tortures shall prevail.
[*Exeunt* CHALDEANS.

FIRST PROPHET.

Why, let them come, one good remains to cheer;
We fear the Lord, and know no other fear.

CHORUS OF CHALDEANS.

Can whips or tortures hurt the mind
On God's supporting breast reclined?
Stand fast, — and let our tyrants see
That fortitude is victory.

ACT II.

Air.

CHORUS OF ISRAELITES.

O peace of mind, angelic guest!
Thou softest soother of the breast,
Dispense thy balmy store.

Wing all our thoughts to reach the skies,
Till earth, diminished to our eyes,
Shall vanish as we soar.

FIRST PRIEST. — RECITATIVE.

No more! Too long has justice been delayed —
The king's commands must fully be obeyed:
Compliance with his will your peace secures,
Praise but our gods, and every good is yours.
But if, rebellious to his high command,
You spurn the favors offered at his hand,
Think, timely think, what ills remain behind;
Reflect, nor tempt to rage the royal mind.

SECOND PRIEST.

Air.

Fierce is the whirlwind howling
O'er Afric's sandy plain,
And fierce the tempest rolling,
Along the furrowed main:

But storms that fly
To rend the sky,
Every ill presaging —
Less dreadful show
To worlds below
Than angry monarchs raging.

ISRAELITISH WOMAN.— RECITATIVE.

Ah me! what angry terrors round us grow!
How shrinks my soul to meet the threatened blow!
Ye prophets, skilled in Heaven's eternal truth,
Forgive my sex's fears, forgive my youth!

If, shrinking thus when frowning power appears,
I wish for life and yield me to my fears.
Let us one hour, one little hour obey;
To-morrow's tears may wash the stain away.

Air.

The wretch, condemned with life to part,
  Still, still on hope relies;
And every pang that rends the heart
  Bids expectation rise.

Hope, like the glimmering taper's light,
  Adorns and cheers our way;
And still, as darker grows the night,
  Emits a brighter ray.

SECOND PRIEST. — RECITATIVE.

Why this delay? At length for joy prepare.
I read your looks, and see compliance there.
Come raise the strain, and grasp the full-toned ly
The time, the theme, the place, and all conspire.

Air.

CHALDEAN WOMAN.

See the ruddy morning smiling,
Hear the grove to bliss beguiling;
Zephyrs through the valley playing,
Streams along the meadow straying.

FIRST PRIEST.

While these a constant revel keep,
Shall reason only bid me weep?
Hence, intruder! we'll pursue
Nature, a better guide than you.

SECOND PRIEST.

Air.

Every moment, as it flows,
Some peculiar pleasure owes;
Then let us, providently wise,
Seize the debtor as it flies.

Think not to-morrow can repay
The pleasures that we lose to-day;
To-morrow's most unbounded store
Can but pay its proper score.

FIRST PRIEST. — RECITATIVE.

But hush! see, foremost of the captive choir,
The master prophet grasps his full-toned lyre;
Mark where he sits, with executing art,
Feels for each tone, and speeds it to the heart.
See, inspiration fills his rising form,
Awful as clouds that nurse the growing storm!
And now his voice, accordant to the string,
Prepares our monarch's victories to sing.

FIRST PROPHET.

Air.

From north, from south, from east, from west,
  Conspiring foes shall come;
Tremble, thou vice-polluted breast,
  Blasphemers, all be dumb.

The tempest gathers all around,
  On Babylon it lies;
Down with her! down — down to the ground:
  She sinks, she groans, she dies.

SECOND PROPHET.

Down with her, Lord, to lick the dust,
Ere yonder setting sun;
Serve her as she has served the just:
'T is fixed — it shall be done.

FIRST PRIEST. — RECITATIVE.

Enough! when slaves thus insolent presume,
The king himself shall judge, and fix their doom.
Short-sighted wretches! have not you and all
Beheld our power in Zedekiah's fall?
To yonder gloomy dungeon turn your eyes —
Mark where dethroned your captive monarch lies;
Deprived of sight, and rankling in his chain,
He calls on Death to terminate his pain.
Yet know, ye slaves, that still remain behind
More ponderous chains, and dungeons more confined.

CHORUS.

Arise, all-potent Ruler, rise,
And vindicate thy people's cause, —
Till every tongue, in every land,
Shall offer up unfeigned applause.

[*Exeunt.*

ACT III.

FIRST PRIEST. — RECITATIVE.

Yes, my companions, Heaven's decrees are past.
And our fixed empire shall forever last:
In vain the maddening prophet threatens woe,
In vain Rebellion aims her secret blow:
Still shall our fame and growing power be spread,
And still our vengeance crush the guilty head.

Air.

Coëval with man
Our empire began,
And never shall fall,
Till ruin shakes all.
With the ruin of all,
Shall Babylon fall.

FIRST PROPHET. — RECITATIVE.

'T is thus that pride triumphant rears the head,
A little while, and all her power is fled:
But ha! what means yon sadly plaintive train,
That this way slowly bends along the plain?
And now, methinks, a pallid corse they bear
To yonder bank, and rest the body there.
Alas! too well mine eyes observant trace
The last remains of Judah's royal race:
Our monarch falls, and now our fears are o'er,
The wretched Zedekiah is no more!

Air.

Ye wretches who by fortune's hate
  In want and sorrow groan —
Come, ponder his severer fate,
  And learn to bless your own.

Ye sons, from fortune's lap supplied,
  A while the bliss suspend;
Like yours, his life began in pride —
  Like his, your lives may end.

SECOND PROPHET.

Behold his squalid corse with sorrow worn,
His wretched limbs with ponderous fetters torn;
Those eyeless orbs that shock with ghastly glare,
Those ill-becoming robes, and matted hair.
And shall not Heaven for this its terrors show,
And deal its angry vengeance on the foe?
How long, how long, Almighty Lord of all,
Shall wrath vindictive threaten ere it fall!

ISRAELITISH WOMAN.

Air.

As panting flies the hunted hind,
  Where brooks refreshing stray;
And rivers through the valley wind,
  That stop the hunter's way:

Thus we, O Lord, alike distressed,
  For streams of mercy long;
Those streams that cheer the sore-oppressed,
  And overwhelm the strong.

FIRST PROPHET. — RECITATIVE.

But, whence that shout? Good Heavens! Amazement all!
See yonder tower just nodding to the fall:
See where an army covers all the ground,
Saps the strong walls, and pours destruction round!
The ruin smokes, destruction pours along —
How low the great, how feeble are the strong!
The foe prevails, the lofty walls recline —
O, God of hosts, the victory is Thine!

CHORUS OF ISRAELITES.

Down with them, Lord, to lick the dust —
  Thy vengeance be begun;

Serve them as they have served the just,
  And let thy will be done.

FIRST PRIEST. — RECITATIVE.

All, all is lost! The Syrian army fails;
Cyrus, the conqueror of the world, prevails!
The ruin smokes, the torrent pours along —
How low the proud, how feeble are the strong!
Save us, O Lord! to Thee, though late, we pray
And give repentance but an hour's delay.

FIRST AND SECOND PRIEST.

Air.

Thrice happy, who in happy hour
  To Heaven their praise bestow,
And own his all-consuming power
  Before they feel the blow.

FIRST PROPHET. — RECITATIVE.

Now, now's our time! ye wretches bold and blind,
Brave but to God, and cowards to mankind,
Too late you seek that power unsought before —
Your wealth, your pride, your kingdom, are no more!

Air.

O Lucifer! thou son of morn,
Alike of Heaven and man the foe,—
  Heaven, men, and all,
  Now press thy fall,
And sink thee lowest of the low.

FIRST PROPHET.

O Babylon, how art thou fallen!
Thy fall more dreadful from delay!

Thy streets forlorn
To wilds shall turn,
Where toads shall pant, and vultures prey!

SECOND PROPHET. — RECITATIVE.

Such be her fate. But listen! from afar
The clarion's note proclaims the finished war!
Cyrus, our great restorer, is at hand,
And this way leads his formidable band.
Give, give your songs of Zion to the wind,
And hail the benefactor of mankind:
He comes, pursuant to divine decree,
To chain the strong, and set the captive free

CHORUS OF YOUTHS.

Rise to raptures past expressing,
Sweeter from remembered woes;
Cyrus comes, our wrongs redressing,
Comes to give the world repose.

CHORUS OF VIRGINS.

Cyrus comes, the world redressing,
Love and Pleasure in his train;
Comes to heighten every blessing,
Comes to soften every pain.

CHORUS OF YOUTHS AND VIRGINS.

Hail to him with mercy reigning,
Skilled in every peaceful art;
Who, from bonds our limbs unchaining,
Only binds the willing heart.

LAST CHORUS.

But chief to Thee, our God, defender, friend,
Let praise be given to all eternity;
O Thou, without beginning, without end —
Let us and all begin and end in Thee!

THE DOUBLE TRANSFORMATION

A TALE.

SECLUDED from domestic strife,
Jack Bookworm led a college life;
A fellowship, at twenty-five,
Made him the happiest man alive;
He drank his glass, and cracked his joke,
And freshmen wondered as he spoke.
Such pleasures, unalloyed with care,
Could any accident impair?
Could Cupid's shaft at length transfix
Our swain, arrived at thirty-six?
O, had the archer ne'er come down
To ravage in a country town;
Or Flavia been content to stop
At triumphs in a Fleet-street shop!
O! had her eyes forgot to blaze;
Or Jack had wanted eyes to gaze.
O! — but let exclamation cease;
Her presence banished all his peace:
So, with decorum all things carried,
Miss frowned, and blushed, and then was — married
Need we expose to vulgar sight
The raptures of the bridal night?
Need we intrude on hallowed ground,
Or draw the curtains closed around?
Let it suffice that each had charms:
He clasped a goddess in his arms;
And, though she felt his usage rough,
Yet in a man 't was well enough.

The honey-moon like lightning flew;
The second brought its transports too,
A third, a fourth, were not amiss;
The fifth was friendship mixed with bliss;
But when a twelvemonth passed away,
Jack found his goddess made of clay:
Found half the charms that decked her face
Arose from powder, shreds, or lace;
But still the worst remained behind —
That very face had robbed her mind.
Skilled in no other arts was she
But dressing, patching, repartee;
And, just as humor rose or fell,
By turns a slattern or a belle.
'T is true she dressed with modern grace —
Half-naked at a ball or race;
But when at home, at board or bed,
Five greasy night-caps wrapped her head.
Could so much beauty condescend
To be a dull domestic friend?
Could any curtain-lectures bring
To decency so fine a thing?
In short — by night 't was fits or fretting;
By day, 't was gadding or coquetting.
Fond to be seen, she kept a bevy
Of powdered coxcombs at her levee;
The squire and captain took their stations,
And twenty other near relations.
Jack sucked his pipe, and often broke
A sigh in suffocating smoke;
While all their hours were past between
Insulting repartee or spleen.

Thus, as her faults each day were known,
He thinks her features coarser grown:
He fancies every vice she shows
Or thins her lip or points her nose;
Whenever rage or envy rise,
How wide her mouth, how wild her eyes!
He knows not how, but so it is,
Her face is grown a knowing phiz —
And, though her fops are wondrous civil,
He thinks her ugly as the devil.
Now, to perplex the ravelled noose,
As each a different way pursues —
While sullen or loquacious strife
Promised to hold them on for life —
That dire disease, whose ruthless power
Withers the beauty's transient flower,
Lo! the small-pox — whose horrid glare
Levelled its terrors at the fair;
And, rifling every youthful grace,
Left but the remnant of a face.

The glass, grown hateful to her sight,
Reflected now — a perfect fright;
Each former art she vainly tries
To bring back lustre to her eyes;
In vain she tries her pastes and creams
To smooth her skin, or hide its seams:
Her country beaux and city cousins,
Lovers no more, flew off by dozens:
The squire himself was seen to yield —
And even the captain quit the field.
Poor madam, now condemned to hack
The rest of life with anxious Jack,

Perceiving others fairly flown,
Attempted pleasing him alone.
Jack soon was dazzled to behold
Her present face surpass the old.
With modesty her cheeks are dyed;
Humility displaces pride:
For tawdry finery is seen
A person ever neatly clean:
No more presuming on her sway,
She learns good nature every day:
Serenely gay, and strict in duty,
Jack finds his wife — a perfect beauty.

A NEW SIMILE.

IN THE MANNER OF SWIFT.

Long had I sought in vain to find
A likeness for the scribbling kind —
The modern scribbling kind, who write
In wit, and sense, and nature's spite —
Till reading, I forgot what day on,
A chapter out of Tooke's Pantheon,
I think I met with something there
To suit my purpose to a hair.
But let us not proceed too furious,
First please to turn to god Mercurius:
You 'll find him pictured at full length
In book the second, page the tenth.
The stress of all my proofs on him I lay,
And now proceed we to our simile.

Imprimis, pray observe his hat,
Wings upon either side — mark that.
Well! what is it from thence we gather?
Why these denote a brain of feather.
A brain of feather! very right —
With wit that's flighty, learning light;
Such as to modern bards decreed:
A just comparison — proceed.
In the next place, his feet peruse;
Wings grow again from both his shoes;
Designed, no doubt, their part to bear,
And waft his godship through the air.
And here my simile unites —
For, in a modern poet's flights,
I'm sure it may be justly said,
His feet are useful as his head.
Lastly, vouchsafe to observe his hand,
Filled with a snake-encircled wand;
By classic authors termed caduceus,
And highly famed for several uses;
To wit — most wondrously endued,
No poppy-water half so good —
For let folks only get a touch,
Its soporific virtue's such,
Though ne'er so much awake before,
That quickly they begin to snore:
Add, too, what certain writers tell —
With this he drives men's soul's to hell.
Now to apply, begin we then:
His wand's a modern author's pen;
The serpents round about it twined
Denote him of the reptile kind —

Denote the rage with which he writes,
His frothy slaver, venomed bites;
An equal semblance still to keep,
Alike, too, both conduce to sleep —
This difference only, as the god
Drove souls to Tartarus with his rod,
With his goose-quill the scribbling elf
Instead of others damns himself.
  And here my simile almost tripped,
Yet grant a word by way of postscript.
Moreover, Mercury had a failing;
Well! what of that? out with it — stealing;
In which all modern bards agree,
Being each as great a thief as he.
But even this deity's existence
Shall lend my simile assistance:
Our modern bards! why what a-pox
Are they — but senseless stones and blocks?

THE HERMIT.

"Turn, gentle hermit of the dale,
  And guide my lonely way
To where yon taper cheers the vale
  With hospitable ray;

"For here, forlorn and lost, I tread,
  With fainting steps and slow —
Where wilds, immeasurably spread,
  Seem lengthening as I go."

"Forbear, my son," the hermit cries,
  "To tempt the dangerous gloom:
For yonder faithless phantom flies
  To lure thee to thy doom.

"Here to the houseless child of want
  My door is open still;
And, though my portion is but scant,
  I give it with good will.

"Then turn, to-night, and freely share
  Whate'er my cell bestows —
My rushy couch and frugal fare,
  My blessing and repose.

"No flocks that range the valley free
  To slaughter I condemn —
Taught by that power that pities me,
  I learn to pity them;

"But from the mountain's grassy side
  A guiltless feast I bring —
A scrip with herbs and fruits supplied,
  And water from the spring.

"Then, pilgrim, turn, thy cares forego;
  All earth-born cares are wrong:
Man wants but little here below,
  Nor wants that little long."

Soft as the dew from heaven descends,
  His gentle accents fell;
The modest stranger lowly bends,
  And follows to the cell.

Far, in a wilderness obscure,
The lonely mansion lay,
A refuge to the neighboring poor,
And strangers led astray.

No stores beneath its humble thatch
Required a master's care;
The wicket, opening with a latch,
Received the harmless pair.

And now, when busy crowds retire
To take their evening rest,
The hermit trimmed his little fire,
And cheered his pensive guest;

And spread his vegetable store,
And gayly pressed, and smiled;
And, skilled in legendary lore,
The lingering hours beguiled.

Around, in sympathetic mirth,
Its tricks the kitten tries —
The cricket chirrups in the hearth,
The crackling fagot flies;

But, nothing could a charm impart
To soothe the stranger's woe —
For grief was heavy at his heart,
And tears began to flow.

His rising cares the hermit spied —
With answering care oppressed;
"And whence, unhappy youth," he cried,
"The sorrows of thy breast?

"From better habitations spurned,
Reluctant dost thou rove?
Or grieve for friendship unreturned,
Or unregarded love?

"Alas! the joys that fortune brings
Are trifling, and decay —
And those who prize the paltry things,
More trifling still than they;

"And what is friendship but a name,
A charm that lulls to sleep —
A shade that follows wealth or fame,
But leaves the wretch to weep?

"And love is still an emptier sound —
The modern fair-one's jest;
On earth unseen, or only found
To warm the turtle's nest.

"For shame, fond youth, thy sorrows hush —
And spurn the sex," he said:
But, while he spoke, a rising blush
His love-lorn guest betrayed.

Surprised he sees new beauties rise,
Swift mantling to the view —
Like colors o'er the morning skies,
As bright, as transient too.

The bashful look, the rising breast,
Alternate spread alarms:
The lovely stranger stands confessed,
A maid in all her charms.

"And, ah! forgive a stranger rude,
A wretch forlorn," she cried —
"Whose feet unhallowed thus intrude
Where Heaven and you reside·

"But let a maid thy pity share,
Whom love has taught to stray —
Who seeks for rest, but finds despair
Companion of her way.

"My father lived beside the Tyne —
A wealthy lord was he;
And all his wealth was marked as mine;
He had but only me.

"To win me from his tender arms
Unnumbered suitors came;
Who praised me for imputed charms,
And felt or feigned a flame.

"Each hour a mercenary crowd
With richest proffers strove;
Among the rest young Edwin bowed —
But never talked of love.

"In humble, simplest habit clad,
No wealth nor power had he;
Wisdom and worth were all he had —
But these were all to me.

"And when beside me in the dale
He carolled lays of love,
His breath lent fragrance to the gale,
And music to the grove.

"The blossom opening to the day,
  The dews of heaven refined,
Could naught of purity display
  To emulate his mind.

"The dew, the blossom on the tree,
  With charms inconstant shine;
Their charms were his; but, woe to me,
  Their constancy was mine.

"For still I tried each fickle art,
  Importunate and vain;
And while his passion touched my heart,
  I triumphed in his pain.

"Till, quite dejected with my scorn,
  He left me to my pride;
And sought a solitude forlorn,
  In secret, where he died.

"But mine the sorrow, mine the fault,
  And well my life shall pay;
I'll seek the solitude he sought,
  And stretch me where he lay.

"And there, forlorn, despairing, hid —
  I'll lay me down and die;
'T was so for me that Edwin did,
  And so for him will I."

"Forbid it, Heaven!" the hermit cried,
  And clasped her to his breast:
The wondering fair one turned to chide —
  'T was Edwin's self that pressed.

"Turn, Angelina! ever dear—
  My charmer, turn to see
Thy own, thy long-lost Edwin, here,
  Restored to love and thee.

"Thus let me hold thee to my heart,
  And every care resign;
And shall we never, never part,
  My life—my all that 's mine?

"No, never from this hour to part,
  We 'll live and love so true;
The sigh that rends thy constant heart
  Shall break thy Edwin's too."

AN ELEGY

ON THE DEATH OF A MAD DOG.

Good people all, of every sort,
  Give ear unto my song;
And if you find it wondrous short—
  It cannot hold you long.

In Islington there was a man,
  Of whom the world might say,
That still a godly race he ran—
  Whene'er he went to pray.

A kind and gentle heart he had,
  To comfort friends and foes;
The naked every day he clad—
  When he put on his clothes.

And in that town a dog was found,
As many dogs there be,
Both mongrel, puppy, whelp, and hound,
And curs of low degree.

This dog and man at first were friends;
But, when a pique began,
The dog, to gain some private ends,
Went mad, and bit the man.

Around from all the neighboring streets
The wondering neighbors ran;
And swore the dog had lost his wits,
To bite so good a man.

The wound it seemed both sore and sad
To every Christian eye;
And while they swore the dog was mad,
They swore the man would die.

But soon a wonder came to light,
That showed the rogues they lied:
The man recovered of the bite,
The dog it was that died.

STANZAS

ON WOMAN.

When lovely woman stoops to folly,
And finds too late that men betray —
What charm can soothe her melancholy?
What art can wash her guilt away?

The only art her guilt to cover,
To hide her shame from every eye,
To give repentance to her lover,
And wring his bosom—is to die.

EPITAPH

ON EDWARD PURDON.

HERE lies poor Ned Purdon, from misery freed,
Who long was a bookseller's hack;
He led such a damnable life in this world—
I don't think he 'll wish to come back.

VERSES

IN REPLY TO AN INVITATION TO DINNER.

"This *is* a poem! This *is* a copy of verses!"

YOUR mandate I got—
You may all go to pot;
Had your senses been right,
You 'd have sent before night.
As I hope to be saved,
I put off being shaved—
For I could not make bold,
While the matter was cold,
To meddle in suds,
Or to put on my duds;
So tell Horneck and Nesbitt,
And Baker and his bit,
And Kauffman beside,
And the Jessamy bride,

With the rest of the crew,
The Reynoldses two,
Little Comedy's face,
And the Captain in lace.
By the by, you may tell him
I have something to sell him;
Of use, I insist,
When he comes to enlist.
Your worships must know
That a few days ago
An order went out,
For the foot-guards so stout
To wear tails in high taste,
Twelve inches at least;
Now I 've got him a scale
To measure each tail;
To lengthen a short tail,
And a long one to curtail.
  Yet how can I, when vext,
Thus stray from my text?
Tell each other to rue
Your Devonshire crew,
For sending so late
To one of my state.
But 't is Reynolds's way
From wisdom to stray,
And Angelica's whim
To be frolic like him —

But, alas! your good worships, how could they be wiser,
When both have been spoiled in to-day's *Advertiser?*

OLIVER GOLDSMITH.

EPITAPH

ON THOMAS PARNELL.

THIS tomb, inscribed to gentle Parnell's name,
May speak our gratitude, but not his fame.
What heart but feels his sweetly-moral lay,
That leads to truth through pleasure's flowery way!
Celestial themes confessed his tuneful aid;
And Heaven, that lent him genius, was repaid.
Needless to him the tribute we bestow—
The transitory breath of fame below;
More lasting rapture from his works shall rise,
While converts thank their poet in the skies.

THE HAUNCH OF VENISON.

AN EPISTLE TO LORD CLARE.

THANKS, my lord, for your venison, for finer or fatter
Never ranged in a forest, or smoked in a platter;
The haunch was a picture for painters to study—
The fat was so white, and the lean was so ruddy.
Though my stomach was sharp, I could scarce help regretting
To spoil such a delicate picture by eating;
I had thoughts, in my chambers, to place it in view,
To be shown to my friends as a piece of *virtù;*
As in some Irish houses, where things are so-so,
One gammon of bacon hangs up for a show—
But, for eating a rasher of what they take pride in,
They 'd as soon think of eating the pan it is fried in.

But hold — let me pause — don't I hear you pronounce
This tale of the bacon a damnable bounce?
Well, suppose it a bounce — sure a poet may try,
By a bounce now and then, to get courage to fly.
  But, my lord, it 's no bounce; I protest, in my turn,
It 's a truth — and your lordship may ask Mr. Byrne.
To go on with my tale — as I gazed on the haunch,
I thought of a friend that was trusty and staunch —
So I cut it, and sent it to Reynolds undrest,
To paint it, or eat it, just as he liked best.
Of the neck and a breast I had next to dispose —
'T was a neck and a breast that might rival Monroe's —
But in parting with these I was puzzled again,
With the how, and the who, and the where, and the when;
There 's Howard and Coley, and Hogarth and Hiff —
I think they love venison — I know they love beef;
There 's my countryman, Higgins — O, let him alone
For making a blunder, or picking a bone.
But hang it — to poets who seldom can eat,
Your very good mutton 's a very good treat;
Such dainties to them, their health it might hurt —
It 's like sending them ruffles when wanting a shirt.
While thus I debated, in revery centred,
An acquaintance, a friend as he called himself, entered;
An under-bred, fine-spoken fellow was he,
And he smiled as he looked at the venison and me.
"What have we got here? — why, this is good eating!
Your own, I suppose — or is it in waiting?"
"Why, whose should it be?" cried I, with a flounce;
"I get these things often," — but that was a bounce;
"Some lords, my acquaintance, that settle the nation,
Are pleased to be kind — but I hate ostentation."

"If that be the case then," cried he, very gay,
"I 'm glad I have taken this house in my way.
To-morrow you take a poor dinner with me;
No words — I insist on 't — precisely at three.
We 'll have Johnson, and Burke; all the wits will be there;
My acquaintance is slight, or I 'd ask my Lord Clare.
And, now that I think on 't, as I am a sinner!
We wanted this venison to make out the dinner.
What say you — a pasty? — it shall, and it must;
And my wife, little Kitty, is famous for crust.
Here, porter! — this venison with me to Mile-end;
No stirring, I beg — my dear friend — my dear friend!"
Thus snatching his hat, he brushed off like the wind,
And the porter and eatables followed behind.
Left alone to reflect, having emptied my shelf,
And "nobody with me at sea but myself,"
Though I could not help thinking my gentleman hasty,
Yet Johnson, and Burke, and a good venison pasty,
Were things that I never disliked in my life —
Though clogged with a coxcomb, and Kitty his wife;
So next day, in due splendor to make my approach,
I drove to his door in my own hackney-coach.
When come to the place where we all were to dine —
(A chair-lumbered closet just twelve feet by nine,)
My friend bade me welcome, but struck me quite dumb
With tidings that Johnson and Burke would not come;
"For I knew it," he cried, "both eternally fail,
The one with his speeches, and t' other with Thrale.
But no matter; I 'll warrant we 'll make up the party
With two full as clever, and ten times as hearty.
The one is a Scotchman, the other a Jew,
They both of them merry, and authors like you.

The one writes the *Snarler*, the other the *Scourge;*
Some think he writes *Cinna*,— he owns to *Panurge*."
While thus he described them by trade and by name,
They entered, and dinner was sèrved as they came.
At the top a fried liver and bacon were seen;
At the bottom was tripe in a swinging tureen;
At the sides there were spinach and pudding made hot;
In the middle a place where the pasty — was not.
Now, my lord, as for tripe, it's my utter aversion,
And your bacon I hate like a Turk or a Persian;
So there I sat stuck like a horse in a pound,
While the bacon and liver went merrily round.
But what vexed me most was that d—d Scottish rogue,
With his long-winded speeches, his smiles and his brogue;
And, "Madam," quoth he, "may this bit be my poison,
A prettier dinner I never set eyes on!
Pray, a slice of your liver, though may I be cursed,
But I've ate of your tripe till I'm ready to burst."
"The tripe," quoth the Jew, with his chocolate cheek,
"I could dine on this tripe seven days in a week;
I like these here dinners so pretty and small,—
But your friend there, the Doctor, eats nothing at all."
"O, ho!" quoth my friend, "he'll come on in a trice;
He's keeping a corner for something that's nice.
There's a pasty!" "A pasty!" repeated the Jew;
"I don't care if I keep a corner for 't too."
"What the de'il, mon, a pasty!" reëchoed the Scot;
"Though splitting, I'll still keep a corner for that."
"We'll all keep a corner," the lady cried out;
"We'll all keep a corner," was echoed about.
While thus we resolved, and the pasty delayed,
With looks that quite petrified, entered the maid;

A visage so sad, and so pale with affright,
Waked Priam, in drawing his curtains by night.
But we quickly found out — for who could mistake her?—
That she came with some terrible news from the baker;
And so it fell out, for that negligent sloven
Had shut out the pasty on shutting his oven.
Sad Philomel thus,— but let similes drop,—
And, now that I think on 't, the story may stop.
To be plain, my good Lord, it 's but labor misplaced,
To send such good verses to one of your taste.
You 've got an odd something,— a kind of discerning,—
A relish,— a taste,— sickened over by learning,—
At least it 's your temper, as very well known,
That you think very slightly of all that 's your own;
So, perhaps, in your habits of thinking amiss,
You may make a mistake, and think slightly of this.

THRENODIA AUGUSTALIS.

SACRED TO THE MEMORY OF HER LATE ROYAL HIGHNESS THE PRINCESS DOWAGER OF WALES, 1772.

Overture. — A solemn dirge.

Air. — Trio.

ARISE, ye sons of worth, arise,
And waken every note of woe;
When truth and virtue reach the skies,
'T is ours to weep the want below!

Chorus.

When truth and virtue reach the skies,
'T is ours to weep the want below!

MAN *speaker.*

The praise attending pomp and power,
The incense given to kings,
Are but the trappings of an hour —
Mere transitory things!
The base bestow them; but the good agree
To spurn the venal gifts as flattery.
But when to pomp and power are joined
An equal dignity of mind —
When titles are the smallest claim —
When wealth, and rank, and noble blood,
But aid the power of doing good —
Then all their trophies last; and flattery turns to fame.
Blessed spirit thou, whose fame, just born to bloom,
Shall spread and flourish from the tomb,
How hast thou left mankind for heaven!
Even now reproach and faction mourn,
And, wondering how their rage was borne,
Request to be forgiven.
Alas! they never had thy hate;
Unmoved, in conscious rectitude,
Thy towering mind self-centred stood,
Nor wanted man's opinion to be great.
In vain, to charm thy ravished sight,
A thousand gifts would fortune send;
In vain, to drive thee from the right,
A thousand sorrows urged thy end:
Like some well-fashioned arch thy patience stood,
And purchased strength from its increasing load.
Pain met thee like a friend that set thee free;
Affliction still is virtue's opportunity!

Song. — *By a* MAN.

Virtue, on herself relying,
  Every passion hushed to rest,
Loses every pain of dying,
  In the hopes of being blest.

Every added pang she suffers
  Some increasing good bestows,
Every shock that malice offers
  Only rocks her to repose.

WOMAN *speaker.*

Yet, ah! what terrors frowned upon her fate —
  Death, with its formidable band,
Fever, and pain, and pale consumptive care,
  Determined took their stand.

Nor did the cruel ravagers design
  To finish all their efforts at a blow;
  But, mischievously slow,
They robbed the relic and defaced the shrine.

      With unavailing grief,
      Despairing of relief,
    Her weeping children round
      Beheld each hour
      Death's growing power,
    And trembled as he frowned.

As helpless friends who view from shore
The laboring ship, and hear the tempest roar,
  While winds and waves their wishes cross —
They stood, while hope and comfort fail,

Not to assist, but to bewail
The inevitable loss.
Relentless tyrant, at thy call
How do the good, the virtuous, fall!
Truth, beauty, worth, and all that most engage,
But wake thy vengeance, and provoke thy rage!

Song. — *By a* MAN.

When vice my dart and scythe supply,
How great a king of terrors I!
If folly, fraud, your hearts engage,
Tremble, ye mortals, at my rage!

Fall, round me fall, ye little things;
Ye statesmen, warriors, poets, kings!
If virtue fail her counsel sage,
Tremble, ye mortals, at my rage!

MAN *speaker.*

Yet let that wisdom, urged by her example,
Teach us to estimate what all must suffer;
Let us prize death as the best gift of nature;
As a safe inn, where weary travellers,
When they have journeyed through a world of cares,
May put off life and be at rest forever.
Groans, weeping friends, indeed, and gloomy sables,
May oft distract us with their sad solemnity:
The preparation is the executioner.
Death, when unmasked, shows me a friendly face,
And is a terror only at a distance;
For as the line of life conducts me on
To death's great court, the prospect seems more fair.
'T is nature's kind retreat, that 's always open

To take us in when we have drained the cup
Of life, or worn our days to wretchedness.
    In that secure, serene retreat,
    Where all the humble, all the great,
        Promiscuously recline;
    Where, wildly huddled to the eye,
    The beggar's pouch and prince's purple lie,
        May every bliss be thine!
And, ah! blessed spirit, wheresoe'er thy flight,
Through rolling worlds, or fields of liquid light,
May cherubs welcome their expected guest;
May saints with songs receive thee to their rest:
May peace, that claimed while here thy warmest love,
May blissful, endless peace, be thine above!

Song. — *By a* WOMAN.

Lovely, lasting peace below,
Comforter of every woe,
Heavenly born, and bred on high,
To crown the favorites of the sky —
Lovely, lasting peace appear;
This world itself, if thou art here,
Is once again with Eden blessed,
And man contains it in his breast.

WOMAN *speaker.*

Our vows are heard! long, long to mortal eyes,
Her soul was fitting to its kindred skies:
Celestial-like her bounty fell,
Where modest want and patient sorrow dwell;
Want passed for merit at her door,
  Unseen the modest were supplied,

Her constant pity fed the poor —
  Then only poor, indeed, the day she died.
And, O! for this, while sculpture decks thy shrine,
  And art exhausts profusion round,
The tribute of a tear be mine,
  A simple song, a sigh profound.
There faith shall come, a pilgrim gray,
To bless the tomb that wraps thy clay;
And calm religion shall repair,
To dwell a weeping hermit there.
Truth, Fortitude, and Friendship shall agree,
To blend their virtues while they think of thee.

Air. — Chorus.

Let us, let all the world agree,
To profit by resembling thee.

Part II.

Overture. — Pastorale.

MAN *speaker.*

Fast by that shore where Thames' translucent stream
  Reflects new glories on his breast,
Where, splendid as the youthful poet's dream,
  He forms a scene beyond Elysium blest —
Where sculptured elegance and native grace
Unite to stamp the beauties of the place,
  While sweetly blending still are seen
  The wavy lawn, the sloping green;
While novelty, with cautious cunning,
Through every maze of fancy running,
  From China borrows aid to deck the scene: —

There, sorrowing by the river's glassy bed,
  Forlorn, a rural band complained,
All whom Augusta's bounty fed,
  All whom her clemency sustained;
The good old sire, unconscious of decay,
The modest matron, clad in home-spun gray,
The military boy, the orphaned maid,
The shattered veteran, now first dismayed:
These sadly join beside the murmuring deep;
And, as they view
The towers of Kew,
Call on their mistress — now no more — and weep.

Chorus.

Ye shady walks, ye waving greens.
Ye nodding towers, ye fairy scenes
Let all your echoes now deplore
That she who formed your beauties is no more!

MAN *speaker.*

First of the train the patient rustic came,
  Whose callous hand had formed the scene,
Bending at once with sorrow and with age,
  With many a tear and many a sign between;
"And where," he cried, "shall now my babes have bread
  Or how shall age support its feeble fire?
No lord will take me now, my vigor fled,
  Nor can my strength perform what they require;
Each grudging master keeps the laborer bare —
A sleek and idle race is all their care.
My noble mistress thought not so:
  Her bounty, like the morning dew,

Unseen, though constant, used to flow;
 And as my strength decayed, her bounty grew."

WOMAN *speaker.*

In decent dress, and coarsely clean,
The pious matron next was seen —
Clasped in her hand a godly book was borne,
By use and daily meditation worn;
That decent dress, this holy guide,
Augusta's care had well supplied.
"And, ah!" she cries, all woe-begone,
"What now remains for me?
O! where shall weeping want repair,
 To ask for charity?
Too late in life for me to ask,
 And shame prevents the deed,
And tardy, tardy are the times
 To succor, should I need.
But all my wants, before I spoke,
 Were to my Mistress known;
She still relieved, nor sought my praise,
 Contented with her own.
But every day her name I'll bless,
 My morning prayer, my evening song;
I'll praise her while my life shall last,
 A life that cannot last me long."

Song. — *By a* WOMAN

Each day, each hour, her name I'll bless —
 My morning and my evening song;
And when in death my vows shall cease,
 My children shall the note prolong.

MAN *speaker.*

The hardy veteran after struck the sight,
Scarred, mangled, maimed in every part;
Lopped of his limbs in many a gallant fight,
In naught entire — except his heart.
Mute for a while, and sullenly distressed,
At last the impetuous sorrow fired his breast.
"Wild is the whirlwind rolling
O'er Afric's sandy plain,
And wild the tempest howling
Along the billowed main;
But every danger felt before —
The raging deep, the whirlwind's roar —
Less dreadful struck me with dismay,
Than what I feel this fatal day.
O! let me fly a land that spurns the brave —
Oswego's dreary shores shall be my grave;
I 'll seek that less inhospitable coast,
And lay my body where my limbs were lost."

Song. — *By a* MAN.

Old Edward's sons, unknown to yield,
Shall crowd from Crécy's laurelled field,
To do thy memory right;
For thine and Britain's wrongs they feel,
Again they snatch the gleamy steel,
And wish the avenging fight.

WOMAN *speaker.*

In innocence and youth complaining,
Next appeared a lovely maid —
Affliction, o'er each feature reigning,
Kindly came in beauty's aid;

Every grace that grief dispenses,
Every glance that warms the soul,
In sweet succession charmed the senses,
While pity harmonized the whole.
"The garland of beauty" — 't is thus she would say —
"No more shall my crook or my temples adorn,
I 'll not wear a garland — Augusta 's away,
I 'll not wear a garland until she return;
But, alas! that return I never shall see,
The echoes of Thames shall my sorrows proclaim,
There promised a lover to come — but, O me!
'T was death — 't was the death of my mistress that came.
But ever, forever, her image shall last,
I 'll strip all the spring of its earliest bloom;
On her grave shall the cowslip and primrose be cast,
And the new-blossomed thorn shall whiten her tomb."

Song. — By a WOMAN.

With garlands of beauty the queen of the May
No more will her crook or her temples adorn;
For who 'd wear a garland when she is away,
When she is removed, and shall never return?

On the grave of Augusta these garlands be placed,
We 'll rifle the spring of its earliest bloom;
And there shall the cowslip and primrose be cast,
And the new-blossomed thorn shall whiten her tomb.

Chorus.

On the grave of Augusta this garland be placed,
We 'll rifle the spring of its earliest bloom;
And there shall the cowslip and primrose be cast,
And the tears of her country shall water her tomb.

LETTER

IN PROSE AND VERSE TO MRS. BUNBURY.

MADAM: I read your letter with all that allowance which critical candor could require; but, after all, find so much to object to, and so much to raise my indignation, that I cannot help giving it a serious answer. I am not so ignorant, Madam, as not to see there are many sarcasms contained in it, and solecisms also, (solecism is a word that comes from the town of Soleis, in Attica, among the Greeks, built by Solon, and applied as we use the word Kidderminster for curtains from a town also of that name; but this is learning you have no taste for.) — I say, Madam, there are sarcasms in it, and solecisms also. But, not to seem an ill-natured critic, I'll take leave to quote your own words, and give you my remarks upon them as they occur. You begin as follows:

"I hope, my good Doctor, you soon will be here,
And your spring velvet coat very smart will appear,
To open our ball the first day in the year."

Pray, Madam, where did you ever find the epithet "good" applied to the title of doctor? Had you called me learned doctor, or grave doctor, or noble doctor, it might be allowable, because they belong to the profession. But, not to cavil at trifles, you talk of my spring velvet coat, and advise me to wear it the first day in the year, — that is, in the middle of winter; — a spring velvet in the middle of winter!!! That would be a solecism, indeed; and yet, to increase the inconsistence, in another part of your letter you call me a beau. Now, on one side or other, you must be wrong. If I am a beau, I can never think of wearing a spring velvet in winter; and if I am not a beau — why — then — that explains itself. But let me go on to your two next strange lines:

"And bring with you a wig that is modish and gay,
To dance with the girls that are making of hay."

The absurdity of making hay at Christmas you yourself seem sensible of; you say your sister will laugh, and so indeed she well may. The Latins have an expression for a contemptuous sort of laughter, *Naso contemnere adunco;* that is, to laugh with a crooked nose; she may laugh at you in the manner of the ancients, if she thinks fit. But now I am come to the most extraordinary of all extraordinary propositions, which is to take you and your sister's advice in playing at loo. The presumption of the offer raises my indignation beyond the bounds of prose; it inspires me at once with verse and resentment. I take advice! and from whom? You shall hear.

First let me suppose, what may shortly be true,
The company set, and the word to be — loo;
All smirking and pleasant, and big with adventure,
And ogling the stake which is fixed in the centre.
Round and round go the cards, while I inwardly damn
At never once finding a visit from Pam.
I lay down my stake, apparently cool,
While the harpies about me all pocket the pool;
I fret in my gizzard — yet, cautious and sly,
I wish all my friends may be bolder than I:
Yet still they sit snug; not a creature will aim,
By losing their money, to venture at fame.

'T is in vain that at niggardly caution I scold,
'T is in vain that I flatter the brave and the bold,
All play their own way, and they think me an ass;
"What does Mrs. Bunbury?" "I, sir? — I pass."
"Pray what does Miss Horneck? Take courage, come, do."
"Who — I? Let me see, sir; why, I must pass too."
Mrs. Bunbury frets, and *I* fret like the devil,
To see them so cowardly, lucky, and civil;
Yet still I sit snug, and continue to sigh on,
Till, made by my losses as bold as a lion,
I venture at all; while my avarice regards
The whole pool as my own. "Come, give me five cards."
"Well done!" cry the ladies; "ah! doctor, that's good —
The pool's very rich. Ah, the doctor is looed."
Thus foiled in my courage, on all sides perplexed,
I ask for advice from the lady that's next.
"Pray, ma'am, be so good as to give your advice;
"Don't you think the best way is to venture for't twice?"
"I advise," cries the lady, "to try it, I own —
Ah, the doctor is looed: come, doctor, put down."
Thus playing and playing, I still grow more eager,
And so bold, and so bold, I'm at last a bold beggar.
Now, ladies, I ask — if law matters you're skilled in,—
Whether crimes such as yours should not come before Fielding;
For, giving advice that is not worth a straw
May well be called picking of pockets in law;
And picking of pockets, with which I now charge ye,
Is, by *quinto Elizabeth*, death without clergy.
What justice! when both to the Old Bailey brought;
By the gods! I'll enjoy it, though 't is but in thought.

Both are placed at the bar with all proper decorum,
With bunches of fennel and nosegays before them ;
Both cover their faces with mobs and all that,
But the judge bids them, angrily, take off their hat.
When uncovered, a buzz of inquiry runs round ;
"Pray, what are their crimes ?" "They 've been pilfering found."
"But pray whom have they pilfered ?" "A doctor, I hear."
"What, yon solemn-faced, odd-looking man that stands near ?"
"The same." "What a pity ! How does it surprise one !
Two handsomer culprits I never set eyes on !"
Then their friends all come round me, with cringing and leering,
To melt me to pity, and soften my swearing.
First Sir Charlés advances, with phrases well strung:
"Consider, dear doctor, the girls are but young."
"The younger the worse," I return him again ;
"It shows that their habits are all died in grain."
"But then they 're so handsome ; one's bosom it grieves."
"What signifies handsome, when people are thieves ?"
"But where is your justice ? their cases are hard."
"What signifies justice ? I want the reward."

"There 's the parish of Edmonton offers forty pounds — there 's the parish of St. Leonard Shoreditch, offers forty pounds — there 's the parish of Tyburn, from the Hog-in-the-pound to St. Giles's watch-house, offers forty pounds: I shall have all that, if I convict them.

"But consider their case : it may yet be your own ;
And see how they kneel : is your heart made of stone ?"
This moves : so, at last, I agree to relent,
For ten pounds in hand, and ten pounds to be spent.

I challenge you all to answer this: I tell you, you cannot It cuts deep. But now for the rest of the letter; and next -- but I want room — so I believe I shall battle the rest out at Barton some day next week.

I don't value you all!

O. G.

SONG,

INTENDED TO HAVE BEEN SUNG, IN THE COMEDY OF "SHE STOOPS TO CONQUER," BY MISS HARDCASTLE.

Air. — "*The Humors of Ballamagairy.*"

AH me! when shall I marry me?
Lovers are plenty, but fail to relieve me;
He, fond youth, that could carry me,
Offers to love, but means to deceive me.

But I will rally and combat the ruiner;
Not a look, not a smile, shall my passion discover:
She that gives all to the false one pursuing her
Makes but a penitent, and loses a lover.

SONG,

IN THE COMEDY OF "SHE STOOPS TO CONQUER."

SCENE — *A room in the alehouse, the* "*Three Jolly Pigeons.*"

LET schoolmasters puzzle their brains
With grammar, and nonsense, and learning —
Good liquor, I stoutly maintain,
Gives *genus* a better discerning.

Let them brag of their heathenish gods;
  Their Lethes, their Styxes, and Stygians;
Their *quis*, and their *quæs*, and their *quods:*
  They 're all but a parcel of pigeons.

When Methodist preachers come down,
  A preaching that drinking is sinful,
I 'll wager the rascals a crown,
  They always preach best with a skinful;
But when you come down with your pence,
  For a slice of their scurvy religion,
I 'll leave it to all men of sense —
  But you, my good friend, are the pigeon.

Then come, put the jorum about,
  And let us be merry and clever;
Our hearts and our liquors are stout —
  Here 's the *Three Jolly Pigeons* forever.
Let some cry up woodcock and hare;
  Your bustards, your ducks, and your widgeons;
But of all the birds in the air —
  Here 's a health to the *Three Jolly Pigeons.*

FRAGMENTARY TRANSLATIONS.

I.

THE shouting army cried with joy extreme:
He sure must conquer who himself can tame!

II.

THEY knew and owned the monarch of the main.
The sea, subsiding, spreads a level plain;

The curling waves before his coursers fly,
The parting surface leaves his brazen axle dry.

III.

SAY, heavenly muse, their youthful frays rehearse,
Begin, ye daughters of immortal verse.
Exulting rocks have owned the power of Song,
And rivers listened as they flowed along.

IV.

THUS, when soft love subdues the heart
 With smiling hopes and chilling fears,
The soul rejects the aid of art,
 And speaks in moments more than years.

V.

OF all the fish that graze beneath the flood,
He, *only*, ruminates his former food.

VI.

CHASTE are their instincts, faithful is their fire,
No foreign beauty tempts to false desire;
The snow-white vesture and the glittering crown,
The simple plumage, or the glossy down,
Prompt not their love; the patriot bird pursues
His well-acquainted tints and kindred hues.
Hence through their tribes no mixed polluted flame,
No monster-breed to mark the groves with shame;
But the chaste black-bird, to its partner true,
Thinks black alone is beauty's favorite hue;
The nightingale, with mutual passion blest,
Sings to its mate, and nightly charms the nest;
While the dark owl to court his partner flies,
And owns his offspring in their yellow eyes.

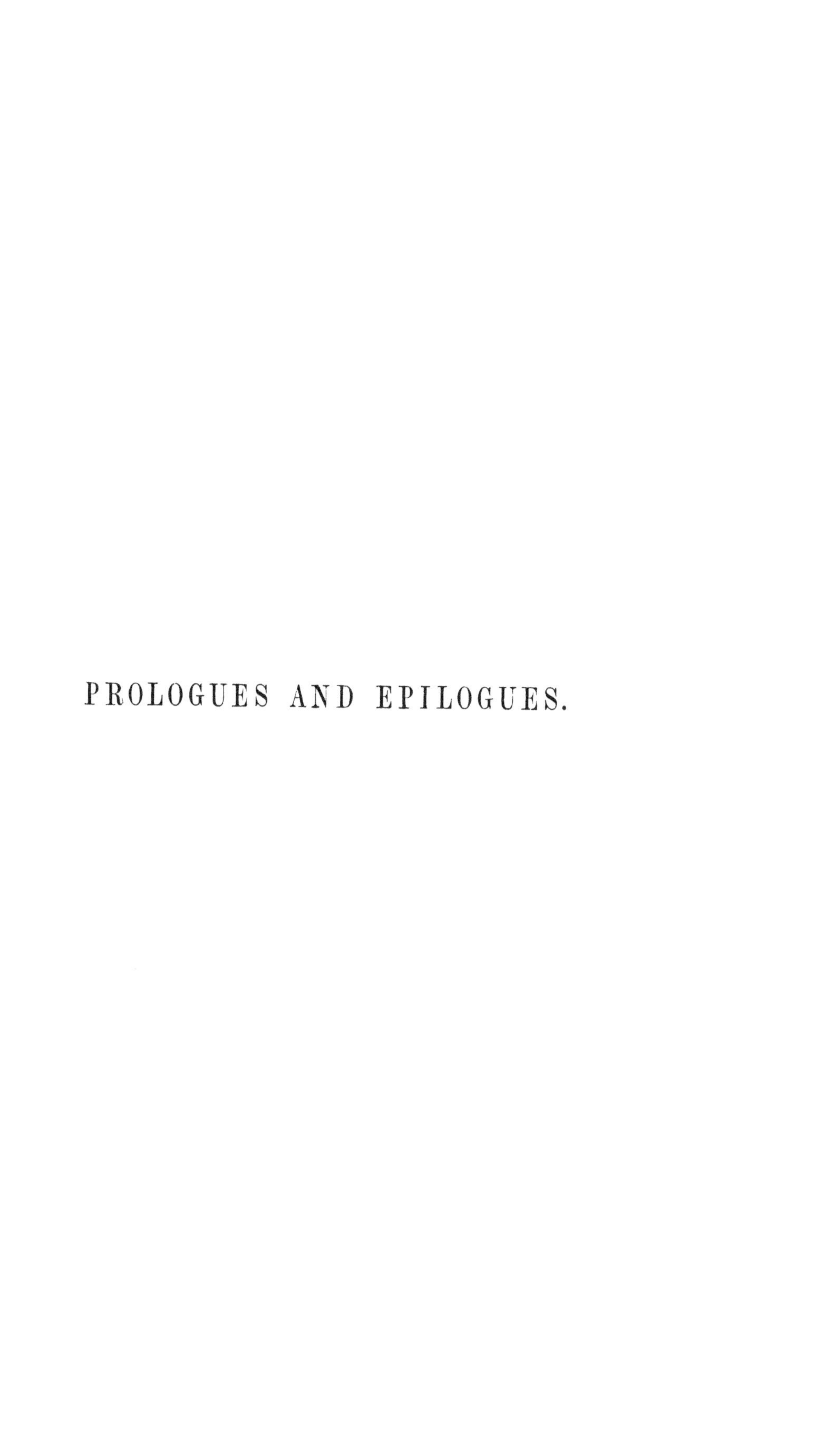

PROLOGUES AND EPILOGUES.

PROLOGUES AND EPILOGUES.

THE PROLOGUE

OF LABERIUS, A ROMAN KNIGHT AND FARCE-WRITER.

From the Latin, preserved by Macrobius.

WHAT ! no way left to shun the inglorious stage,
And save from infamy my sinking age ?
Scarce half alive, oppressed with many a year,
What in the name of dotage drives me here ?
A time there was, when glory was my guide —
Nor force nor fraud could turn my steps aside ;
Unawed by power, and unappalled by fear,
With honest thrift I held my honor dear :
But this vile hour disperses all my store,
And all my hoard of honor is no more —
For, ah ! too partial to my life's decline,
Cæsar persuades, submission must be mine !
Him I obey, whom heaven itself obeys ;
Hopeless of pleasing, yet inclined to please.
Here, then, at once I welcome every shame,
And cancel at three-score a life of fame ;
No more my titles shall my children tell ;
The old buffoon will fit my name as well ;
This day beyond its term my fate extends,
For life is ended when our honor ends.

*　　*　　*　　*　　*　　*

EPILOGUE

TO THE GOOD-NATURED MAN.

As puffing quacks some caitiff wretch procure
To swear the pill, or drop, has wrought a cure —
Thus, on the stage, our play-wrights still depend,
For epilogues and prologues, on some friend
Who knows each art of coaxing up the town;
And make full many a bitter pill go down.
Conscious of this, our bard has gone about
And teased each rhyming friend to help him out.
"An epilogue — things can't go on without it;
It could not fail, would you but set about it."
"Young man," cries one — a bard laid up in clover —
"Alas! young man, my writing days are over;
Let boys play tricks and kick the straw; not I:
Your brother doctor there perhaps may try."
"What, I! dear sir," the doctor interposes;
"What, plant my thistles, sir, among his roses!
No, no; I've other contests to maintain;
To-night I head our troops at Warwick-lane:
Go, ask your manager." "Who, me? — your pardon;
These things are not our forte at Covent Garden."
Our author's friends, thus placed at happy distance,
Give him good words, indeed, but no assistance:
As some unhappy wight, at some new play,
At the pit-door stands elbowing away,
While oft, with many a smile, and many a shrug,
He eyes the centre, where his friends sit snug —
His simpering friends, with pleasure in their eyes,
Sink as he sinks, and as he rises rise:
He nods, they nod; he cringes, they grimace;
But not a soul will budge to give him place.

Since, then, unhelped, our bard must now conform
To bide the "pelting of this pitiless storm" —
Blame where you must, be candid where you can.
And be each critic the *good-natured man.*

EPILOGUE

TO THE SISTER, A COMEDY, BY MRS. CHARLOTTE LENNOX.

WHAT ! five long acts — and all to make us wiser !
Our authoress sure has wanted an adviser.
Had she consulted me, she should have made
Her moral play a speaking masquerade ;
Warmed up each bustling scene, and in her rage
Have emptied all the green-room on the stage :
My life on 't, this had kept her play from sinking ;
Have pleased our eyes, and saved the pain of thinking.
Well, since she thus has shown her want of skill,
What if I give a masquerade ? — I will,
But how ? ay, there 's the rub ! [*pausing*] — I 've got my cue :
The world 's a masquerade ! the maskers, you, you, you.
[*To Boxes, Pit, and Gallery.*
Lud ! what a group the motley scene discloses —
False wits, false wives, false virgins, and false spouses !
Statesmen with bridles on ; and, close beside them,
Patriots in party-colored suits that ride them.
There Hebes, turned of fifty, try once more
To raise a flame in Cupids of three-score.
These in their turn, with appetites as keen,
Deserting fifty, fasten on fifteen.
Miss, not yet full fifteen, with fire uncommon,
Flings down her sampler, and takes up the woman ;

The little urchin smiles, and spreads her lure,
And tries to kill, ere she 's got power to cure.
Thus 'tis with all — their chief and constant care
Is to seem everything but what they are.
Yon broad, bold, angry spark, I fix my eye on,
Who seems to have robbed his visor from the lion;
Who frowns, and talks, and swears, with round parade,
Looking, as who should say, damme! who's afraid?
[*Mimicking.*
Strip but this visor off, and sure I am
You'll find his lionship a very lamb.
Yon politician, famous in debate,
Perhaps, to vulgar eyes, bestrides the state;
Yet, when he deigns his real shape to assume,
He turns old woman, and bestrides a broom.
Yon patriot, too, who presses on your sight,
And seems to every gazer all in white,
If with a bribe his candor you attack,
He bows, turns round, and whip — the man 's a black!
Yon critic, too — but whither do I run?
If I proceed, our bard will be undone!
Well, then, a truce, since she requests it too:
Do you spare her, and I 'll for once spare you.

PROLOGUE TO ZOBEIDE.

A TRAGEDY, BY JOSEPH CRADOCK.

IN these bold times, when learning's sons explore
The distant climate, and the savage shore —
When wise astronomers to India steer,
And quit for *Venus* many a brighter here —

While botanists, all cold to smiles and dimpling,
Forsake the fair, and patiently go simpling —
When every bosom swells with wondrous scenes,
Priests, cannibals, and *hoity-toity* queens—.
Our bard into the general spirit enters,
And fits his little frigate for adventures.
With Scythian stores, and trinkets, deeply laden,
He this way steers his course, in hopes of trading —
Yet ere he lands he has ordered me before,
To make an observation on the shore.
Where are we driven? our reckoning sure is lost!
This seems a barren and a dangerous coast.
Lord! what a sultry climate am I under!
Yon ill-foreboding cloud seems big with thunder,
[*Upper gallery*
There mangroves spread, and larger than I've seen them—
[*Pit.*
Here trees of stately size—and turtles in them—
[*Balconies.*
Here ill-conditioned oranges abound— [*Stage.*
And apples, [*takes up one and tastes it*] *bitter* apples strew the ground.
The place is uninhabited, I fear;
I heard a hissing—there are serpents here!
O! there the natives are — a dreadful race!
The men have tails, the women paint the face.
No doubt they're all barbarians — yes, 'tis so;
I'll try to make palaver with them, though;
[*Making signs.*
'T is best, however, keeping at a distance.
Good savages, our Captain craves assistance:
Our ship 's well stored—in yonder creek we've laid her;
His honor is no mercenary trader:

This is his first adventure ; lend him aid,
Or you may chance to spoil a thriving trade.
His goods, he hopes, are prime and brought from far —
Equally fit for gallantry and war.
What ! no reply to promises so ample ?
I'd best step back — and order up a sample.

INTENDED EPILOGUE

TO SHE STOOPS TO CONQUER.

Enter Mrs. Bulkley, *who curtseys very low as beginning to speak. Then enter Miss* Catley, *who stands full before her, and curtseys to the audience.*

MRS. BULKLEY.

Hold, Ma'am, your pardon. What 's your business here ?

MISS CATLEY.

The Epilogue.

MRS. BULKLEY.

The Epilogue ?

MISS CATLEY.

Yes, the Epilogue, my dear.

MRS. BULKLEY.

Sure you mistake, Ma'am. The Epilogue ? *I* bring it.

MISS CATLEY.

Excuse me, Ma'am. The author bid *me* sing it.

Recitative.

Ye beaux and belles, that form this splendid ring,
Suspend your conversation while I sing.

MRS. BULKLEY.

Why, sure the girl 's beside herself ! an Epilogue of singing ?
A hopeful end indeed to such a blessed beginning.

Besides, a singer in a comic set!
Excuse me, Ma'am, I know the etiquette.

MISS CATLEY.

What if we leave it to the House?

MRS. BULKLEY.

The House! — Agreed.

MISS CATLEY.

Agreed.

MRS. BULKLEY.

And she, whose party 's largest, shall proceed.
And first, I hope, you 'll readily agree,
I 've all the critics and the wits for me.
They, I am sure, will answer my commands;
Ye candid-judging few, hold up your hands;
What! no return? I find too late, I fear,
That modern judges seldom enter here.

MISS CATLEY.

I 'm for a different set. — Old men, whose trade is
Still to gallant and dangle with the ladies.

Recitative.

Who mump their passion, and who, grimly smiling,
Still thus address the fair with voice beguiling:

Air — Cotillon.

Turn, my fairest, turn, if ever
Strephon caught thy ravished eye;
Pity take on your swain so clever,
Who without your aid must die.
Yes, I shall die, hu, hu, hu, hu,
Yes, I must die, ho, ho, ho, ho,
Da Capo.

MRS. BULKLEY.

Let all the old pay homage to your merit:
Give me the young, the gay, the men of spirit
Ye travelled tribe, ye macaroni train
Of French friseurs, and nosegays justly vain,
Who take a trip to Paris once a year
To dress and look like awkward Frenchmen here;
Lend me your hands. O, fatal news to tell,
Their hands are only lent to the Heinel.

MISS CATLEY.

Ay, take your travellers — travellers indeed!
Give me my bonny Scot, that travels from the Tweed.
Where are the chiels? Ah! ah, I well discern
The smiling looks of each bewitching bairn.

Air — A bonny young lad is my Jockey.

I 'll sing to amuse you by night and by day,
And be unco merry when you are but gay;
When you with your bagpipes are ready to play,
My voice shall be ready to carol away
With Sandy, and Sawney, and Jockey,
With Sawney, and Jarvie, and Jockey.

MRS. BULKLEY.

Ye gamesters, who, so eager in pursuit,
Make but of all your fortune one *va toute:*
Ye jockey tribe, whose stock of words are few,
"I hold the odds — done, done, with you, with you."
Ye barristers so fluent with grimace —
"My Lord, — your Lordship misconceives the case."
Doctors, who cough and answer every misfortuner —
"I wish I 'd been called in a little sooner,"
Assist my cause with hands and voices hearty,
Come, end the contest here, and aid my party.

MISS CATLEY.

Air — Ballinamony.

Ye brave Irish lads, hark away to the crack,
Assist me, I pray, in this woful attack;
For sure I don't wrong you, you seldom are slack,
When the ladies are calling, to blush and hang back.
For you 're always polite and attentive,
Still to amuse us inventive,
And death is your only preventive:
Your hands and your voices for me.

MRS. BULKLEY.

Well, Madam, what if, after all this sparring,
We both agree, like friends, to end our jarring?

MISS CATLEY.

And, that our friendship may remain unbroken,
What if we leave the Epilogue unspoken?

MRS. BULKLEY.

Agreed.

MISS CATLEY.

Agreed.

MRS. BULKLEY.

And, now with late repentance,
Un-epilogued the poet waits his sentence:
Condemn the stubborn fool who can't submit
To thrive by flattery — though he starves by wit.

[*Exeunt.*

ANOTHER INTENDED EPILOGUE

TO SHE STOOPS TO CONQUER.

To be spoken by Mrs. Bulkley.

THERE is a place — so Ariosto sings —
A treasury for lost and missing things;

Lost human wits have places there assigned them,
And they who lose their senses, there may find them
But where 's this place, this storehouse of the age ?
The moon, says he; but I affirm, the stage:
At least, in many things I think I see
His lunar and our mimic world agree.
Both shine at night, for, but at Foote's alone
We scarce exhibit till the sun goes down.
Both prone to change, no settled limits fix,
And sure the folks of both are lunatics.
But in this parallel my best pretence is,
That mortals visit both to find their senses:
To this strange spot rakes, macaronies, cits,
Come thronging to collect their scattered wits.
The gay coquette, who ogles all the day,
Comes here at night, and goes a prude away.
Hither the affected city dame advancing,
Who sighs for operas and dotes on dancing,
Taught by our art her ridicule to pause on,
Quits the *Ballet*, and calls for *Nancy Dawson.*
The gamester, too, whose wit 's all high or low,
Oft risks his fortune on one desperate throw,
Comes here to saunter, having made his bets,
Finds his lost senses out, and pays his debts.
The Mohawk, too, with angry phrases stored —
As "Damme, Sir!" and "Sir, I wear a sword!" —
Here lessoned for a while, and hence retreating,
Goes out, affronts his man, and takes a beating.
Here come the sons of scandal and of news,
But find no sense — for they had none to lose.
Of all the tribe here wanting an adviser,
Our Author 's the least likely to grow wiser;

Has he not seen how you your favor place
On sentimental queens and lords in lace?
Without a star, a coronet, or garter,
How can the piece expect or hope for quarter?
No high-life scenes, no sentiment: the creature
Still stoops among the low to copy nature.
Yes, he's far gone: and yet some pity fix,
The English laws forbid to punish lunatics

EPILOGUE

TO THE COMEDY OF SHE STOOPS TO CONQUER.

WELL, having stooped to conquer with success,
And gained a husband without aid from dress,
Still as a barmaid, I could wish it too,
As I have conquered him, to conquer you:
And let me say, for all your resolution,
That pretty barmaids have done execution.
Our life is all a play, composed to please;
"We have our exits and our entrances."
The first Act shows the simple country maid,
Harmless and young, of everything afraid;
Blushes when hired, and with unmeaning action,
"I hopes as how to give you satisfaction."
Her second Act displays a livelier scene —
The unblushing barmaid of a country inn,
Who whisks about the house, at market caters,
Talks loud, coquettes the guests, and scolds the waiters.
Next the scene shifts to town, and there she soars,
The chop-house toast of ogling connoisseurs.

On 'squires and cits she there displays her arts,
And on the gridiron broils her lovers' hearts —
And as she smiles, her triumphs to complete,
Even common-councilmen forget to eat.
The fourth Act shows her wedded to the squire.
And madam now begins to hold it higher;
Pretends to taste, at operas cries *caro*,
And quits her *Nancy Dawson* for *Che Faro*:
Dotes upon dancing, and, in all her pride,
Swims round the room the Heinel of Cheapside;
Ogles and leers with artificial skill,
Till, having lost in age the power to kill,
She sits all night at cards, and ogles at spadille.
Such, through our lives, the eventful history —
The fifth and last Act still remains for me.
The barmaid now for your protection prays;
Turns female barrister, and pleads for Bayes.

EPILOGUE,

SPOKEN BY MR. CHARLES LEE LEWES, IN THE CHARACTER OF HARLEQUIN, AT HIS BENEFIT.

Hold! prompter, hold! a word before your nonsense;
I 'd speak a word or two, to ease my conscience.
My pride forbids it ever should be said,
My heels eclipsed the honors of my head;
That I found humor in a piebald vest,
Or ever thought that jumping was a jest. [*Takes off his mask.*
Whence, and what art thou, visionary birth?
Nature disowns, and reason scorns thy mirth;

In thy black aspect every passion sleeps,
The joy that dimples, and the woe that weeps.
How hast thou filled the scene with all thy brood
Of fools pursuing, and of fools pursued!
Whose ins and outs no ray of sense discloses;
Whose only plot it is to break our noses;
Whilst from below the trap-door demons rise —
And from above, the dangling deities.
And shall I mix in this unhallowed crew?
May rosined lightning blast me if I do!
No, I will act — I 'll vindicate the stage:
Shakspeare himself shall feel my tragic rage.
Off! off! vile trappings! a new passion reigns!
The maddening monarch revels in my veins.
O! for a Richard's voice to catch the theme:
"Give me another horse! bind up my wounds! —soft —
'twas but a dream."
Ay, 't was but a dream — for now there 's no retreating,
If I cease Harlequin, I cease from eating.
'T was thus that Æsop's stag — a creature blameless,
Yet something vain, like one that shall be nameless,
Once on the margin of a fountain stood,
And cavilled at his image in the flood.
"The deuce confound," he cries, "these drumstick shanks!
They neither have my gratitude nor thanks;
They 're perfectly disgraceful! strike me dead!
But for a head — yes, yes, I have a head.
How piercing is that eye! how sleek that brow!
My horns! — I 'm told horns are the fashion now."
Whilst thus he spoke, astonished! to his view,
Near, and more near, the hounds and huntsmen drew.

"Hoicks! hark forward!" came thundering from behind,
He bounds aloft, outstrips the fleeting wind;
He quits the woods, and tries the beaten ways;
He starts, he pants, he takes the circling maze.
At length his silly head, so prized before,
Is taught his former folly to deplore;
Whilst his strong limbs conspire to set him free,
And at one bound he saves himself — like me.

[*Taking a jump through the stage-door*

VIDA'S GAME OF CHESS,

AS IT HAS BEEN FOUND TRANSCRIBED IN THE HANDWRITING

OF

OLIVER GOLDSMITH,

NOW FIRST PRINTED (1854) FROM THE ORIGINAL MS.

IN THE POSSESSION OF

BOLTON CORNEY, ESQ.

ADVERTISEMENT.

MARC JEROME VIDA, a very distinguished modern Latin poet, was born at Cremona, towards the close of the fifteenth century. His *Scacchiæ Ludus*, or *Game of Chess*, introduced him to the notice of LEO X., who was delighted with the novelty of its subject and the felicity with which it was treated. That great patron of letters immediately called Vida to his court, and loaded him with wealth and honors. Among other benefices he presented the poet with the priory of St. Silvestro, near Tivoli, that he might devote his time to study and composition. He died in 1566.

The *Game of Chess* has been translated into Italian, by Masden and Pindemonte, and into French by M. Levée, with the other works of Vida, in 1809. His poem *De Arte Poeticâ*, which Julius Scaliger preferred to that of Horace, has been twice translated into English.

The following translation of the *Scacchiæ Ludus* was not known to Mr. BOLTON CORNEY at the time of publishing his illustrated edition of Goldsmith's Poems, but has since come into his possession. It was communicated by him to Mr. PETER CUNNINGHAM, by whom it was first printed in the beautiful edition of *Goldsmith's Complete Works*, recently issued by Mr. Murray.

Of the manuscript of this translation, Mr. FORSTER, who has drawn largely from it in the last edition of his admirable work on the Life and Times of Goldsmith, gives the following account: "It is a small quarto manuscript of thirty-four pages, containing six hundred and seventy-nine lines, to which a fly-leaf is appended. in which Goldsmith notes the differences of nomenclature between Vida's chessmen and our own. It has occasional interlineations and corrections, but rather such as would occur in transcription than in a first or original copy. Sometimes, indeed, choice appears to have been made (as at page 29) between two words equally suitable to the sense and verse, as 'to' for 'toward;' but the insertions and erasures refer almost wholly to words or lines accidentally omitted and replaced. The triplet is always carefully marked; and though it is seldom found in any other of Goldsmith's poems, I am disposed to regard its frequent recurrence here as even helping in some degree to explain the motive which had led him to the trial of an experiment in rhyme comparatively new to him. If we suppose him, half consciously it may be, taking up the manner of the great master of translation, Dryden, who was at all times so much a favorite with him, he would at least be less apt to fall short in so marked a peculiarity, than to err perhaps a little on the side of excess. Though I am far from thinking such to be the result in the present instance. The effect of the whole translation is very pleasing to me, and the mock heroic effect I think not a little assisted by the reïterated use of the triplet and Alexandrine. As to any evidences of authorship derivable from the appearance of the manuscript, I will only add another word. The lines in the translation have been carefully counted, and the number is marked in Goldsmith's hand at the close of his transcription. Such a fact is, of course, only to be taken in aid of other proof; but a man is not generally at the pains of counting — still less, I should say, in such a case as Goldsmith's, of elaborately transcribing — lines which are not his own."

VIDA'S GAME OF CHESS.

TRANSLATED.

ARMIES of box that sportively engage,
And mimic real battles in their rage,
Pleased I recount; how, smit with glory's charms,
Two mighty Monarchs met in adverse arms,
Sable and white: assist me to explore,
Ye Serian Nymphs, what ne'er was sung before.
No path appears; yet resolute I stray
Where youth undaunted bids me force my way.
O'er rocks and cliffs while I the task pursue,
Guide me, ye Nymphs, with your unerring clue.
For you the rise of this diversion know,
You first were pleased in Italy to show
This studious sport; from Scacchis was its name,
The pleasing record of your Sister's fame.
 When Jove through Ethiopia's parched extent
To grace the nuptials of old Ocean went,
Each god was there; and mirth and joy around
To shores remote diffused their happy sound.
Then when their hunger and their thirst no more
Claimed their attention, and the feast was o'er;
Ocean, with pastime to divert the thought,
Commands a painted table to be brought.

Sixty-four spaces fill the checkered square;
Eight in each rank eight equal limits share.
Alike their form, but different are their dyes,
They fade alternate, and alternate rise,
White after black; such various stains as those
The shelving backs of tortoises disclose.
Then to the gods, that mute and wondering sate,
You see (says he) the field prepared for fate.
Here will the little armies please your sight,
With adverse colors hurrying to the fight:
On which so oft, with silent sweet surprise,
The Nymphs and Nereids used to feast their eyes,
And all the neighbors of the hoary deep,
When calm the sea, and winds were lulled to sleep.
But see, the mimic heroes tread the board;
He said, and straightway from an urn he poured
The sculptured box, that neatly seemed to ape
The graceful figure of a human shape: —
Equal the strength and number of each foe,
Sixteen appeared like jet, sixteen like snow.
As their shape varies various is the name,
Different their posts, nor is their strength the same.
There might you see two Kings with equal pride
Gird on their arms, their Consorts by their side;
Here the Foot-warriors glowing after fame,
There prancing Knights and dexterous Archers came,
And Elephants, that on their backs sustain
Vast towers of war, and fill and shake the plain.
  And now both hosts, preparing for the storm
Of adverse battle, their encampments form.
In the fourth space, and on the furthest line,
Directly opposite the Monarchs shine:

The swarthy on white ground, on sable stands
The silver King; and thence they send commands.
Nearest to thesė the Queens exert their might;
One the left side, and t' other guards the right:
Where each, by her respective armor known,
Chooses the color that is like her own.
Then the young Archers, two that snowy-white
Bend the tough yew, and two as black as night
(Greece called them Mars's favorites heretofore,
From their delight in war and thirst of gore).
These on each side the Monarch and his Queen
Surround obedient; next to these are seen
The crested Knights in golden armor gay;
Their steeds by turns curvet, or snort, or neigh.
In either army on each distant wing
Two mighty Elephants their castles bring,
Bulwarks immense! and then at last combine
Eight of the foot to form the second line,
The vanguard to the King and Queen; from far
Prepared to open all the fate of war.
So moved the boxen hosts, each double-lined,
Their different colors floating in the wind:
As if an army of the Gauls should go,
With their white standards, o'er the Alpine snow,
To meet in rigid fight on scorching sands
The sun-burnt Moors and Memnon's swarthy bands.
  Then Father Ocean thus; you see them here,
Celestial powers, what troops, what camps appear.
Learn now the several orders of the fray,
For even these arms their stated laws obey.
To lead the fight, the Kings from all their bands
Choose whom they please to bear their great commands

Should a black hero first to battle go,
Instant a white one guards against the blow;
But only one at once can charge or shun the foe.
Their general purpose on one scheme is bent,
So to besiege the King within the tent,
That there remains no place by subtle flight
From danger free; and that decides the fight
Meanwhile, howe'er, the sooner to destroy
The imperial Prince, remorseless they employ
Their swords in blood; and whosoever dare
Oppose their vengeance, in the ruin share.
Fate thins their camp; the parti-colored field
Widens apace, as they o'ercome or yield,
But the proud victor takes the captive's post;
There fronts the fury of the avenging host
One single shock: and (should he ward the blow)
May then retire at pleasure from the foe.
The Foot alone (so their harsh laws ordain)
When they proceed can ne'er return again.
 But neither all rush on alike to prove
The terror of their arms: the Foot must move
Directly on, and but a single square;
Yet may these heroes, when they first prepare
To mix in combat on the bloody mead,
Double their sally, and two steps proceed;
But when they wound, their swords they subtly guide
With aim oblique, and slanting pierce his side.
But the great Indian beasts, whose backs sustain
Vast turrets armed, when on the reddening plain
They join in all the terror of the fight,
Forward or backward, to the left or right,

Run furious, and impatient of confine
Scour through the field, and threat the furthest line.
Yet must they ne'er obliquely aim their blows;
That only manner is allowed to those
Whom Mars has favored most, who bend the stubborn bows.
These glancing sidewards in a straight career,
Yet each confined to their respective sphere,
Or white or black, can send the unerring dart
Winged with swift death to pierce through every part.
The fiery steed, regardless of the reins,
Comes prancing on; but sullenly disdains
The path direct, and boldly wheeling round,
Leaps o'er a double space at every bound:
And shifts from white or black to different colored ground.
But the fierce Queen, whom dangers ne'er dismay,
The strength and terror of the bloody day,
In a straight line spreads her destruction wide,
To left or right, before, behind, aside.
Yet may she never with a circling course
Sweep to the battle like the fretful Horse;
But unconfined may at her pleasure stray,
If neither friend nor foe block up the way;
For to o'erleap a warrior, 't is decreed
Those only dare who curb the snorting steed.
With greater caution and majestic state
The warlike monarchs in the scene of fate
Direct their motions, since for these appear
Zealous each hope, and anxious every fear.
While the King 's safe, with resolution stern
They clasp their arms; but should a sudden turn
Make him a captive, instantly they yield,
Resolved to share his fortune in the field.

He moves on slow; with reverence profound
His faithful troops encompass him around,
And oft, to break some instant fatal scheme,
Rush to their fates, their sovereign to redeem;
While he, unanxious where to wound the foe,
Need only shift and guard against a blow.
But none, however, can presume to appear
Within his reach, but must his vengeance fear;
For he on every side his terror throws;
But when he changes from his first repose,
Moves but one step, most awfully sedate,
Or idly roving, or intent on fate.
These are the several and established laws;
Now see how each maintains his bloody cause.
  Here paused the god, but (since whene'er they wage
War here on earth the gods themselves engage
In mutual battle as they hate or love,
And the most stubborn war is oft above)
Almighty Jove commands the circling train
Of gods from favoring either to abstain,
And let the fight be silently surveyed;
And added solemn threats if disobeyed.
Then called he Phœbus from among the Powers,
And subtle Hermes, whom in softer hours
Fair Maia bore: youth wantoned in their face;
Both in life's bloom, both shone with equal grace.
Hermes as yet had never winged his feet;
As yet Apollo in his radiant seat
Had never driven his chariot through the air,
Known by his bow alone and golden hair.
These Jove commissioned to attempt the fray,
And rule the sportive military day;

Bid them agree which party each maintains,
And promised a reward that 's worth their pains.
The greater took their seats; on either hand
Respectful the less gods in order stand,
But careful not to interrupt their play,
By hinting when to advance or run away.
Then they examine who shall first proceed
To try their courage, and their army lead.
Chance gave it for the White, that he should go
First with a brave defiance to the foe.
A while he pondered which of all his train
Should bear his first commission o'er the plain;
And then determined to begin the scene
With him that stood before to guard the Queen.
He took a double step: with instant care
Does the black Monarch in his turn prepare
The adverse champion, and with stern command
Bid him repel the charge with equal hand.
There front to front, the midst of all the field,
With furious threats their shining arms they wield;
Yet vain the conflict,— neither can prevail
While in one path each other they assail.
On every side to their assistance fly
Their fellow-soldiers, and with strong supply
Crowd to the battle, but no bloody stain
Tinctures their armor; sportive in the plain
Mars plays a while, and in excursion slight
Harmless they sally forth, or wait the fight.
But now the swarthy Foot, that first appeared
To front the foe, his ponderous javelin reared
Leftward aslant, and a pale warrior slays,
Spurns him aside, and boldly takes his place.

Unhappy youth, his danger not to spy!
Instant he fell, and triumphed but to die.
At this the sable King with prudent care
Removed his station from the middle square,
And slow retiring to the furthest ground,
There safely lurked, with troops intrenched around.
Then from each quarter to the war advance
The furious Knights, and poise the trembling lance:
By turns they rush, by turns the victors yield,
Heaps of dead Foot choke up the crimsoned field:
They fall unable to retreat; around
The clang of arms and iron hoofs resound.
But while young Phœbus pleased himself to view
His furious Knight destroy the vulgar crew,
Sly Hermes longed to attempt with secret aim
Some noble act of more exalted fame.
For this, he inoffensive passed along
Through ranks of Foot, and midst the trembling throng
Sent his left Horse, that free without confine
Roved o'er the plain, upon some great design
Against the King himself. At length he stood,
And having fixed his station as he would,
Threatened at once with instant fate the King
And the Indian beast that guarded the right wing.
Apollo sighed, and, hastening to relieve
The straitened Monarch, grieved that he must leave
His martial Elephant exposed to fate,
And viewed with pitying eyes his dangerous state.
First in his thoughts, however, was his care
To save his King, whom to the neighboring square
On the right hand he snatched with trembling flight;
At this, with fury springs the sable Knight,

Drew his keen sword, and, rising to the blow,
Sent the great Indian brute to shades below.
O fatal loss! for none except the Queen
Spreads such a terror through the bloody scene.
Yet shall you ne'er unpunished boast your prize,
The Delian god with stern resentment cries;
And wedged him round with foot, and poured in fresh supplies.
Thus close besieged, trembling he cast his eye
Around the plain, but saw no shelter nigh,
No way for flight; for here the Queen opposed,
The Foot in phalanx there the passage closed:
At length he fell; yet not unpleased with fate,
Since victim to a Queen's vindictive hate.
With grief and fury burns the whitened host,
One of their Towers thus immaturely lost.
As when a bull has in contention stern
Lost his right horn, with double vengeance burn
His thoughts for war, with blood he 's covered o'er,
And the woods echo to his dismal roar,
So looked the flaxen host, when angry fate
O'erturned the Indian bulwark of their state.
Fired at this great success, with double rage
Apollo hurries on his troops to engage,
For blood and havoc wild; and, while he leads
His troops thus careless, loses both his steeds:
For, if some adverse warriors were o'erthrown,
He little thought what dangers threat his own.
But slyer Hermes with observant eyes
Marched slowly cautious, and at distance spies
What moves must next succeed, what dangers next arise.

Often would he, the stately Queen to snare,
The slender Foot to front her arms prepare,
And to conceal his scheme he sighs and feigns
Such a wrong step would frustrate all his pains.
Just then an Archer, from the right-hand view,
At the pale Queen his arrow boldly drew,
Unseen by Phœbus, who, with studious thought,
From the left side a vulgar hero brought.
But tender Venus, with a pitying eye,
Viewing the sad destruction that was nigh,
Winked upon Phœbus (for the goddess sat
By chance directly opposite); at that
Roused in an instant, young Apollo threw
His eyes around the field his troops to view;
Perceived the danger, and with sudden fright
Withdrew the Foot that he had sent to fight,
And saved his trembling Queen by seasonable flight
But Maia's son with shouts filled all the coast:
The Queen, he cried, the important Queen is lost!
Phœbus, howe'er, resolving to maintain
What he had done, bespoke the heavenly train.
What mighty harm, in sportive mimic fight,
Is it to set a little blunder right,
When no preliminary rule debarred?
If you henceforward, Mercury, would guard
Against such practice, let us make the law:
And whosoe'er shall first to battle draw,
Or white, or black, remorseless let him go,
At all events, and dare the angry foe.
He said, and this opinion pleased around:
Jove turned aside, and on his daughter frowned,

Unmarked by Hermes, who, with strange surprise.
Fretted and foamed, and rolled his ferret eyes.
And but with great reluctance could refrain
From dashing at a blow all off the plain.
Then he resolved to interweave deceits,—
To carry on the war by tricks and cheats.
Instant he called an Archer from the throng,
And bid him like the courser wheel along:
Bounding he springs, and threats the pallid Queen.
The fraud, however, was by Phœbus seen;
He smiled, and, turning to the gods, he said:
Though, Hermes, you are perfect in your trade,
And you can trick and cheat to great surprise,
These little sleights no more shall blind my eyes;
Correct them if you please, the more you thus disguise.
The circle laughed aloud; and Maia's son
(As if it had but by mistake been done)
Recalled his Archer, and with motion due
Bid him advance, the combat to renew.
But Phœbus watched him with a jealous eye,
Fearing some trick was ever lurking nigh,
For he would oft, with sudden sly design,
Send forth at once two combatants to join
His warring troops, against the law of arms,
Unless the wary foe was ever in alarms.
Now the white Archer with his utmost force
Bent the tough bow against the sable Horse,
And drove him from the Queen, where he had stood
Hoping to glut his vengeance with her blood.
Then the right Elephant with martial pride
Roved here and there, and spread his terrors wide:

Glittering in arms from far a courser came,
Threatened at once the King and Royal Dame;
Thought himself safe when he the post had seized,
And with the future spoils his fancy pleased.
Fired at the danger, a young Archer came,
Rushed on the foe, and levelled sure his aim;
(And though a Pawn his sword in vengeance draws,
Gladly he'd lose his life in glory's cause).
The whistling arrow to his bowels flew,
And the sharp steel his blood profusely drew;
He drops the reins, he totters to the ground,
And his life issued murmuring through the wound.
Pierced by the Foot, this Archer bit the plain;
The Foot himself was by another slain;
And with inflamed revenge, the battle burns again.
Towers, Archers, Knights, meet on the crimson ground,
And the field echoes to the martial sound.
Their thoughts are heated, and their courage fired,
Thick they rush on with double zeal inspired;
Generals and Foot, with different colored mien,
Confusedly warring in the camps are seen,—
Valor and Fortune meet in one promiscuous scene.
Now these victorious lord it o'er the field;
Now the foe rallies, the triumphant yield:
Just as the tide of battle ebbs or flows.
As when the conflict more tempestuous grows
Between the winds, with strong and boisterous sweep
They plough the Ionian or Atlantic deep!
By turns prevails the mutual blustering roar,
And the big waves alternate lash the shore.
But in the midst of all the battle raged
The snowy Queen, with troops at once engaged;

She felled an Archer as she sought the plain,—
As she retired an Elephant was slain;
To right and left her fatal spears she sent,
Burst through the ranks, and triumphed as she went:
Through arms and blood she seeks a glorious fate.
Pierces the furthest lines, and nobly great
Leads on her army with a gallant show,
Breaks the battalions, and cuts through the foe.
At length the sable King his fears betrayed,
And begged his military consort's aid:
With cheerful speed she flew to his relief,
And met in equal arms the female chief.
  Who first, great Queen, and who at last did bleed?
How many Whites lay gasping on the mead?
Half dead, and floating in a bloody tide,
Foot, Knights, and Archer lie on every side.
Who can recount the slaughter of the day?
How many leaders threw their lives away?
The checkered plain is filled with dying box,
Havoc ensues, and with tumultous shocks
The different-colored ranks in blood engage,
And foot and horse promiscuously rage.
With nobler courage and superior might
The dreadful Amazons sustain the fight,
Resolved alike to mix in glorious strife,
Till to imperious fate they yield their life.
  Meanwhile each Monarch, in a neighboring cell,
Confined the warriors that in battle fell,
There watched the captives with a jealous eye,
Lest slipping out again to arms they fly.
But Thracian Mars, in stedfast friendship joined
To Hermes, as near Phœbus he reclined,

Observed each chance, how all their motions bend,
Resolved if possible to serve his friend.
He a Foot-soldier and a Knight purloined
Out from the prison that the dead confined;
And slyly pushed them forward on the plain;
The enlivened combatants their arms regain,
Mix in the bloody scene, and boldly war again.
  So the foul hag, in screaming wild alarms
O'er a dead carcass muttering her charms,
(And with her frequent and tremendous yell
Forcing great Hecaté from out of hell)
Shoots in the corpse a new fictitious soul;
With instant glare the supple eyeballs roll,
Again it moves and speaks, and life informs the whole
  Vulcan alone discerned the subtle cheat;
And, wisely scorning such a base deceit,
Called out to Phœbus. Grief and rage assail
Phœbus by turns; detected Mars turns pale.
Then awful Jove with sullen eye reproved
Mars, and the captives ordered to be moved
To their dark caves; bid each fictitious spear
Be straight recalled, and all be as they were.
  And now both Monarchs with redoubled rage
Led on their Queens, the mutual war to wage.
O'er all the field their thirsty spears they send,
Then front to front their Monarchs they defend.
But, lo! the female White rushed in unseen,
And slew with fatal haste the swarthy Queen;
Yet soon, alas! resigned her royal spoils,
Snatched by a shaft from her successful toils.
Struck at the sight, both hosts in wild surprise
Poured forth their tears, and filled the air with cries;

They wept and sighed, as passed the funeral train,
As if both armies had at once been slain.
And now each troop surrounds its mourning chief,
To guard his person or assuage his grief.
One is their common fear; one stormy blast
Has equally made havoc as it passed.
Not all, however, of their youth are slain;
Some champions yet the vigorous war maintain.
Three Foot, an Archer, and a stately Tower,
For Phœbus still exert their utmost power.
Just the same number Mercury can boast,
Except the Tower, who lately in his post
Unarmed inglorious fell, in peace profound,
Pierced by an Archer with a distant wound;
But his right Horse retained its mettled pride,—
The rest were swept away by war's strong tide.
But fretful Hermes, with despairing moan,
Grieved that so many champions were o'erthrown,
Yet reässumes the fight; and summons round
The little straggling army that he found,—
All that escaped from fierce Apollo's rage,—
Resolved with greater caution to engage
In future strife, by subtle wiles (if fate
Should give him leave) to save his sinking state.
The sable troops advance with prudence slow,
Bent on all hazards to distress the foe.
More cheerful Phœbus, with unequal pace,
Rallies his arms to lessen his disgrace.
But what strange havoc everywhere has been!
A straggling champion here and there is seen;
And many are the tents, yet few are left within.

The afflicted Kings bewail their consorts dead,
And loathe the thoughts of a deserted bed;
And though each monarch studies to improve
The tender memory of his former love,
Their state requires a second nuptial tie.
Hence the pale ruler with a love-sick eye
Surveys the attendants of his former wife,
And offers one of them a royal life.
These, when their martial mistress had been slain.
Weak and despairing tried their arms in vain;
Willing, howe'er, amidst the Black to go,
They thirst for speedy vengeance on the foe.
Then he resolves to see who merits best,
By strength and courage, the imperial vest;
Points out the foe, bids each with bold design
Pierce through the ranks, and reach the deepest line:
For none must hope with monarchs to repose
But who can first, through thick-surrounding foes,
Through arms and wiles, with hazardous essay,
Safe to the furthest quarters force their way.
Fired at the thought, with sudden joyful pace
They hurry on; but first of all the race
Runs the third right-hand warrior for the prize,—
The glittering crown already charms her eyes.
Her dear associates cheerfully give o'er
The nuptial chase; and swift she flies before,
And glory lent her wings, and the reward in store.
Nor would the sable King her hopes prevent,
For he himself was on a Queen intent;
Alternate therefore through the field they go;
Hermes led on, but by a step too slow,

His fourth left Pawn : and now the adventurous White
Had marched through all, and gained the wished-for site.
Then the pleased King gives orders to prepare
The crown, the sceptre, and the royal chair,
And owns her for his Queen : around exult
The snowy troops, and o'er the Black insult.
  Hermes burst into tears,— with fretful roar
Filled the wide air, and his gay vesture tore.
The swarthy Foot had only to advance
One single step ; but, O ! malignant chance !
A towered Elephant, with fatal aim,
Stood ready to destroy her when she came :
He keeps a watchful eye upon the whole,
Threatens her entrance, and protects the goal.
Meanwhile the royal new-created bride,
Pleased with her pomp, spread death and terror wide ;
Like lightning through the sable troops she flies,
Clashes her arms, and seems to threat the skies.
The sable troops are sunk in wild affright,
And wish the earth opening snatched 'em from her sight.
In burst the Queen, with vast impetuous swing :
The trembling foes come swarming round the King,
Where in the midst he stood, and form a valiant ring.
So the poor cows, straggling o'er pasture-land,
When they perceive the prowling wolf at hand,
Crowd close together in a circle full,
And beg the succor of the lordly bull ;
They clash their horns, they low with dreadful sound,
And the remotest groves reëcho round.
  But the bold Queen, victorious, from behind
Pierces the foe ; yet chiefly she designed

Against the King himself some fatal aim,
And full of war to his pavilion came.
Now here she rushed, now there; and had she been
But duly prudent, she had slipped between,
With course oblique, into the fourth white square,
And the long toil of war had ended there;
The King had fallen, and all his sable state,
And vanquished Hermes cursed his partial fate.
For thence with ease the championess might go,
Murder the King, and none could ward the blow.
With silence, Hermes, and with panting heart,
Perceived the danger, but with subtle art
(Lest he should see the place) spurs on the foe,
Confounds his thoughts, and blames his being slow.
For shame! move on; would you forever stay?
What sloth is this, what strange perverse delay?—
How could you e'er my little pausing blame?—
What! you would wait till night shall end the game?
Phœbus, thus nettled, with imprudence slew
A vulgar Pawn, but lost his nobler view.
Young Hermes leaped, with sudden joy elate;
And then, to save the monarch from his fate,
Led on his martial Knight, who stepped between,
Pleased that his charge was to oppose the Queen —
Then, pondering how the Indian beast to slay,
That stopped the Foot from making further way.—
From being made a Queen; with slanting aim
An Archer struck him; down the monster came,
And dying shook the earth: while Phœbus tries
Without success the monarch to surprise.
The Foot, then uncontrolled, with instant pride,
Seized the last spot, and moved a royal bride.

And now with equal strength both war again,
And bring their second wives upon the plain;
Then, though with equal views each hoped and feared,
Yet, as if every doubt had disappeared,
As if he had the palm, young Hermes flies
Into excess of joy; with deep disguise,
Extols his own Black troops, with frequent spite
And with invective taunts disdains the White.
Whom Phœbus thus reproved with quick return —
As yet we cannot the decision learn
Of this dispute, and do you triumph now?
Then your big words and vauntings I 'll allow,
When you the battle shall completely gain;
At present I shall make your boasting vain.
He said, and forward led the daring Queen;
Instant the fury of the bloody scene
Rises tumultuous, swift the warriors fly
From either side to conquer or to die.
They front the storm of war; around them Fear,
Terror, and Death, perpetually appear.
All meet in arms, and man to man oppose,
Each from their camp attempts to drive their foes;
Each tries by turns to force the hostile lines;
Chance and impatience blast their best designs.
The sable Queen spread terror as she went
Through the mid ranks: with more reserved intent
The adverse dame declined the open fray,
And to the King in private stole away:
Then took the royal guard, and bursting in,
With fatal menace close besieged the King.
Alarmed at this, the swarthy Queen, in haste,
From all her havoc and destructive waste

Broke off, and, her contempt of death to show,
Leaped in between the monarch and the foe,
To save the King and state from this impending blow.
But Phœbus met a worse misfortune here:
For Hermes now led forward, void of fear,
His furious horse into the open plain,
That onward chafed, and pranced, and pawed amain.
Nor ceased from his attempts until he stood
On the long-wished-for spot, from whence he could
Slay King or Queen. O'erwhelmed with sudden fears,
Apollo saw, and could not keep from tears.
Now all seemed ready to be overthrown;
His strength was withered, every hope was flown.
Hermes, exulting at this great surprise,
Shouted for joy, and filled the air with cries;
Instant he sent the Queen to shades below,
And of her spoils made a triumphant show.
But in return, and in his mid career,
Fell his brave Knight, beneath the Monarch's spear.
  Phœbus, however, did not yet despair,
But still fought on with courage and with care.
He had but two poor common men to show,
And Mars's favorite with his ivory bow.
The thoughts of ruin made them dare their best
To save their King, so fatally distressed.
But the sad hour required not such an aid;
And Hermes breathed revenge where'er he strayed.
Fierce comes the sable Queen with fatal threat,
Surrounds the monarch in his royal seat;
Rushed here and there, nor rested till she slew
The last remainder of the whitened crew.

Sole stood the King, the midst of all the plain,
Weak and defenceless, his companions slain.
  As when the ruddy morn ascending high
Has chased the twinkling stars from all the sky,
Your star, fair Venus, still retains its light,
And, loveliest, goes the latest out of sight,
No safety 's left, no gleams of hope remain;
Yet did he not as vanquished quit the plain,
But tried to shut himself between the foe,—
Unhurt through swords and spears he hoped to go,
Until no room was left to shun the fatal blow.
For if none threatened his immediate fate,
And his next move must ruin all his state,
All their past toil and labor is in vain,
Vain all the bloody carnage of the plain,—
Neither would triumph then, the laurel neither gain.
Therefore through each void space and desert tent
By different moves his various course he bent:
The Black King watched him with observant eye,
Followed him close, but left him room to fly.
Then when he saw him take the furthest line,
He sent the Queen his motions to confine,
And guard the second rank, that he could go
No further now than to that distant row.
The sable monarch then with cheerful mien
Approached, but always with one space between.
But as the King stood o'er against him there,
Helpless, forlorn, and sunk in his despair,
The martial Queen her lucky moment knew,
Seized on the furthest seat with fatal view,
Nor left the unhappy King a place to flee unto.

At length in vengeance her keen sword she draws,
Slew him, and ended thus the bloody cause:
And all the gods around approved it with applause.
  The victor could not from his insults keep,
But laughed and sneered to see Apollo weep.
Jove called him near, and gave him in his hand
The powerful, happy, and mysterious wand
By which the Shades are called to purer day,
When penal fire has purged their sins away;
By which the guilty are condemned to dwell
In the dark mansions of the deepest hell;
By which he gives us sleep, or sleep denies,
And closes at the last the dying eyes.
Soon after this, the heavenly victor brought
The game on earth, and first the Italians taught.
  For (as they say) fair Scacchis he espied
Feeding her cygnets in the silver tide,
(Scacchis, the loveliest Seriad of the place)
And as she strayed, took her to his embrace.
Then, to reward her for her virtue lost,
Gave her the men and checkered board, embossed
With gold and silver curiously inlaid;
And taught her how the game was to be played.
Even now 't is honored with her happy name;
And Rome and all the world admire the game.
All which the Seriads told me heretofore,
When my boy-notes amused the Serian shore.

NOTES TO GOLDSMITH.

The Traveller.

Page 23. — This poem was first published in December, 1764, by John Newbery, price 1*s*. 6*d*. It went through nine editions in his lifetime, and is here reprinted from the 9th 4to, 1774, compared with the 1st, and with the 6th corrected 4to, 1770.

Page 23, line 1. — "Chamier once asked him what he meant by 'slow,' — the last word in the first line of 'The Traveller,' —

'Remote, unfriended, melancholy, slow.'

Did he mean tardiness of locomotion? Goldsmith, who would say something without consideration, answered, 'Yes.' I was sitting by, and said, 'No, sir; you do not mean tardiness of locomotion; you mean that sluggishness of mind which comes upon a man in solitude.'" — Johnson, *in Boswell.*

Page 23, line 3. — *Carinthia* was visited by Goldsmith in 1755, and still (1854) retains its character for inhospitality.

Page 36, line 12.

"To stop too fearful, and too faint to go."

This line was written by Dr. Johnson.

Page 36, line 20. — The concluding ten lines, except the last couplet but one, were written by Dr. Johnson.

Page 36, line 28.

"Luke's iron crown, and Damiens' bed of steel."

When Tom Davies, at the request of Grainger, asked Goldsmith about this line, he was referred for an explanation of Luke's iron crown to a book called *Geographie Curieuse*; the poet added, that by Damiens' bed of steel he meant the rack.

Mr. Bolton Corney states that the names of the brothers were *Zeck*, Luke and George; following, probably, the passage to that effect in Boswell's Johnson, referring to the "*Respublica Hungarica*." We presume that the volume to which Boswell alludes is one cited as *Respublica et Status Hungariæ* (Elzevir, 1634), in a number of the *European Magazine* for February, 1790. The passage there cited we translate as follows, placing explanatory words in brackets:

"In the year 1514 a great insurrection broke out in Hungary; for while the Cardinal of Strigonium [Gran] was preaching a crusade [against the Turks] to the people, and many thousands had enrolled their names under him, an embassy of Ulasdislaus meanwhile concludes a treaty with Selim the Sultan. Those who had enlisted, however, by no means laid aside their arms on this account: but make Captain George Zeck, who had several times routed the Turks, their king: and first throughout Hungary, as if inflamed by madness, break into numerous castles and monasteries. As many nobles as they can, with their wives and children, they butcher; lay waste their property; violate their virgins; transfix the

Bishop of Chonad with a wooden stake driven through his body; and threaten the same fate to the Archbishop of Strigonium and others. But after the new king George, with his generals, was taken by Count John [Zapolya], the woiwode [governor of Transylvania], he was subjected to a hitherto unheard of and horrible punishment. First the king himself is crowned with an iron crown, white-hot; then his blood is drawn from two veins cut, and is given to his brother Luke to drink. Then thirty peasants, starved for three days, were thereby driven to such a pitch of savageness that they tore with their teeth and swallowed the entrails of their king while he was yet alive. The king himself, however, maintaining meanwhile a wonderful firmness, neither groaned nor shrank from any kind of torture: beseeching only that his brother Luke might be spared, as he had been compelled by him to take part in the war. At length, when almost all his limbs had been severed, they eviscerated him; and his body, cut into small pieces, partly roasted on spits, and partly boiled in a kettle, they set before his soldiers to eat: whom, thus fed, together with Luke Zeck, and variously tormented by the executioner, they put to death. Ulasdislaus, the king, died at Buda, in 1516, and is buried at Alba Regalis [Stuhlweissenburg]."

From this it would appear that the name of the brothers was *Zeck*, and that Mr. Corney might be correct in the substitution (a little trenching on editorial privilege) of *Zeck* for *Luke*. But the real name of the rebels was *Dosa*, George and Luke, who were of the *Zeckler* race, one of the native races of Transylvania. See the title "Dosa, George," in the 7th volume of the *Universal Lexicon* (Halle and Leipzig, 1734), in which it is stated that George was seated on a glowing hot iron throne, and invested with a crown and sceptre of the same fashion. This horrible account corresponds in substance to that given, under the same title, in the *Biographie Universelle*: "Dosa fut livré aux plus horribles supplices par ses impitoyables vainqueurs: on le fit asseoir sur un trône de fer rouge, une couronne sur la tête, un sceptre à la main, l'un et l'autre également rougis au feu, puis on lui ouvrit les veines et l'on fit avaler un verre de son sang à son frére Lucas, qui l'avait secondé dans sa révolte." S.

Robert Francois Damiens was put to death with revolting barbarity, in the year 1757, for an attempt to assassinate Louis XV.

The Deserted Village.

Page 39. — This poem was published by W. Griffin, at Garrick's Head, in Catharine-street, Strand, in May, 1770, in a two-shilling 4to, and ran through six editions in the same year. The sum that Goldsmith received for it is unknown.

Page 40, line 11. — The tyrant alluded to is said to have been Lieutenant-General Robert Napier, an English gentleman, who purchased an estate near Ballymahon, and ejected many of his tenants for the non-payment of rent.

Page 42, line 22. — Sir Joshua Reynolds painted a fine picture of "Resignation," which was engraved by Watson. The print bears the following inscription: "This attempt to express a character in *The Deserted Village* is dedicated to Dr. Goldsmith, by his sincere friend and admirer, Joshua Reynolds."

Page 52, line 17. — "Dr. Johnson favored me * * by marking the lines which he furnished to Goldsmith's *Deserted Village*, which are only the last four." — Boswell.

Retaliation.

Page 55—60.

First published on the 18th of April, 1774, a fortnight after the death of the author. We have seven nominal editions of it in the same year.

Scarron — Paul Scarron, a popular French writer of burlesque. Died in 1660. Goldsmith translated his *Roman Comique*.

Our Dean — Thomas Barnard, then Dean of Derry; a scholar and wit. He wrote a sarcastic epitaph on Goldsmith, but followed it by an apology, which was read at the club.

Our Burke — Edmund Burke.

Our Will — William Burke — a kinsman of Edmund Burke — some time under-secretary of state, and member of the House of Commons. He afterwards passed fifteen years in India, and died 1798.

Dick — Richard Burke, a barrister, younger brother of Edmund Burke. He died recorder of Bristol, 1794.

Cumberland — Richard Cumberland, the dramatist. Died 1811.

Douglas — Doctor Douglas, Canon of Windsor, an ingenious Scotch gentleman, distinguished for detecting several literary forgeries of his countrymen; particularly Lauder on Milton, and Bower's History of the Popes.

Garrick — David Garrick, Esq., the incomparable actor.

Ridge — Counsellor John Ridge, of the Irish bar.

Reynolds — Sir Joshua Reynolds.

Hickey — An eminent attorney, whose hospitality and good humor acquired him in his club the title of "Honest Tom Hickey."

Tommy Townshend — Mr. T. Townshend, member from Whitchurch, of whom Junius gives a portrait. Died 1803.

Honest Richard — Mr. Richard Burke. This gentleman had slightly fractured one of his arms and legs, at different times. Barry the painter observed of him, that no one was better stocked with good nature.

Dodd — The Rev. Dr. Dodd, afterwards hanged for forgery.

Kenrick — Dr. Kenrick, who read lectures at the Devil Tavern, under the title of "The School of Shakspeare," — lexicographer, reviewer, dramatist, and the bitter enemy of Goldsmith. Died 1779. Johnson said that he was one of the many who have made themselves public without making themselves known.

Macpherson — James Macpherson, Esq., who had published a miserable translation of Homer.

Kelly — Mr. Hugh Kelly, dramatist; died 1777.

Woodfall — Mr. William Woodfall, printer of the *Morning Chronicle*; a matchless reporter and able theatrical critic. Died 1803.

Postscript. — It seems that Goldsmith designed to extend his plan. Besides the epitaph on Whitefoord, the poet left a fragment on Topham Beauclerc, which has perished. The word *Postscript*, in the early editions, alludes to a memorandum of Mr. Kearsly, the publisher.

Whitefoord — Mr. Caleb Whitefoord — so notorious a punster that Goldsmith used to say that it was impossible to keep his company without being infected with the itch of punning. He was a man of varied attainments, and a frequent writer in the *Public Advertiser*, which was edited by his friend, Mr. Henry Sampson Woodfall. His *Cross Readings* were published in that journal under the signature of *Papyrius Cursor*.

To an Impertinent Musician.

Page 63. — Oliver, while a pupil at Elphin, was requested to dance a hornpipe. The musician, a youth also, compared him to Æsop, and this was the young poet's impromptu reply.

The Clown's Reply.

Page 63. — From the "Poems and Plays, Dublin, Price &c., 1777." The verses are dated Edinburgh, 1753. No authority is cited for assigning them to Goldsmith.

The Logicians Refuted.
Page 64—65.

Bob — Sir Robert Walpole.

"No *judges*, fiddlers, dancing-masters."

Some of the editions have "jugglers," — which would seem the true reading, from the company in which the word is found. It is probable, however, that Goldsmith intended by this an allusion to Swift's aversion to lawyers.

Elegy on Mrs. Blaize.

From the *Bee*. An imitation of a noted French song of fifty stanzas, each of which ends with a ludicrous truism, — "Le fameux la Gallisse, homme imaginaire," printed in the *Menagiana*, iv. 191.

Description of an Author's Bed-Chamber.

Page 68. — These lines first appeared in *The Citizen of the World.* They purport to have been read at a club of authors by a poet in shabby finery, as part of "an heroic poem, *which he had composed the day before.*" Afterwards, with some variation, they appeared in *The Deserted Village.* A letter of Goldsmith to his brother gives four lines additional:

"And now imagine, after his soliloquy, the landlord to make his appearance in order to dun him for the reckoning:

'Not with that face, so servile and so gay,
That welcomes every stranger that can pay,
With sulky eye he smoked the patient man,
Then pulled his breeches tight and thus began.'

On seeing Mrs. *** Perform.

Page 69. — From the *Citizen of the World.* A specimen furnished by the Chinese philosopher of the "flaunting newspaper verses" then current in the composition of panegyrics on the players.

Elegy on the Death of the Right Hon. ***.

Page 70. — From the *Citizen of the World.* "An elegy," in which the Chinese philosopher unfolds the secret of flattering the worthless, and yet preserving a safe conscience.

Translation of a South American Ode.

Page 71. — From the *Citizen of the World.* In a conversation which turned on love, the philosopher affirmed it to be *merely a name;* a female orator insisted that it was a natural and universal passion, — that it had flourished "even in the sultry wilds of Southern America," — in proof whereof she recited this ode.

The Captivity.

Page 71. — Written in 1764, but never set to music or published by its author. The original MS. was sold to Mr. Dodsley for ten guineas, and afterwards came into the hands of Mr. John Murray, of Albermarle-street. Two of the songs were printed in 1776, with some emendations which are adopted in the present version.

The Hermit.

Page 89. — First published in the *Vicar of Wakefield* 1766. It is now printed from the amended text, with an additional stanza, the 30th, which was given by the author to Richard Archdale, Esq.

Epitaph on Edward Purdon.

Page 97. — Composed while the author was proceeding from his chambers in the Temple to the Club at the Globe Tavern. Purdon was a college friend of Goldsmith, and assisted him in translating the *Memoirs of a Protestant*. It was for his unpublished translation of the *Henriade* that Goldsmith wrote his *Life of Voltaire*.

REPLY TO AN INVITATION TO DINNER.

Page 97. — Written about the year 1769, in reply to an invitation to dinner at Dr., afterwards Sir George Baker's (died 1809), to meet Angelica Kauffman, Miss Reynolds, Sir Joshua Reynolds, Mrs. Horneck, widow of Captain Kane Horneck, her son Charles, or the *captain in lace*; her daughter Mary, or the *Jessamy bride*, afterwards Mrs. Gwyn, and Catherine, or *little Comedy*, afterwards Mrs. Bunbury. For these verses, first published in 1837, the reader is indebted to Sir Henry Bunbury.

The following is the compliment alluded to:

"While fair Angelica, with matchless grace,
Paints Conway's lovely form and Stanhope's face,
Our hearts to beauty willing homage pay,—
We praise, admire, and gaze our souls away.
But when the likeness she hath done for thee,
O Reynolds! with astonishment we see,
Forced to submit, with all our pride we own
Such strength, such harmony excelled by none,
And thou art rivalled by thyself alone."

EPITAPH ON THOMAS PARNELL.

Page 99. — From *The Haunch of Venison*, etc., 1776. This epitaph is supposed to have been written about 1770, but was never inscribed over Parnell's grave.

THE HAUNCH OF VENISON.

Page 99. — Lord Clare was Robert Nugent, of Carlanstown, Westmeath, a politician, and a poet above mediocrity — in 1766 created Viscount Clare, and in 1776 Earl Nugent. He was a jolly, voluptuous Irishman.

Monroe — Dorothy Monroe, whose charms are celebrated in verse by Lord Townshend; *Howard* — author of the Choice Spirits' Museum, 1765; *Coley* — Colman, says Horace Walpole; *Hogarth*, a surgeon of Golden Square; *Hiff*, Paul Hiffernan, an obscure medical practitioner, also a theatrical critic and author of several volumes; *Higgins* — Captain Higgins? He made a blunder by drawing our poet into a foolish affray.

The leading idea of this clever epistle is taken from Boileau's third Satire.

THRENODIA AUGUSTALIS.

Augusta, relict of Frederic Prince of Wales, and mother of George III., died February 8th, 1770, and this piece was performed at Mrs. Cornely's, Soho Square, on the 20th. The poet depicts her character with historical exactness. We transcribe the advertisement prefixed to it:

"The following may more properly be termed a compilation than a poem. It was prepared for the composer in little more than two days; and may therefore rather be considered as an industrious effort of gratitude than of genius. In justice to the composer, it may likewise be right to inform the public that the music was adapted in a period of time equally short."

It was first printed in small quarto, by W. Woodfall, in 1772. The composer was Signor Vento; the speakers, Mr. Lee and Mrs. Bellamy; and the singers, Mr. Champness, Mr. Dine, and Miss Jameson.

The mere statement that the piece is a "compilation" is hardly sufficient to justify the free use of Collins's poems, without a more particular acknowledgment. The lines referred to are now familiar to all readers, but they were little known at the time Goldsmith wrote.

LETTER TO MRS. BUNBURY.

Page 113. — This is an answer to an invitation to Barton, the residence of Henry Bunbury, Esq.; and appeared in the correspondence of Sir Thomas Hanmer, Bart., 1838.

Henry, second son of Sir W. Bunbury, was celebrated in early life as an amateur artist.

He married Catherine Horneck in 1771, and died at Keswick in 1811. These lines were written about the year 1772, in answer to a versified invitation from Mrs. Bunbury to pass the Christmas at Barton, and to take the advice of herself and her sister in playing at loo. Miss Horneck, afterwards the wife of General Gwyn, survived till 1840, and cherished to her latest day the memory of her friendship with Goldsmith. Sir John Fielding, half-brother to the novelist, held the office of justice for Westminster. Sir Charlés — Sir Thomas Charles Bunbury, the elder brother — died in 1820.

Song.

Page 117. — This song was omitted in the representation, because Mrs. Bulkley, who played Miss Hardcastle, did not sing. Goldsmith sang it himself, very agreeably, as we are told by Boswell.

Fragmentary Translations.

Page 118. — " In some recent editions of our poet," says Mr. Bolton Corney, " we have more than a hundred lines translated from Horace, etc. I have traced about a third part to Philip Francis, and therefore submit a new collection." Fragment 1, *The Shouting Army*, from a French version of Homer ; 2, From Homer ; 3, From the Latin of Vida ; 4, From Scarron ; 5, From Ovid ; 6, From the Latin of Addison, *Spectator*, No. 412.

The Prologue of Laberius.

Page 123. — From an *Enquiry into the Present state of Polite Learning in Europe*, 1759. Laberius, when in his sixtieth year, was commanded by Julius Cæsar to act in one of his numerous farces. He complied, but expressed his feelings on the occasion with much point and dignity, in a prologue, a part of which Goldsmith has imitated.

Epilogue to The Sister.

Page 125. — This comedy was acted at Covent Garden, on the 18th of February, 1769, but was never repeated. Charlotte Ramsay, a native of America, went to England in early life, married a Mr. Lennox, and devoted herself to authorship. She wrote *The Sister*, and The Female Quixote, a clever novel, but died in reduced circumstances in 1804.

Prologue to Zobeide.

Page 126. — *Zobeide* was translated from *Les Scythes* of Voltaire, by Joseph Cradock, a literary gentleman, a friend of Goldsmith, who wrote his own *Memoirs*, and died in 1826. This prologue was spoken by Mr. Quick, in the character of a sailor. Lieut. Cook had been sent out to observe the transit of Venus at Otaheite. The astronomers alluded to are Cook and Green ; the botanists, Banks and Solander.

Epilogues to She Stoops to Conquer.

Page 128 to 134. — The history of the several epilogues written for this comedy is preserved in the following extract of a letter from Goldsmith to his friend Mr. J. Cradock :

" Murphy sent me rather the outline of an Epilogue than an Epilogue, which was to be sung by Mrs. Catley, and which she approved. Mrs. Bulkley, hearing this, insisted on throwing up her part, unless, according to the custom of the theatre, she was permitted to speak the Epilogue. In this embarrassment, I thought of making a quarrelling Epilogue between Catley and her, debating who should speak the Epilogue ; but then Mrs. Catley refused, after I had taken the trouble of drawing it out. I was then at a loss indeed : an Epilogue was to be made, and for none but Mrs. Bulkley. I made one, and Coleman thought it too bad to be spoken : I was obliged, therefore, to try a fourth time, and I made a very mawkish thing, as you 'll shortly see."

Epilogue for Mr. C. Lee Lewes.

Page 134. — Spoken at Covent Garden, on the 7th of May, 1773. Lewes was the original Young Marlow in *She Stoops to Conquer*. He died in 1803.

www.ingramcontent.com/pod-product-compliance
Lightning Source LLC
LaVergne TN
LVHW011157110826
845150LV00006B/1249

* 9 7 8 1 4 2 5 5 4 5 7 4 1 *